3 H 23 $2⁰⁰
James F. Delaney.

D1061808

Three Popes
and a
Cardinal

Books by Malachi Martin

THE PILGRIM (under the pseudonym, Michael Serafian)

THE ENCOUNTER

THREE POPES AND A CARDINAL

Malachi Martin

THREE POPES AND A CARDINAL

Hart-Davis, MacGibbon   London

Granada Publishing Limited
First published in Great Britain 1973 by Hart-Davis, MacGibbon Ltd
Frogmore, St Albans, Hertfordshire AL2 2NF, and
3 Upper James Street, London W1R 4BP

ISBN 0 246 10607 7

Printed in Great Britain by Fletcher & Son Ltd, Norwich.

CONTENTS

Preface

Well before the year 2000, there will no longer be a religious institution recognizable as the Roman Catholic and Apostolic Church of today. In the religious history of man, this is the Age of Human Pathology. It is the Passion, not of Jesus, but of man. It was about four hundred years in the making. It has taken just forty years to become an active reality.

If such an event is considered a disaster, one can easily find scapegoats among all those who tear at the Roman Church's fabric in order to make their own ideas prevail: the priests who rebel against bishops; the bishops who undermine the authority of the pope; the black Catholics who insist that their will be done in the name of their particular racism and under threat of total fission; nuns who refuse to work except as they will, because as women they have long been oppressed by men; lay folk who desert religious practice because those in charge are either confused or idiotic. Particular scapegoats could be sought. Cardinals Suenens of Belgium and Alfrink of Holland could be faced with the reproach that they are playing with fire. Cardinals Heenan of Westminster, Conway of Ireland, and Ruffini of Palermo could be equally taxed for inaction. The most effective action, at times, is sheer inaction. Those Catholic conservative financial groups who are exercising their economic sinews to effect the election of their candidate to the Throne of Peter in succession to Paul VI could be severely criticized for playing God. The Jesuit Order, both in its superiors and ranks, could be chided for the tatterdemalion condition of its performance as "Pope's men" and rational beings.

Blame, in other words, is easy. For it is characteristic of all involved that they will not listen, but only consent to be heard; that they are persuaded they know the answers, but they will not bother to ask the questions; and that they are willing to tamper with a delicate structure, merely because they can muster centers of disruption or maintain rigidities, but are not formally saddled with ultimate responsibility for that which they destroy by disruption and rigidity. But, in fact, all are sincere; and, in the final analysis, all are overtaken by events they did not plan and faced with crises they cannot surmount. They are all gripped in the logic of an inexorable momentum which has taken its head. Like Peter, in the words of Jesus, Peter's Church has grown old and is being led where it would not go.

It is not so much that the active membership and the number of the people baptized into the Roman Church will be reduced considerably. Rather it is that there will be, instead of the Church we know, a series of independent "churches," in addition to one hard-core group clustered around the Bishop of Rome, the traditional claimant to be the successor of St. Peter and sole head of the Church which Jesus of Nazareth founded in the first century of this era. But we cannot really call them churches. There will be no central authority for teaching and jurisdiction. There will be a general—but virtually nominal—similarity among all groups. But there will be no centralized control, no uniformity in teaching, no universality in practice of worship, prayer, sacrifice, and priesthood. Churches, cathedrals, schools, convents, monasteries, seminaries, and such, these groups will not have. Nor will they desire them. They will have no use for them.

The rise of such groupings will not occur, as of old, through formal heresy or schism, through dynastic ambitions or nationalistic partisanship. Nor will they resemble the autonomous churches of Eastern Orthodox Christianity or the various "Rites" (Armenian, Maronite, Melchite, etc.) which the Roman Church includes in its fold today. They will not be "autocephalous" churches. They will be autozoic groups, with their own life-cycles, their own styles of living, their own rules, their own prides and ambitions and strifes and disruptions, their own births and their own deaths. This will be so because they will have renounced the ancient fact which gave birth to every local church of which we have knowledge: foundation by an Apostle or on his tradition. The autozoic groups of tomorrow will claim no descendance from the original group of men Jesus formed, his Twelve Apostles and the other disciples. Nor will they feel any need for such a descendance. Apostolic succession, as a mark of accepted authenticity, is out.

The break-point or dawn of this vast change came with the Second Vatican Council (1962–1965). It was the occasion which provided an opening. Out through this opening there poured, first as a trickle, then as a stream, finally as a flood, the clamor of human spirits long held down and imprisoned. Those who had suffered from the oppression of power sought to grasp the compassion embodied in Angelo Roncalli as John XXIII and seemingly offered by his Council. But Roncalli's Council was a majestic gamble which failed in its essential purpose. The human spirits, however, were out and free, never to return again. One dates from that point onwards the death agony of the old and the emergence of the new groups and the seeming madness which possesses them.

Except in the opinion of the very ultra- and dyed-in-the-wool conservative mind, this Vatican Council is considered to have been a boon to Christianity, a vast advance for Roman Catholicism, and an unmitigated success as an expression of the popular will. It, together with Roncalli's name and memory, is invoked as justification for the most extraordinary and diverse actions: a guerrilla massacre in Colombia, homosexual marriages in Manhattan, denials of the Virgin Birth, of the Resurrection, of the pope's infallibility, the exit of whole groups from religious communities, tactile prayer, Satan-Jesus cults, masses celebrated by women in drawing rooms, rock masses, confetti resurrections, groupie encounters, nude altarboys, polygamous unions, communal yoga, Communist governments, black revolutionary Jesuses, female Holy Spirits, full-blooded revolt by Northern European theologians, and a whole litany of clerical posturings and theological asininities which an earlier narrow-minded age would have consigned to the flames of a faggot fire but which today are considered to be legitimate exercises of human rights.

The motives animating the different autozoic groups and holding them together as separate entities will be among six possible pathologies. *Ethnic pathology* will motivate all those groups which spring up as a reaction to racism, real or presumed, in the past history and the present administration and teaching of the Roman Church. Of necessity, they must substitute their own brand of racism for the antecedent racism. But the obvious rule is: two wrong racisms add up to one right racism. *Doctrinal pathology* will provide the motivation for those groups which organize themselves on the basis of concept and ideology as distinct from the traditional religious life and experience of the Church. A blueprint for such groups is provided in the writings of Hans Kung, well-known Swiss theologian. Nowhere in the thicket of concept and ideology can the spirit of Jesus move and animate men. *Economic pathology* will be the motivation for all those who rise up in reaction to the economic oppression, industrial monopolism, and social stratification with which the Church has accommodated for too long to be able now to disassociate itself. Today the prime examples of this are to be found in Latin America; to a lesser degree in Spain, Portugal, and Italy. The poor are no longer blessed because they are poor, and the Kingdom of Heaven is seen through the barrel of a gun. *Psychophysical pathology* will motivate those who are drawn together because of a mutually shared psychophysical characteristic: the Gay Church, Women's Lib, Christian Yogis, Pentecostalists, Processeans, and others. These are to mainstream Roman Catholicism what the Dancing Dervishes were to mainstream Islam. *Ecumenical pathology* will supply motivation for all those who are engaged in that form of ecclesiastical "musical chairs" called the ecumenical movement, and who place in it their future hopes for Christianity. The distinct advantage of ecumenism is that it gives the firm illusion of forward movement, of doing something, being about something. Like the wheel, it turns on its own axis in the same place. *Political pathology* will motivate all those who make political events into religious issues, assume for themselves a quasi-Messianic or almost-Jesus identity, and propagate their political ideas by words and actions that deliberately ape and savor of Jesus and his utterly a-political mission. For many, gone dead in themselves because of a passive religious training and background, it is a liberation. Calvaries, mob scenes, trials, visions, and heroics are possible on every side.

All the autozoic groups will share a set of common characteristics. They will be modeled on socio-political entities of their day. They will have their primary areas of activity in the socio-political and economic fields. They will use socio-political means to achieve their aims. They will not aim at spreading a message received from beyond the stars and the knowable bounds of the human dimension, but will strive merely and exclusively for placement within that human dimension. And, instead of injecting transcendent principles into their ambient society, thus to transform it, they will be injected with the principles of that society and be transformed by it. They will be genuine members of the human mainstream wherever it goes. They will not be professedly Christians. They will be men, not sons of God. They will strive to be human, not to be holy. Each will have a Jesus of its making and its like. There will always be, of course, a hardcore group spread throughout the globe and strictly Romanist in sympathy.

There will be, finally, a body of churchmen and laity who are quite comfortable and snug within the status quo, who are opposed to all change as inherently bad, and who hope (and sometimes believe) that, because of God's promises which they understand in their way, they can ride out the storm. Once upon a time, as they remember, they claimed to be uniquely acquainted with the precincts where God walked the earth in human shape, and to disburse his salvation. Primarily found today in the clerical circles of Ireland, Spain, Portugal, and Italy, but also rampant among some American bishops, it is the prime target of the dissolution now let loose in the Roman Church. For what cannot change must go. Such seems to be the irrevocable decision of contemporary history, to speak figuratively. More and more, like unbelieving mourners beside the dead body of a great leader, they are too preoccupied with the flesh of their Church. The spirit has fled its prison, but they huddle together unknowingly, gazing on the gray walls that once contained that spirit.

But there is no room for pessimism or doomsday prophecies in this picture. Nor is there any consolation in it for those who for a long time have yearned to see the end of Roman Catholicism, if not of Christianity itself. It is not a coming Armageddon, or the reign of Antichrist, or a world without followers of Jesus and quite rid of his presence. It is not the end of the world or even the end of the Christian world. It is merely the end of a situation which has become intolerable for the human spirit and totally unsuitable for the word of God as it was revealed to men once upon a time, in past human history. There is no room for any pessimism, precisely because without this fragmentation and precipitation of all elements, there does not seem, humanly speaking, to be any chance that the word of God, the Good News, can reach man as man, as God surely intended it to do. And without pessimism, there need be no fear.

There is room, however, for regret of a limited kind, when one remembers the irredentism of the Roman mind. It is capable of almost infinite compromise on many matters. In its long history, it has exhibited killing patience and interminable perdurance, cohabiting temporarily with almost everything: exile, persecution, indifference, rebellion, syncretism, scorn, hate, ostracism, war, slander, calumny, corruption, weakness, greed, laxity, cruelty, hypocrisy, slavery. But on the question of its privilege in teaching authority and jurisdiction, it has never yielded one jot or tittle. Not to the Arians in the earlier centuries. Not to the Eastern Churches in the Middle Ages. Not to Luther and the Reformers in the sixteenth century or the Modernists of the nineteenth century. Faced, however, with an unacceptable choice —renunciation of that privilege or severe revolt, it will categorically refuse the choice, and thus initiate the sundering of a body already racked with strains and stresses. The regret is not for the sundering but for the quickened pain of passing, and, summarily, for the needlessness of it all, were men to act as sons of God.

This book is not concerned with that near-future condition of Roman Catholicism but with that break-point in the early sixties of this century, the Vatican Council organized by John XXIII. Within the certain limits of my information and experience, it expresses what took place.

Eugenio Pacelli, as Pius XII, was the Prince of Power and the last pope in the traditional sense. He insisted that he, as man, was Pope. He was a model of what popes thought popes should be, a papal archetype toward which forty-one popes had striven since the middle of the sixteenth century. When he died nineteen years after his accession, the charisma of power died with him.

Angelo Roncalli, as John XXIII, was the Prince of Compassion. He insisted, as pope, that he was man. He inherited the dry rot of Pacelli's Church and undertook a great gamble with gargantuan faith and with the desperation of love. Roncalli started from an intuition of a certain change in the human dimension of twentieth-century man. He saw already emergent a new identity and new conditions for men. Further, he saw this change as inexorable. In the rushing stream of human time, the waters of human fortunes had, he felt, already passed through a trap-gate of history carrying all human things with them beyond the point of no return. He was not a professional historian but he had a profound sense of history. He was the head of a Church which had been an active participant in more than one such trap-gate of change over a period of almost two thousand years. There is no understanding of Roncalli's basic intuition without a historical perspective of those changes, for one had led into another. Roncalli's gamble failed. With his end, at the age of eighty-one, there ended the charisma of compassion. But his death agony and his end were uncompassionately long, as if time had been delayed and his mortality was taking a toll for the compassion which he had wrested from its hands for other men. In his Church and throughout the major portions of Christianity, there was left the illusion of unity, of a getting-together, and of a new spirit.

Giovanni Battista Montini, as Paul VI, entered the papacy as the Prince of that Unity, wearing the illusion of that charisma. For a time some promise hovered around his figure but, within seven years of his accession, it had evaporated. This was inevitable. He presided over the conclusion of John's Ecumenical Council, which by now had been transformed merely into a forum for fresh legislation. The spirit was gone, but the minds of the participants were divagated into febrile discussions, attempted refurbishing of long-dead concepts, folio-length decrees, politicking caucuses, infighting commissions, and intermittent theological cockpits, complete with quarreling onlookers.

This too would have passed, if the bitterness of frustration had not followed the Johannine illusion. John had proffered a heady wine, and it had been drunk to the lees. The bitterness affected high and low. Paul's infallibility was attacked coldly and analytically by an Indian bishop and theologically by a Swiss theologian. A cardinal, without nod or say-so from Paul (the only legitimate proposer), proposed a fresh ecumenical council to be held in Jerusalem. A plethora of organizations sprang into existence. Priests organized themselves against their bishops. Nuns in large groups and whole communities "secularized" themselves. Congregations rose in the middle of their cardinal-bishop's sermon and left the church.

The malaise had surfaced. Suffering had been replaced with disgust and indifference. Paul, mindful of John's gamble and its failure, refused to excommunicate, to excise, even to excoriate. He protested, chided, pleaded, wept, warned. He traveled as a pilgrim of protest against poverty, against abortion, against contraception, against war, against religious revolt. But the charisma of unity was gone. The agony had set in. He became the Prince of Agony, stripped of power, dry of compassion and the object of no compassion, locked in a fervid maze of circumstances which he had not created, over which he had no control, and from which there was no escape. Paul himself has been unpoped. His Church is undergoing a "churching." But the truth is that something had died at some point in the past. It had been buried without pomp or human cognizance. Only in this period has it been revealed and recognized.

Interwoven with the tragedies of these three Popes is the shadow of Augustin Cardinal Bea. His is the most tragic figure in recent Church history: he died the most disappointed, embittered, disillusioned, and misrepresented member of Roman Catholic leadership in the twentieth century. Yet he could die saying most sincerely, "God has been extraordinarily generous with me." Earlier and in his heyday with Pacelli, he learned power and experienced its vicious and vicarious exhilaration. "Even if we haven't got virtue, we do have the power here. Don't forget it, my son," said Bea as rector of the Pontifical Biblical Institute as he dismissed a recalcitrant Belgian student, Gustave Lambert. That was in the thirties. Father Bea was at the height of power. But eventually he suffered from the corruption of power and, as Pacelli's confessor, walked around with thirteen years of Pacelli's conscience on his own conscience. Late in life, with Roncalli, he learned to love with compassion and to judge without cavil or pretension. "I am neither optimist nor pessimist. I am a realist," Cardinal Bea kept repeating. He had thus a brief springtime of achievement. But with Montini he saw unity dissolve; and he, together with his hopes, ambitions, and his lately won lessons, was swallowed up in the darkness and agony of Montini's reign and the inevitable decline of Christianity as presently organized.

To understand Roncalli's decision, we must understand the changing human dimension as he did. This change is most manifest in the United States. Americans are the guinea pigs of history. What Roncalli thought about this change applies par excellence to the United States. Understanding Roncalli's failure, we will understand the plight of Paul, presiding over the visible and the invisible forces of his Church.

Part I

THE POPES AND THE CARDINAL

1

The Three Popes

The first time that the three Popes—Pacelli, Roncalli, Montini —came into focus for me was during a conversation with Augustin Bea—the Cardinal-to-be—in late December 1958 in Rome. Bea had come to greet me in my new quarters. I was a new arrival from Louvain, Belgium, and about to take up a post at Rome's Pontifical Biblical Institute. It was evening time, and we were both waiting for the community supper bell to ring. "Come, sit in my room and let us chat until supper," he said. "There is much to talk about, and a great time is dawning." He answered some questions of mine about the factors which led to the election of Roncalli as Pope John XXIII. Pacelli had been dead for some two months, and Roncalli was pope only a little over a month. In Louvain, Roncalli's election had been greeted with groans by some, with laughter by others.

When Bea spoke of "a new effort to be made," I asked why such a new effort was necessary. To illustrate his meaning, he plunged into an incisively delivered account of a meeting among the three men. His summations of the three, together with what I knew of their lives, provided a study in contrasts. It also made his mind clear: after Pacelli, a vast change was essential. He fully expected Montini to be pope some day; but the success of Montini's pontificate depended on the extent of the change which Roncalli could effect.

The three men, Pacelli, Roncalli, Montini, had met together in 1954. "By routine, as it were," remarked Bea with a slow smile, "and not by any clearly fateful cause, or by any deliberately fate-

3

ful move on their part." It was in Pacelli's study, at morning time. Pacelli, then seventy-eight, was seemingly at the zenith of his power. "Petrified in his glory," remarked President René Coty of France. Actually, the hard crust of his power was worn thin; it was about to split and fission. But in those late days of May he was preoccupied with another matter. He was about to declare to all men that one of his predecessors, Pius X, was truly in heaven: Pius X had practiced "heroic virtue" on the planet earth; he was a perfect Roman; he now "beheld the face of God." All this Pacelli would do with infallibility and freedom from any possible error. "*Che Romano!*" Pacelli would cry repeatedly and exultingly over Vatican Radio to listening millions. Pacelli was in triumph and celebration. He progressed in stateliness and majesty, acting with the offhand dexterousness which only comes with absolute power wielded absolutely. He suspected nothing disastrous. He feared merely the ancient fears: decline of the "Christian West," Soviet Bolshevism; heresy and deviationism in the Church of God.

Roncalli, aged seventy-three, was a cardinal and Patriarch of Venice. Most people said of him: Roncalli is now as far as he can go in the hierarchy. By reputation a conservative; yet he talked with the nasty Socialists of the northern provinces and towns. Seemingly at the extremest point in his life achievement; actually, at the beginning of a third decisive phase of his life. Roncalli was not a man at ease. For the first time in his life he was in a hurry. For the first time he was brooding. Personally, he venerated Pacelli. Outsiders and onlookers sensed a change. They concluded: he has raised his sights. Roncalli is a remote possibility as next pope. Roncalli is thus *papabile*.

Montini, the youngest at fifty-seven, was the heir apparent. Seemingly a destined figure inevitably groomed for succession— some said for immediate succession—to Pacelli's throne. Actually, he was a puzzled man sharing a Pacellist power he knew vaguely as impotent, and bedeviled by a keen political instinct which told him that some subtly violent change had already taken place outside the ken of the power he shared. Montini was a patient man, serving without the overheat of undue ambition, and submitting without the overreaction of disappointment. He also venerated Pacelli.

It was early morning when Cardinal Roncalli was announced in the papal study. Papa Pacelli was already in consultation with Monsignore Montini. A routine visit had been planned. Yet this was a final nodal point in these three separate but interconnected lives. Pacelli was still Prince of that Power to which, men said, he was born in 1876. His life was unitary, single-track, of one piece.

Saddled with ill health from his birth, marked by a deep propensity for study, favored by ecclesiastical preferment, Eugenio Pacelli was not required to live in a seminary for young ecclesiastics in training. Having performed all his studies at home, he became a priest in 1899. Immediately he was co-opted into the Vatican Secretariat of State. His career had been decided. It was, as they said, "predestined." He belonged. He was somebody special from the beginning. After sixteen years of apprenticeship with veterans in Vatican diplomacy and politics, he was made bishop and sent to Munich as the Pope's Nuncio. World War I was in its dreadful twilight: the Kaiser's Germany was crumbling; the Russian campaign was a failure; America was entering the war. Industry was in fragments; hunger was rampant. After World War I, with the birth of the Weimar Republic, he was sent as Papal Nuncio to Berlin. He lived through the attempted Communist takeover, saw the rise of Hitler's Brownshirts and eventually the emergence of Hitler's Third Reich. In 1929 he was recalled to Rome, became a cardinal, and was appointed Vatican Secretary of State. In his retinue Pacelli now had a German Jesuit secretary, Heinrich; a German Jesuit adviser, Leiber; and a German Franciscan housekeeper, Suora Pasqualina, a small, rotund little nun whom he had met at Einsiedeln and who had been with him since 1918.

As Bea spoke of Pacelli, I looked around the room: bare white walls, high ceiling, a table, a typewriter covered with a white linen towel, bookcases, a closet, an iron bedstead, a washbasin, and one large window giving onto the central *cortile,* where a fountain splashed. It all spoke of Bea's dedication, of an untrammeled spirit provided with only the instruments and the most necessary conditions for frugal physical survival. "You must be thinking of the special glass," he jokingly said, breaking off his monologue for one moment. Fresh arrivals at the Institute were treated to a special glass of wine at their first meal. Then he continued. "When I became the Pope's confessor in 1945, I felt I was entering a family. As in every family, I assumed a responsibility. Its weight has never left me. And now there is much work to be done."

"Why do you stress his stay in Germany?" I asked. "The years Pius spent in Germany," Bea answered, "were capital in the formation of his mentality and policy as pope. Neither changed after that stay. The whole of Church policy was accordingly frozen." Pacelli's years in Germany had left two indelible marks on him: a fear and foreboding of Soviet Bolshevism as direful as the fear and foreboding of Christians in the fifth century for Attila and his Huns; and admiration and love of Germany, of Germans, and of Germanic orderliness.

On March 2, 1939, Pacelli was elected pope. War was imminent; great powers were about to clash. His election was quick and sure. "A formality," commented one of them beforehand. It took the participating cardinals fewer ballots than ever before in three preceding centuries of papal elections. Pacelli was the man.

The Prince of Power. From the start, he isolates himself, requiring from his entourage submission, unquestioning service, and distance. Above all, distance. The distance of respect. He never betrayed any real surprise, or ever gave a hint of being profoundly moved. He listened expressionless and wordless to whomever it was who spoke. Then he delivered himself, as he chose. He punished ruthlessly. Cardinal Wyszynski of Poland he refused to see for eight days: the Cardinal had signed an agreement with Dictator Gomulka over Pacelli's head. When Cardinal Tien of China fled before Mao Tse-tung's victorious armies in 1949 and appeared in Rome on Pacelli's doorstep, the Pope let him know that he should have remained with "his flock" and that he was to go and never come back to Rome again. He did. On Pacelli's election, one cardinal remarked that Pacelli was "a bad choice." Summoned to the Pope's library, in front of two inferior clerics, he was told to renew his obeisance and submission. The Cardinal bowed low and did so. "No," Pacelli said, "you will kneel and kiss the toe of my right foot." He did.

Pacelli had his pet bogies. He hated tobacco and flies as much as insubordination, independence, or ill-taste. He rejected any attempt to force his hand. In 1938, Hitler on state visit to Mussolini in Rome was refused an audience with Pacelli at Castel Gandolfo.

Pacelli distrusted the French, feared the British, kept the Spaniards at a distance because of their forthright dogmatism and pride, and regarded the Americans as infants in the comity of nations and members of a culture which was in a state of decline without ever having enjoyed an apogee. Mrs. Myron Taylor did not help when she presented His Holiness with a box of chocolates on her first visit. Nor did Franklin D. Roosevelt, writing to him for the first time as "My dear old friend." Pacelli regarded Germany as the political and economic heartland of Europe. Now, Pacelli's Europe was the center of the world.

Initially, he saw the Rome-Berlin Axis as a bulwark against the Soviet threat and a possible breeding ground for a new Roman Catholic humanism and for a renewal of Christian power in the socio-political order. Herr Hitler and Signor Mussolini were trying to build a new order, in spite of Anglo-Saxon back teeth. Even with the Allied victory in 1945, the occupation of Eastern Europe by Soviet Russia by 1949, and the rise of Communist China by 1950, Pacelli read the signs differently. Civilization and Christianity depended on the Central European band running from the Baltic to the Mediterranean. For the moment the signs were propitious: Roman Catholics were prominent in or headed the governments in Germany (Adenauer), France (de Gaulle, Schuman), and Italy (De Gasperi). American Catholics were generous with money and men, very active in good works, obedient, submissive, and with an almost myopic cult of the European Catholic mind.

American hegemony surprised him. It had to be accepted. It was to be acknowledged. But upon it the Christian West could not rely. America could not hold. For the future, Pacelli bent his influence toward rebuilding the broken bulwarks of traditional Christendom. He enabled the Christian Democrats to rule in Italy. He fostered Adenauer in Germany. He set about overcoming the repugnance which Paris felt for the Vatican. Roncalli, as his envoy in Paris, effected this with his charisma, his utterly inoffensive dignity, and the absence of any duplicity in his behavior. Roncalli had accomplished Pacelli's will. He was rewarded with an-end-of-a-career plum: the Patriarchate of Venice and the cardinalate.

Here now on that May morning in 1954 was Roncalli advancing toward the outstretched hand of the Pope, his face wreathed in the same smile, his wide-open eyes, pudgy arms, and swaying gait displacing any former atmosphere of conventional correctitude and rigid protocol. "When Nuncio Roncalli enters my room," the late Menderes of Turkey once said, "the room does not receive him; he takes in the entire room." Roncalli knelt, kissed the Pope's ring, and turned to greet Monsignore Montini. When Montini was Pacelli's aide, Pacelli had formed the habit of calling Montini for a preliminary discussion before making a decision on some difficult problem. Montini understood affairs, had been at the Pope's side throughout the difficult years of Fascism, of the Nazi occupation, and at the arrival of the Allied Liberators in 1944. As second to Pacelli, Montini was in his element. Indeed, it had been remarked of him that he was born to serve. Like Pacelli's, his life was of a piece.

Paul was born in Concesio, near Brescia, on September 26, 1897. Like Pacelli's, his studies for the priesthood were not performed in a seminary but at home, where his health could be fostered. A priest in 1920, he entered the Vatican Secretariat in 1922. Of him, as of Pacelli, men said "predestined." By birth, family, friends, he was somebody. He belonged. He served here for thirty-two years, becoming Archbishop of Milan in this year 1954. He spent a few months in 1923 at the Vatican nunciature in Warsaw. He functioned as chaplain to university students. But his work was at the Secretariat. He was popular with the diplomatic corps in Rome, always being accessible, always to be found in his office, always ready to listen, always knowledgeable about Italian politics, for which he had a passion, and always informed as to Pacelli's mind on international questions. Rome was his home. Politics was his passion. In a true sense, his appointment in 1954 as Archbishop of Milan was a banishment from that home on account of his passion: Pius feared his political sympathies for the far left. But Pius left a sting in the appointment. He refused Montini the cardinal's hat. He was the first Archbishop of Milan in six hundred years not to be a cardinal. This was a punishment dictated by Pacelli's relatives, who occupied high posts in the Vatican State. Montini had uncovered some unpleasant facts in their regard.

The conversation among the three men that May morning centered on the main topic of Pacelli's interest: the threat of an alliance between Italian Socialists and Christian Democrats. Such an alliance would interrupt the rule of the Christian Democrats. For Pacelli, this rupture would open the door to a Socialist, perhaps eventually a Communist, government. The Italian Communist Party had the largest number of card-carrying members (over six million) of all the Western European Communist parties. The danger of this rupture appeared acute in the industrial north of Italy. Pacelli wanted his two principal churchmen from the north to discuss this matter.

Discussion of the problem inevitably led to the "European" question. Here Pacelli could make no headway. Yes, Roncalli agreed with the Holy Father: Europe should be fostered as a unity. Indeed, it could even be a greater unity. Yes, Germany would be the heart of that unity. But under one condition only: that Germany was reunited. As things stand now? queried Pacelli. As things stand now, Roncalli answered, there is no practical probability that the two Germanies would be united again—or soon—in the foreseeable future. Therefore? Therefore, the Europe of which His Holiness is speaking does not exist and will not exist in the foreseeable future. The Europe of 1954 was a different entity. Yes, there is a Soviet threat. Precisely because of this, the two Germanies will not be united in the foreseeable future. And precisely because of this, papal policy should veer in a different direction both as regards Europe and as regards the political future of Italy. What direction? That would depend, Roncalli ventures, on one's analysis of the change which has already taken place. Pacelli nodded when change was first mentioned. But then he looked at Roncalli curiously. What change? Here Roncalli was vague.

Pacelli probably sensed something else. Roncalli was not the same man Pacelli had sent to Paris in 1944 after a five-minute audience; and he had evolved considerably since his early days in Bergamo, where he was born as Angelo Giuseppe on November 25, 1881, to dirt-farmer parents with a large family of six daughters and five sons. Roncalli's life, in fact, had been a series of laborious beginnings. Even now, although by human reckoning his life is over, he is, unknowingly, about to start the most significant part of his life.

Roncalli's life fell into three distinct phases. There was a first phase of thoughtlessness and conventional career-seeking. His piety was as simplistic, as stylized, as artificial as anyone's. His cultivation of ecclesiastical superiors who could help him on in his career was as self-serving, as tireless, and as single-minded as anyone's. His acceptance of the status quo was as thoughtless as any minor cleric's, and not any more venal than in a majority of major clerics and ecclesiastics of his day. After all, he was a nobody who wanted so desperately to belong. Except when his long life was almost over, men and contemporaries would never in his regard breathe that word of awe and reverence: "predestined." No. Young Angelo Roncalli made friends wisely, did all the expected things, accepted the domineering and domination of others, preserved all the letters of introduction, took all the rebuffs, performed all the chores, and never stepped out of line. It all began for him at the age of eleven in the minor seminary at Bergamo. There, he put on the clothes of a "little cleric"; black broad-rimmed hat, black soutane, culottes, black stockings, black boots. Twelve years later he became a priest.

A series of appointments followed: secretary to the Bishop of

Bergamo; military chaplain; president of a Catholic Action group; founder of a students' hostel; professor and spiritual director at Bergamo; director of a fund-raising organization, and professor of pathology at Rome. He met four Popes: Leo XIII, Pius X, Benedict XV, and Pius XI. He watched two emperors come and go in procession: Edward VII of England and Kaiser William II of Germany. He saw war for three years (1915–18). He traveled in Germany, Austria, France, Switzerland, Poland, and Palestine. He said all the right things, did all the right things, published the right kind of books. But he leaped no thought barriers. His piety was manifest but boring. His self-control was acquired: no women, no boys, no hard liquor. His probity was above reproach. He had a fine stentorian voice which could fill the largest cathedral. But he symbolized neither the Church militant nor the Church suffering nor the Church triumphant. He was rather the Church comfortable.

The second phase begins in 1925. He is sent by Pius XI to Bulgaria as Apostolic Visitor. He is made bishop only for this purpose. He is lonely at Ulitza Lioulin 3, Sofia. He travels in Greece, Turkey, Slovenia. He meets and wins Greek Orthodox, Russian Orthodox, Armenian Orthodox dignitaries. Surprise. In spite of their multiple heresies, they are as good, as sincere, as human as any Roman. One of his Vatican friends solicits from Pius XI Roncalli's appointment to the nunciature in Rumania. A leg-up for the young careerist. But Pius XI is in one of his black moods. He refuses. In 1934, Roncalli is appointed Apostolic Delegate to Turkey and Greece. He resides at Istanbul, in the shadow of the Golden Horn, near the Bosporus. With Turks and Greeks he has the same experience: he reaches them, touches their minds and hearts, not by his archbishop's dignity, not in virtue of his diplomatic status, not by Vatican wealth or power, not even by his piety and pietistic practices. Some of his decisions even contravene all he has been taught, as when he issued false baptismal certificates to some four thousand Jews, thus enabling them to escape as Christians the Nazi Holocaust. Theologically, canonically, diplomatically, pietistically, it was wrong. Humanly, as a unique means, it was right. All in all, it was a charisma of human feeling and of what was good. It worked, it produced love, it had to be of God. Or so he came to reason.

The same experience was his as Apostolic Nuncio to Paris. The appointment was a thorny thicket of Pacellist maneuvers and of French resentments for recent misguided Vatican support of Fascist Italy. The purpose of the appointment was twofold, in Pacelli's mind: reconciliation with Paris, as a first stage, and the overcoming of French opposition to Pacelli's dream of a unified Western Europe. Blocking achievement of this ultimate purpose stood the tall figure of Charles de Gaulle, a unique being consumed with the vision of French preeminence and French glory. Monsignor Valerio Valeri, scion of a noble house, Pacelli's aristocratic Nuncio in Paris, is told by the General: go home. "Very well," commented a Vatican official of the Secretariat of State. "They don't want a lordly prince. We shall send them a peasant." Summoned to Rome by a ciphered telegram, Roncalli is granted a five-minute interview by Pacelli between two other, more pressing affairs of state; and then Roncalli departs for Paris. To everybody's surprise, the peasant succeeds. Roncalli manages to reconcile Gaullists, Socialists, Communists, radicals, and—that form of human protest peculiar to the French—professional unbelievers. But nobody, not even Roncalli, can get the French to cooperate toward a unified Europe. Roncalli travels extensively and notes in detail the conditions in Belgium, Holland, Germany, Spain, North Africa. He talks, chats, questions, visits, watches, reads incessantly.

The second phase of his life is drawing to a close with a slow awakening. Everywhere he finds the same things: the Church is not an integral part of society; the Church stands aside; human society at all levels, economic, social, political, intellectual, artistic, personal, seems to have been subtly transformed in the blackness of some night and to be moving beyond the reach of the Church and of Christianity. His awakening becomes jolting in 1950. He is in Rome. Pacelli insists on defining infallibly a new dogma: Mary the Virgin was taken in body and soul by God to heaven after she died. *"Ma perche adesso?"* Roncalli asked a friend. Why this definition, and why make it now? Pacelli of course is convinced that the Virgin requires this definition as a condition for saving the world from the red and yellow perils of Soviet and Chinese Communism. This was communicated to him by a vision. He does consult the Church; a majority believe in the dogma. But this, for Roncalli, is not the point. The point is, the Virgin's assumption into heaven and Pacelli's infallible declaration that it so happened cannot make a whit of difference. It will be as effective in Roncalli's real world as a balloon barrage against an atomic blast or the sprinkling of rosewater against bubonic plague.

The third phase begins in 1953 with his cardinalate and appointment to Venice. It is one of quickening perception, of reali-

zation that time has run out, of consciousness that he can most
probably do nothing. He is a man in a hurry. He broods on his
achievements and his reputation, and on the apparent close of
his career with the Venice appointment. As a Vatican person, he
has known only power to prevail. He has none. As a career man,
he has learned that the near-impossible is needed. He cannot
achieve it. Pacelli is wrong about the Italian political situation,
wrong about the unity of Europe, wrong about the health of the
Church. In the five years until Pacelli's death, figures much more
imposing than Roncalli will gyrate as *papabili:* Siri of Genoa;
Ruffini of Palermo; Lercaro of Bologna; Ottaviani, Valeri, and
Agagianian, all the Roman Curia; Montini of Milan.

Roncalli loved Montini and eyed him speculatively this particular morning as Pacelli talked on. In this conversation, it was
clear that Montini was a part of the Pacellist image. Discussions
between Papa Pacelli and Montini as his Pro-Secretary of State
were habitually a one-way stream poured out in quiet incisive
Italian by the Pope and returning from Montini renewed in
vigor and clarity but unchanged in substance. Pacelli was an
upper source; Montini was a fitting receptacle. Both men were
carved in an antique mold but furbished in a modern setting. All
the seas of thought and emotion and reaction which orginated in
the older man were received in perfect accord by the younger
prelate. In him they were held echoingly, recorded accurately,
and sang harmoniously. There was, in addition, a precious quality in Montini. Things were never quite black and never quite
white. Discussion never became desiccated and forbidding.
"Yes" and "no" were infrequent answers to a request for an opinion. "One could get the impression," "a first reading of this problem," "neither extreme of opinion" were the ready formulas to
introduce the delicate balance of pro and con upon which rested
Montini's enunciations. After all, there were always darknesses
to be noted on the angular shapes of harsh decisions. There were
always dull-gray or whitish patches to be noted on the surfaces
of an apparently peremptory event.
    Now Roncalli stands as a solitary rock washed by the twin
tides of opinion and suggestion that come from the two men
with him. And neither ecclesiastical relationships nor bureaucratic submission nor personal piety can change the patent facts
of character differences. They are written by nature across the
countenances of all three. Pacelli and Montini are the same,
with a certain individual difference. Roncalli is quite different.

But he has a certain acquired sameness with the other two. Physically and culturally, Pacelli and Montini conform to a classical Italian papal type. Both have slender frames, delicate skins, poor eyesight, graceful hands, and a studied gait. Both eat sparingly, read voraciously, work late into the night, and have a natural grace which adapts itself readily to the papal robes as natural clothing and which seems to be made for protocol reception. Both are highly sensitive. Both are victims of insomnia from their earliest years. Both suffer from bad health all their lives.

There are certain physiognomic differences. Pacelli has the straight Roman nose humped slightly in the center of the bridge. Montini has the heavy, slightly aquiline nose of the Lombard conquerors. Pacelli's brown eyes, set narrowly behind his nose, belong to a southern Italianate strain. Montini has the fair eyes of the northern peoples. Pacelli's mouth is small, symmetrical, full-lipped, set in noble, imperial resolve. Montini's mouth is a thin-lipped swath clenched in resistant determination. In spite of these differences, the fundamental sameness subsists. Pacelli is a classical Renaissance ruler in the mode of El Greco but seen through twentieth-century eyes. Montini is the classical Renaissance city diplomat stalking out of Tintoretto's city-state.

John sleeps healthfully, eats gargantuously, retires early, wearily and thankfully, rises with natural repugnance and difficulty, wears his ceremonial robes as if he were doing precisely that—acting out faithfully an artificially created part—and maintains all his life a healthy animal reaction which can be sanctified by a good intention but not mitigated by the phrases of piety. "Eleven years of seminary food would blunt the taste buds of the Archangel Michael," he once said plaintively and sympathetically to a group of seminarists. His face is, in a sense, the face of Everyman. It could be that of a Munich beer leader, a County Cork plowman, a Greek sea captain, a North Country English farmer, a Ukrainian peasant, a French winegrower, or a Sicilian workman. When later it appeared in newspapers or on television, it was not alien to European or American or Asian. For the accepted traits of any human being are there in enormous proportions: big eyes, large ears, a big mouth, an unmistakable nose, full neck. Physiognomically, he could be anybody from almost any race. Years of ecclesiastical life and diplomatic activity endowed him with those useful exterior habits that make for smooth relations with his opposite number. He was, after all, Italian like Pacelli and Montini.

A correspondingly deep cleavage in character sets the two

other men apart from Roncalli. Their physical lineaments convey totally different messages to an onlooker. Pacelli's face is a carefully etched monochromed marble rectangle placed on a delicate frame, which, from shoulders to feet, gives the impression of a subtly fashioned shell housing a transcendent spirit. The Spirit. Montini's face is a multi-angle oval weight of tempered steel balanced slightly awry on a body which seems barely capable of supporting the overborne intellect. The Intellect. Roncalli's face is a shadowless human bronze set solidly on a massive torso, a wide girth of hip and thigh, and four-square legs. The Man.

When Pacelli had a rather disagreeable interview with Joachim von Ribbentrop, Hitler's Foreign Minister, on the eve of World War II, he reported to Cardinal Maglione afterwards that "our spirits met, although our words clashed. I pray that God will open his eyes." Maglione's quick-witted Neapolitan retort: "Let's hope God closes them soon." Pacelli saw what he wanted to see. When Montini was forced by protocol to sit between the German and British ambassadors at a ceremonial Vatican banquet during the course of the war (otherwise, the representatives of the two warring nations would have been side by side), he chose to address neither of them or pay any attention to their wants during the meal, thus emphasizing his official neutrality. "How could he bear it?" asked one monsignore who saw this display of strategy and self-control. "Montini?" answered his companion. "He is like St. Joan of Arc, he has his voices." Montini hears always the voices of history. When Roncalli was asked once in Paris whether he was disturbed by the décolletage of the ladies present at diplomatic functions, he answered: "Not at all, I assure you. And you don't have to worry about the imaginations of the other diplomats present—they are too busy watching my reactions to get too preoccupied with these manifestations of fashion and beauty." Roncalli always perceived the human element. The Spirit, the Intellect, and the Man.

There could never be any doubt about the spiritual motives which animated Pius XII. Whether he was engrossed with a delicate diplomatic problem or closeted with a visiting ruler or addressing a group of Italian Vespa riders or lecturing an international congress of gynecologists, Pacelli not only sprinkled his discourse with quotations from the choral odes of Sophocles, the Easter Poem of Sedulius, and the risorgimento writers—he breathed the spiritual and the supernal. When he stood with outspread hands to give the papal blessing *urbi et orbi* to the thousands crowded into St. Peter's Square, man felt that the thin white-clad figure was surrounded by a mystic aura, that somehow the gates of heaven were open here, and that on a new Jacob's ladder the Angels of the Almighty descended and ascended, bringing man's pleas to God and God's graces to men. One had to overcome the impressive exterior façade, the practical reserve due to physical delicacy, the velvet Italian with its inherent authoritarianism due to the self-conscious *Romanità* and imperial-mindedness of its user, the constant dwelling on the plane of utterly self-justifying generality due to its lack of any specificity. Only then could one perceive the structured spirit of a bygone world from which the soul of Pacelli had come.

It was afflicted with a congenital myopia condemnable on no specific issue (because it did not join with any specific issue). It was as noble and as outworn as the intransigency of the last rulers of Byzantium, who died nobly on the walls of Constantinople in 1453 for a system which was already dead. Central to the Pacellist conception of the world was Rome, the Roman version of Christianity, the awesome authority of a Sacristy built over the bones of a Galilean who had perished hung upside down on a Roman cross on the Appian Way, and the waiting wisdom of a Chancellery that preserved in its dust-free archives parchment-clear memories: Constantine in the fourth century, Attila the Hun in the fifth century, Islam hammering at the doors of Europe at Tours in the eighth century, the Spanish in 1527, the Piedmontese in 1870, the Nazis in 1942.

Polarity was essential to Pacelli: the inner, divinely consecrated authority of the City of God, and the outer besieging force of the "world," of "evil," of "antichrist." This polarity spelled intransigency and unremitting rejection of all parleying, all dialogue, for dialogue meant a moratorium with the forces of evil. Parleying meant compromise with the truth. Cardinal Stepinac, who remained in Yugoslavia and died in a Titoist prison, and Cardinal Mindszenty, who ended up as refugee in the United States Legation of Budapest—these were the heroes for Pacelli. Pacelli had sharp memories of Cardinal Innitzer and his deathly compromise with Hitler at the time of the Austrian *Anschluss*.

Pacelli was, thus, the last embodiment of the ancient City of God. In him was found that practical combine of traditional Roman imperialism and Augustinian intransigency enunciated by Pope Damasus and shouted triumphantly in the *Song of Roland: "Chrétiens ont raison, païens ont tort."* Pacelli was a Pius IX who had succeeded. His coffin was not bespattered with mud

by the Romans when he died; his name was affixed to a Roman
square as the Liberator of the City. Between his exercise of spiritual primacy and Vatican power-politics there was absolutely no
distinction—in his own mind.

Europe was still the center of the world. Christianity was still
the ideology of Europe. Rome was the center of Christianity. The
fine network of nationalities and local patriotisms had to be re-
established. The pillars of its strength, France, Spain, Germany,
and Italy, had to be reinstated. The head of Europe's political,
military, and commercial vigor, Germany, had to be reinte-
grated. Outside stood the threatening presence of Russian Bolshevism. Inside was the creeping evil of secularism, of atheism.
Outside stood the various "splinter" forms of Christianity: inside
there flowed the multiple evils of religious lapse, theological
heresy, philosophical errors, sociological diseases. Pacelli's
world, therefore, was the world of the two Static Circles of which
one had to disappear, because it was the flesh, and one had to
persevere until the end of time, because it was the spirit. In that
world of the spirit where power prevailed, there was a humanism, an ethic, and a religion peculiar to it. Together, the three
covered and included the entire dimension of human existence.
They and they only gave an understanding of what man was, as
an individual and as a member of society. The human dimension, as Pacelli conceived it, lay in the tension between the two
Static Circles. To understand this conception is to understand
Pacelli's failure at midcentury, Roncalli's problem once he became pope, and Montini's helplessness in the twilight of his
reign.

Roncalli, however, had none of the traits which made Pacelli.
No lineal spiritual descendant of Leo the Great; no ecclesiastical
protégé of the Roman aristocracy; no political *arrivista* backed
up by family finances or local politics. He was the *uomo nuovo*.
He possessed to a supreme degree the formula for success typical of such a character: enter a situation, study its innards, isolate and capture the key to its substance; then turn the key as
hard as can be done. Wherever he worked, he brought the look of
the peasant farmer tempered by continual dependence on the
vagaries of wind, of rain, of sun, of soil, buoyed with the confidence that this was God's world and not a Manichaean kingdom
divided irrevocably between Good and Evil. He was calmed with
the realism which acknowledges facts of life however brutal they
be, and which has learned to sow the seeds of later harvests in

unpromising grounds. A proverb of his native countryside ran, "Where weeds can grow, wheat can flourish."

This innate realism, when focused on the world of his day, refused all artificial divisions in terms of once fiercely propagated ideologies. It could discern in the welter of changing seasons in men's humor, in the gushing torrents of new fashions, in the slow dissolution of sacrosanct structures, the outline of an emerging order of things in which essential human values would be preserved and in which the Gospel of Love would be of supreme importance. Roncalli's world was the Unique Circle of Man. He began with an initial, all-embracing diameter of patient understanding and confidence that everything within that diameter, being human, was neither alien to his Gospel nor ultimately repugnant to its message. Only the Old Order had changed. More accurately, it had perished, throttled by historical events. The New Order was not to be penetrated as if it were an alien and separated body lodged beside the Old. It was a new dimension in human affairs. Not a genetic mutation; not a creeping sickness or a mortal illness in men's minds and lives; not an incurable disease corroding human society. Another understanding of man had arisen among men. It was alien to and irreconcilable with the Pacellist, the traditional one. It was vehicled by man's fresh structuring of his world. It evacuated all the ancient concepts of any practical value and appeal for man. Working with Bea during the four years following my conversation with him, I was to get to know him and, through him, Roncalli as Pope John XXIII.

If Pacelli was the last authentic papal representative of a tradition no longer valid, and Roncalli was the initiator of a new era separated by a gulf of unknowing from the world of Pacelli, Montini was a soul hovering over the gulf. "He will surely be pope some day," was Bea's opinion, "but much must happen before that, or he will be the Pope of Agony." These are the three men, Popes all, who mark the decline and fall of Roman Catholicism as a religious organization. One man, Augustin Bea, moved through the lives of all three. He was to be the Cardinal.

"There was no real exchange of views on that day between the three men," Bea remarked as he finished recounting the elements of that May meeting just four years previously. "But the future Holy Father [Roncalli] was like a man who could not take his eyes off a sight neither of the other two could see. He repeated several times that 'events have overtaken all of us.'"

2

The Cardinal

The event took place in 1943 at five o'clock in the evening. A Sardinian saying goes like this: Men sip the wine of life in the light of the morning, they parley with destiny in noonday heat, they grimace at death in the darkness of the night, but they are trapped by their fate in the long shadows of the evening. So it was on this evening.

The place: St. Peter's Square, sloping gently up Vatican Hill to the Dome of the Basilica which Buonarrotti designed as a hooded symbol signifying for all generations man's permanent possession of Absolute Truth. The day: October 23, 1943, when guarded convoys of army trucks rumbled through the streets on both sides of the Tiber, fulfilling errands designed in Berlin. The reigning Pope: Eugenio Pacelli, sixty-six years of age, now self-named Pius because he wished to work for world peace, at this moment praying in his private chapel.

The masters of the city: Germany's Wehrmacht, gripping with military armor all of Italy and all but one of Rome's seven hills and maintaining a round-the-clock vigil on the seventh, the Vatican Hill. No refugee from the writ of the Third Reich must seek sanctuary within, nor must any of the wanted persons inside Vatican territory emerge with impunity.

Only two sounds broke the silence: the noise of sporadic traffic beyond the white line dividing Vatican City from Greater Rome, and the soothing murmur of the waters that sprayed up to two shining peaks from the twin fountains on either side of the obelisk in the center of the Square and fell flashing, splashing,

18

down on the wide stone basins. The waters sang ceaselessly to the Swiss Guards standing in the shadow of Bernini's colonnades, and it whispered up as far as the windows of the Secretariat of State and the papal apartments on the right.

Standing motionless below and just outside the white dividing line were three hunched, bulky figures: three German army trucks, their forms clothed in menace that ruined the tranquillity, in threat that marred the godliness, in silence that shattered the evening peace, in earthiness that offended the air of eternity which hung over the Square. The scene resembled a William Blake etching of demonic presence, of malignity abroad in daylight. It was evening and the shadows were long.

On the third floor of the papal apartments, a black-cassocked priest, Father Bea, S.J., left the private study of the Pope and directed his steps to the elevator. A guard stopped him and motioned silently to the window. He glanced out, his eyes following the pointing finger. He saw the helmeted soldiers in well-known field-gray with rifles at the ready, the bonnets of the trucks pointing away from the Square and toward the east, the interior of each truck visibly packed with humanity, with men and women, some with kerchiefs around their heads and some with infants in their arms, children of differing ages, all gazing out of the inner darkness in complete silence at the Basilica now a somber red outline against the dying rays of the sun setting behind it in the west.

"*Caspita! Padre,*" said the guard familiarly, "*è una cosa matta!*" He quickly explained the situation. The trucks were part of a task force rounding up some of the eight thousand Roman Jews who were destined for the crematoria of Auschwitz. The Final Solution. As final as the solution reached by the Crusaders massacring every Jew—man, woman, and child—across Europe, on their way to Palestine to defend Christ's Burial Place. The same solution implemented by most Christian rulers and ecclesiastics and most Christian people since the time of Pope Damasus in the fourth century. The deicide, the accursed people . . . Today Bea is helpless. Nothing he can do can save the Jews of Rome. Bea could not foresee it at this moment, but twenty-one years later another event will take place at eleven minutes past noonday. Men parley with destiny in the noonday heat. So it will be at this noonday, and so it would be for two more noons, a parley with a destiny which history was reserving for this moment.

The place: St. Peter's Basilica, lit by yellow rays of sun and furrowed by rows of raised seats along the full length of the long nave, peopled with the prelates of the Second Vatican Ecumenical Council listening, listening. The day: September 25, 1964, the eighty-eighth General Assembly of the Council and the tenth day of its third session. The presiding cardinal of the day: the heavy-lidded Leo Cardinal Suenens from Belgium, Flemish by family, French by education, with Gallic logic on his tongue and Germanic fire on his brain. The reigning pope: Giovanni Battista Montini, sixty-seven years of age, now self-named Paul after the Jew from Tarsus, at this moment watching the proceedings on closed-circuit television from the private study where once Pacelli had sat and suffered. The speaker: Augustin Cardinal Bea, German in nationality, now in his eighty-third year, Jesuit, scholar, confessor of Pius XII, former confidant and adviser of John XXIII, acknowledged leader of the progressive thinkers in the Council. The Cardinal had exactly nineteen minutes for his speech. The subject: the proposed Council declaration on the Jews. Formal discussion was scheduled for Monday and Tuesday of the following week. But the Cardinal had to carry the head of St. Andrew the Apostle back to Greece on Saturday, and he could not be present at the two scheduled sessions. Rome had possessed this mummified head for over eight hundred years. To give it back now would certainly impress Greeks with the Vatican's sincere desire to "get together" and to grant "recognition" to the Greek Orthodox Church. Roncalli has been dead some fourteen months. Now in its third session, the Ecumenical Council has been transformed into another Church council.

Bea's face stood out against the blood-red cardinalitial robes like an oval sheet of ancient parchment unrolled delicately and held up to a reddened sunset for decipherment of its mystery, its discretion, its reserve. His Latin syllables rolled out with the resonance of ancient solid things, like a voice echoing across measureless distances of time from forgotten ages and holding a timeless message. One Italian paper had effusively spoken of his "autumnal wisdom," and the description fitted: he was the master of aging granaries in which the mellowed grains of research and reflection and mature conclusion had been stored with care and deliberation.

"The Council cannot possibly avoid taking a stand on this issue . . . Over six million Jews were killed during the last war . . . There is no doubt that much anti-Semitism has found a basis in certain texts of the New Testament . . . Public opinion will judge us favorably or unfavorably according as we act in this matter . . . Many have felt that this declaration is out of place . . . But there is a close connection between all Christians and the Chosen People . . ."

Bea had stood here on November 19, 1963, and spoken about a Council declaration on the Jews. He would also stand here on September 21, 1965, and speak again on the Council declaration concerning the Jews. It was left to friend and enemy to judge his motives and to decide what were the issues. But there were only a handful of people who knew and realized that Bea had started downhill to the grave of his ambitions. He, like every part of the Council, had been reduced in stature and dynamism. On this day he is fighting for the existence of what appears to be a pet project: a Church declaration telling all and sundry that the Jews are not guilty of the death of Jesus. The apogee of Bea's endeavor was past. Between now and his death in 1968, there was reserved for him a path of petty efforts, ecclesiastical entanglements, humiliating commands from Pope Paul, annoying restrictions from his enemies, a growing disdain in him for the caballing and the chambering concerning his person and his role. All this was in the hidden future.

Now, 1943, Father Bea gazed and thought.

The drivers of the trucks were Bavarians on their first stint in Rome, and they had never prayed in the central church of Christendom. Their Protestant comrades were guarding the condemned while they went and kissed the bronze toe of St. Peter's statue and prayed for their individual families and for Germany, the Fatherland, over the tombs of the Blessed Apostles, Peter and Paul.

It was also the Fatherland of the priest. He had been born Augustin Bea in Riedböhringen (600 inhabitants), South Baden, Germany, on May 28, 1881, almost seven months before Angelo Roncalli (November 25 of the same year). Bea spent the first forty-three years of his life in Germany. Physically: of medium height, mesocephalic, blond, blue-eyed; with rounded cheekbones, thin upper lip, full and overhanging underlip, jutting chin, straight and solid nose, hunched shoulders, deft spatular hands. Mentally: clear, orderly, methodical; a bear for hard work (at his death in 1968, he will have 260 publications to his name); tenacious in memory, at ease in six languages besides German; a stickler for plans and their execution; no light in his heart but a steady glowing fire on his brain burning brightly to the end. He was German, of the Germans.

"*Sono già morti, poveretti*" (They are dead already, poor

people). The guard's remark recalled Bea's attention. Then, with typical well-intentioned Italian irreverence, the guard added: "*Anche per loro è morto Gesù Cristo, padre?*" (Jesus Christ died for them also, Father?). The remark hung for a split second in the air like an embodied question mark. It was a sudden mystery of interrogation. Bea initially refused it recognition because even to recognize it would transform it into a wounding shaft. "*Anche per loro è morto Gesù Cristo, padre?*" Then its force became clear. And it was an arrow.

It stood angularly against his breast. Whichever way he moved, it wounded him over and over again. Pius XII had decided not to speak out against this Final Solution of Hitler's. The decision had been the result of much discussion, pockmarked with little personal agonies and gnawing scruples. He had seen Pius, day after day during one period of three weeks, with doubt and indecision and pain running across his face in mad crisscross lines like malicious field mice scurrying destructively over the stubble of an already harvested wheatfield.

Poveretti? Bea had started off as one. At least in two senses. Bone-poor parents: Karl, his father, the village carpenter; Maria, his mother, helped to till their small plot of land. No cultural or intellectual background. But the young boy was driven by a mind full of curiosity. The villagers paid for his primary schooling. The parish priest taught him a little Latin. All this only whetted his appetite. At the age of seventeen, he entered the Freiburg school of theology with an official declaration, or certificate, of poverty. This was 1900. In 1902, he joins the Jesuits. He follows the Jesuit intellectual and moral training: philosophy at Maastricht in Holland (1904–7); teaching Greek and Latin at Innsbruck, Austria (1907–10); theology at Falkenburg, Germany (1910–12). Ordained in 1912, he spends some months in Rome studying Bible. The next twelve years he spends teaching and directing other Jesuits. In 1924, he is called to Rome as head of a house of international studies and professor of Bible theology. At this time Bea was known to be not merely a "safe theologian" in thought, word, and teaching. He was also reckoned to be a traditionalist, a sincere member of the Establishment such as it was. He was an exemplary Jesuit. He conformed. A professional. He knew the pitfalls and he avoided them.

Bea focused his eyes on the field-gray uniforms of the waiting guards. Fragments of phrases rang in his memory, phrases he heard in those days from Vatican officials. "Certain tendencies

of National Socialism are disturbing, but we must strive for
some sort of *modus vivendi* with it . . . A new world order is in
the making . . . We have to think of the Catholic population
living in occupied countries; reprisals could be taken against
them . . . To speak out now on this subject would draw all
their ire on the rest of the Jews and even on Our Person, thus
stopping whatever We are now doing for peace . . ."

His own explanations and advice to Pius had been measured
according to the latter's receptivity and the horrible options open
to him. "Yes, Holy Father, there are parts of the New Testament
which justify a negative attitude on the part of the Church, but
these cannot be regarded as actual genuine teachings of the
Bible . . . There is no indication of a collective guilt of Jews in
the Gospel . . . The phrase 'His blood be on us and on our children'—probably not an actual phrase used by the populace;
most of them did not know of Christ's existence . . . The world
will never forget or forgive our silence, Holy Father . . . Holiness, the final decision is for Your Holiness . . ."

Bea was already an adviser of Pope Pius XII. In 1930 he had
been made Rector of the Pontifical Biblical Institute in Rome,
thus starting another phase of his career. It was to last almost
thirty years (1930–59). Many scholarly and learned men are
called to Rome by the Roman authorities. Most spend their lives
extending and exercising their scholarship and their learning,
without ever touching the levers of power. Power, as it were,
decrees their lives and the mode of their dying. They never walk
with power. But it was not thus with Augustin Bea, and this for
apparently fortuitous reasons.

First, rectorship of the Pontifical Institute was a prestigious
thing. The Institute was unique. Its exclusive function was to
train future Catholic professors of Bible. As such, it was a sensitive post. On the one hand, it was watched jealously and scrupu-
lously scrutinized by the guardians of doctrinal purity who
resided in the Holy Office and in the other powerful Vatican ministries. Many a Vatican monsignore dreamed of being rector in
the Institute, if the Jesuits could be expelled. On the other hand,
it had a powerful voice. Technically speaking, it was for the pope
the last word in Bible theology. Orthodox Catholic teaching depended on the Institute as on its lifeline, because the Bible was a
chief source of knowledge about the origins and meaning of
Christianity. The most formidable attack against Christianity's
truth had come from scientists—archaeologists, linguists, Semitic scholars, Bible theologians, who had studied the Bible in

the light of the ancient Near East. The Institute was supposed to provide answers to their objections, counter-offensives for their attacks, and new elaborations of Catholic Bible doctrine on the basis of knowledge of the ancient world.

The post of rector, consequently, was a formidable fulcrum of power within the Roman machinery of government and its propagation of belief. Bea had an orthodoxy that could not be questioned and a theological reputation that could not be gainsaid. He was respected in an argument. He was feared because of his ultra-orthodox stance. Over and above this, he was capable of biting sarcasm, a ferocious taste and feel for doing his homework, cold and ruthless dissection of opposing points of view— all this cast over with a subtle and, for onlookers, an almost troubling lack of emphasis or violence in his manner. They felt that he could afford to be so gentle, unobtrusive, self-confident, so compassionate without condescension, and so submissive without subservience, precisely because of some irresistible power in which he partook.

With all this, Bea had one other advantage: his close association with Pacelli. Pacelli knew him from Germany. In Rome, he rapidly joined the group of German Jesuits on whom Pacelli relied for advice and counsel. He became Pacelli's confessor in 1945 and was his confessor until Pacelli's death in 1958. It was small wonder that he became a consultant in the all-powerful Holy Office in 1949. Pacelli was conducting war on a double front at that moment: against the crippling behavior of his own Vatican officials, and against the new ideas that were being broadcast by theologians from France, Holland, Belgium, and Germany. Against the former he needed Bea's loyalty. Against the latter he needed Bea's orthodoxy. Bea spared no one, made many enemies, retained few friends, and walked serenely on his way.

What will always be inexplicable, except on the basis of his character, was the position of power he carved out from the hard, resistant granite of the Vatican monolith. Bea naturally inspired a sense of surety, of rock-bound firmness. He seemed to be denuded of any self-seeking, to be clean of any tarnish, and to be childlike in his piety. He led a regular life, rose early, went to bed early and at the same hour for years, had a marvelous sense of humor, a devastating realism, a hearty laugh, could be brilliantly witty after a Germanic fashion. Once, when some kilt-wearing broad-shouldered members of an Irish pipers band strode in to an audience with Papa Pacelli, Bea whispered to a neighbor: "Do you think that they can talk?"

Not only did Bea always know where power lay, he seemed to be always associated with it. Weakness he understood and aided. Opposition he undermined ruthlessly. Ambition in others he perceived and destroyed as effectively as he could. He could not stand stupidity, did not brook ignorance, feared cunning like the pest, and turned away in disgust from bad taste. He was endowed, finally, with an infinitely delicate sense of timing. He could wait and wait unendingly and exhaustively, wait for the right time in the right place with the right people. He could absorb snubs, humiliations, defeats, plots and counterplots, frustrations, until the time for action arrived. He only tried the impossible once; but that he did because by then he had learned compassion and love and the abandonment of self-security which springs from them. In 1943 his character was in minor key. He was waiting. Besides, he knew Pacelli could not be changed.

The Jewish question had come up in discussion between him and Pacelli before this. Pacelli's attitude to all non-Roman Christians and to all non-Christians had been mooted several times between Pacelli and Bea, between Bea and Vatican officials, between Bea and his students. He could remember the nagging questions put to him (rather aggressively, he had thought at the time) by a student in class: "Would it not be in accord with Holy Scripture to regard persecution of Jews as divine punishment for their sin of rejection? Why otherwise have they always been the object of Christian ire? Is not their relationship to Christian revelation one of recalcitrant rebels, who insist on clinging to a belief and a worship declared obsolete by the Incarnation of Our Lord Jesus?" The student was Spanish, probably from the north —to judge by the accent—and vibrant with the triumphalism of Catholic hispanidad.

Bea had no ready black-and-white answers to such blunt and partisan questions. Many a time, for instance, as Pacelli's confessor, he was strongly inclined to use his awesome power as the man before whom the Pope knelt for absolution, on whose word the Pope depended for his periodic draught of inner peace in conscience. To say: "Holiness, the Church is parched." Or: "Holiness, a deep chasm has opened between Your Holiness and the people." Or: "Holiness, Your Holiness was cruel, or blind, or hasty, or illusioned, or unwise, or ignorant." Bea's will inclined

him so. But his intellect whispered secretly: "No. He will not
accept, because he does not understand. He will not understand,
because his world is a dead world. Wait." Pacelli and Pacellism,
in fact, were a perfect trap for the intellectual that Bea su-
premely was.

He had the weakness of the genuine intellectual: eternal balancing of evidence for and against, and perpetual seeking of
compromise. It was the final undoing of Bea after John's death.
Pacelli and Pacellism were inspired with regnancy, sustained by
the huzzahs and the *evvivas* of the adoring crowds, nourished
themselves on flowery verbality. It provided a safe refuge for the
intellectual. It announced surety. It guaranteed ultimate safety.
Bea had traveled through Russia, Siberia, Korea, Japan, Indone-
sia, India, and the Middle East, during the twenties. Nothing
really registered in him. He was mind-proof and soul-guarded.
He was cradled and contented with the Princedom of Power.

Only his contact with John XXIII provided him for a short
while with the wisdom he had never known and the warmth his
heart had never lived. Roncalli had known Bea before becoming
pope. In March 1959, Bea met John again during an audience
given for the entire staff of the Holy Office. Some time later,
John sent for Bea. The occasion was innocuous. Some matters in
the private papers of Pacelli concerned Bea personally. Others
he alone could explain adequately to the new pope. It was the
beginning of a close association. For many it has always remained an enigma how Roncalli as he was reckoned to be—
simple, pietistic, intuitive, a Vatican official, the bureaucrat's
man—could form such a close bond of trust, friendship, and
understanding with Augustin Bea, the scholar, the sharp intellect, the Jesuit, Pacelli's man.

Bea found that John had one concern: the deteriorating condition both of Roman Catholicism and of Christianity in the
world of the twentieth century. John found in Bea one asset:
stark realism. There was in Bea no trace of partisan views concerning Pacelli, Pacellist views, Pacelli's reign, or the Roman
Church as Pacelli had left it. Did Father Bea wish to receive the
cardinal's hat which Pacelli had wanted him to have? Not really.
Not as a farewell gift. Not as a guarantee of quiet retirement in
ripe old age. What did His Holiness think of Pacelli's onetime
intention—or rather velleity—to recall the unfinished Vatican
Council? (It had started in 1869 and been broken off *sine die* in
1870 at the outbreak of the Franco-Prussian War.) John answered pointedly but with a quip: "We are infallible enough."

That First Vatican Council had declared the Pope of Rome to be infallible. The point was, another Church council of that kind or of the traditional kind would be merely a fruitless exercise, a free and feckless somersault into the thin air of irrealism. Who needed it? Besides, John added, we have not many years to live. There is too much to do in a short time.

The conversation was prolonged. There were further conversations and consultations between the two men. Bea quickly acquired the conviction and the resolve of Roncalli. His horizons became illuminated and enlarged as he began to realize what Roncalli had meant when he stated blandly that it was time for him "to launch out into the deep." The new pope had no intention of staying within the tranquil waters of a traditional ecumenical council of the Roman Catholic Church. He had another intent and a far greater scope to his thought.

With characteristic enthusiasm and methodic work, Bea set about preparing himself. He needed information about the Protestant Churches and Protestant leaders, about the Greek and Russian Orthodox Churches and their Patriarchs, about Israel and Jews and Judaism, about the attitudes of Arab states to any change in the Vatican's viewpoint concerning Jews. He needed a team of his own who could work under his direction. They should have official status in the Vatican. A year later, his Secretariat for the Promotion of Christian Unity was born. By then he had gathered around him other associates, one of whom was myself. There came to his aid for this organization of men, information, and events the natural genius he possessed for human relations and every ounce of experience he had acquired in the various administrative posts he had held during his earlier years. He relied, for the filling out of his ideas and the implementation of his plans, both on an organized and formally constituted team and on a varying number of informal associates to whom he delegated various tasks, confided particular elaboration of plans. To belong to either was to experience the quiet and purposeful way in which he initiated new associates gradually and easefully, but still without ever making molehills out of mountains. But Bea worked thus in watertight compartments, expecting absolute discretion and ultimate self-effacement, never commingling projects or personalities, always maintaining personal lines of communication, keeping larger counsels and individual contributions for his own. Officially, for instance, and as far as the Vatican officialdom and the greater public could know, he saw Roncalli as frequently and infrequently as any other curial cardinal. Unofficial interviews and conversations were off the record, had their own frequency dictated by events, and were quite another thing.

Bea assessed someone from a certain distance, made up his own mind, and proceeded to call on his capabilities bit by bit, drawing him into a close association based on mutual esteem and loyalty to a common cause, and colored by Bea's own brand of enthusiasm, which always had a boyish element. In the beginning, my training in Near East studies interested Bea. These were particularly oriented to the historical period between the emergence of the last book of the Jewish Bible and the first books of the Christian Gospel (called by scholars the inter-Testamentary period). The period fascinated Bea: it was the immediate womb of Christianity, and it bore directly on Bea's personal interest in the relations between Christians and Jews. Bea needed ideas, information, fresh approaches, explanations couched in language understood by non-Catholics and non-Christians, and new assessments of perennial situations, for conversations with Jewish representatives and the mollification of Arab resentments.

But the interest of Bea and Roncalli in this question was part of the larger mosaic; it was part of Roncalli's planned Event with its all-embracing intent; both the Jewish question and Bea's Secretariat filled only one small section of that mosaic. It was in discussing this larger intent and implementing some of its imperatives that I understood Roncalli and Bea as described in this book. There were conversations with participants and delegates at the Council in Rome, information gathering and assessment, the planning of particular events, the leavening of minds, the monitoring of how Council spirits were moving, and the day-to-day caretaking action in ongoing projects. At certain rare moments, Bea felt the need to unburden himself, outside the ambit of his official role and away from official associates, to some others (of whom I was one), in order to deliver his soul of his frustrations, to send his deep vulnerabilities wailing along the margins of nonentity, and to repair what damage had been done by the mockeries, the hurts, and the failures of life. Like many of his fellow Jesuits and many who underwent for many years a strict discipline in self-expression, Bea could not confide such states to paper, much less allow them free commerce in his daily working system.

Working with Bea then and later, I was constantly aware of

something in him which had never aged or withered. He was capable of fresh appraisals. He never lost the inquisitive mind. He was never dismayed. He enunciated the greatest difficulties with an ease and a calm which betokened unshakable confidence. Above all, he could neglect the unessential and put his finger unerringly on the vital element in a given situation. One series of inquiries which I conducted for him on Constantinople in 1960 indicated a strong grass-roots opposition among the clerics surrounding the Patriarch Athenagoras and a deep suspicion in the minds of Protestants as to Vatican intentions in regard to the Eastern Orthodox Churches. "Only the Patriarch matters in the long run," was Bea's commentary after he had listened to the report. "He is genuinely behind the Holy Father's effort because he understands, and he is a supreme politician."

From 1960 onwards, Bea launched into a febrile activity of traveling, lecturing, correspondence, and organization. By the autumn of 1963, when John had been buried and Montini reigned as Paul VI, the Council would become, indeed, just another council. Bea still worked tirelessly, but the original project had failed. Tied up in Council machineries, foiled by the grinding wheels of bureaucracy, frustrated by the arrival and dominance of little men with little ideas, forced to publish views with which he disagreed, inevitably brokenhearted by the corruption which power again wrought, caught in the crossfire between the eternal duo of Vatican existence—theology and politics—Bea lasted until late in 1968.

Whatever consolation he experienced toward the end of his days came from within, from some inner source of tranquillity, for exteriorly his efforts were spent. Perhaps one occasion was granted him when something of the compassion and love of Roncalli's personality hovered over his head and invaded his heart. It was in St. Peter's Basilica, October 1967. The Patriarch of Constantinople, Athenagoras, stood with Pope Paul VI on a platform. The eighty-six-year-old Bea, infirm, limping, breathing with difficulty, climbed the steps and stood with them. Paul put one hand on Bea's shoulder and the other on the Patriarch's shoulder. There was a split second of silence. Bea's face was transfixed as he looked at Athenagoras. Then the audience started to applaud and the magic of the instant fled. Bea was dead within a year. He now lies buried beside his parents in the village of Riedböhringen. His place on the world stage seems, at this distance, to have been nothing more than the flitting circle of a momentary spotlight: two years of brilliance (1961–63), and then five years of holding action, of diminishing afterglow, and of enveloping shadows.

Three figures in gray came out of the Basilica, fastened their helmets, strolled down the steps, and proceeded leisurely to the waiting trucks. German boys, as once he had been. He had seen them, had been one of them, in Coblenz. It was 1917, and he was doing his military service during World War I. Something hurt inside Bea; he was stubbing his toe against an ancient dream. The waiting guards sprang into the trucks. A sharp command sounded across the Square, hitting on the colonnades like tempered steel. The engines started into life, and the trucks filed away down the Via della Conciliazione. A few moments later they had crossed the Victor Emmanuel Bridge and silence reigned. With millions of others, their human cargo would soon be grimacing at death in the darkness of the long night which enveloped Hitler's Europe. The fountains still spouted their gentle waters up into the air and down, sparkling onto the wide, moss-green basins.

3

The Human Dimension

Many people would feel that a book on one pope, let alone on three popes and a cardinal, is or should be primarily religious in character or at least in purpose. At least, they presume, it was written primarily to convey opinions on, or information concerning, religion or religious matters, to condemn or to praise some religious aspect of human things. None of these forms the purposes of the present book. It concerns man in the last third of the twentieth century, as seen through the eyes of one man, Angelo Roncalli.

Generally accepted interpretations of this man, and the events which surround his pontificate, run along well-known lines. He is a Friar Tuck pope bumbling along indomitably with peasant mirth, girth, fellowship, and unwittingly opening up all men's hearts. He is the kindly pope talking with the atheist artist and evoking tears. He is the priest-pope primarily concerned with a pastoral role: babies, women's sodalities, aging priests, and the guardian angels. Alternately, he is presented as an almost Machiavellian character hiding a deeply conniving mind behind an impenetrable wall of adipose tissue. It was all a grand plan, a carefully hatched plot right from his peasant home in Bergamo to the papal throne. There are, also, numerous attempts to fit John into the traditional image of the Supreme Pontiff. These stress the triumphalism, the regalia, the curial surroundings, the glorifications of *L'Ossevatore Romano,* and the plaudits of papal audiences.

The confusion arose and still arises in this matter of John's

31

character for a complex reason. It was that he thought and
therefore acted on a geopolitical plane. So did Pacelli, his prede-
cessor. So does Paul VI, his successor. So did Pacelli's great ancestor, the first Prince of Power, Leo the Great in the fifth century. But John did not act on that plane as they had. He was out
of traditional character. He was the exception to a 1,600-year-old
rule. For the first time in well over a thousand years, a pope did
not act in order to advance papal power. He acted primarily on
behalf of men and in view of their changing dimension.

The human dimension in this context is understood as the
frame of reference or a context of circumstances. Whenever we
speak about a man, we speak about him on the presumption of
such a distinctly human dimension. Many people love dogs, cats,
tortoises, hamsters, pet alligators, fish, birds, horses, and a vari-
ety of other animals. They make pets of them. Sometimes they
prefer these animals to man. But no matter how great and pref-
erential that love, no animal lover and no human being will fail
to distinguish between a man and an animal. And this distin-
guishing goes beyond mere exterior traits. We may call some
man an "animal" in a fit of rage. We may call him a human
animal when speaking clinically. But we acknowledge implicitly
or explicitly the specifically human dimension of this two-legged
animal. That dimension is never just a general and vague
matter. It is always specified. The specifications vary in number,
in intensity, from one age to another, from one group to another,
from one individual to another.

A Montagnard tribesman in Laos and an American doctor living in Idaho have certain vegetable and animal habits in common. In addition, they both speak and think. Their social and
ethical lives bear some resemblance to each other, in rudimen-
tary fundamentals at least. The political frameworks in which
they individually live differ rather totally. Their human dimension is of narrow ambit. On the other hand, throughout the countries of the traditional West, there is a common human dimension which we can recognize more quickly and more easily than
we can define it.

It is a broad band of traits, interlocking and weaving a common web in ways of life, ways of thinking, ways of feeling, ways
of judging people and things, in aspirations and in goals. Whatever major differences there are between the participants, and
they are huge, they seem in their majority to be, ultimately, linguistic, economic, and political. The most expanded form of human aspiration and goal is, admittedly, found in a technologi-

cally prominent country such as the United States; the narrowest, in poor countries such as Portugal and Ireland or in poor regions such as some of the Soviet Socialist Republics, the Appalachian regions of the United States, and in scattered parts of Italy, Spain, and the Soviet satellite countries.

The human dimension in America is broad, but it is not intellectual or pseudo-intellectual. It is not avant-garde, even anachronistically. It cannot really breathe in the village mentality of the Eastern seaboard or the super-ethnic culture of New York in particular. It is concerned only remotely with its thought molds, less with its ego controls, and not at all with the scary search after "one's true self." It rarely if ever suffers psychic anguish over concepts; distrusts both polysyllabic words and "loaded" terms such as "survival," "intellectual freedom," or the "pain of our materialism"; forms opinions mainly from radio and TV; has not set out on a "long trek in the night"; limits its reading to specialist magazines, paperbacks, newspapers; is occasionally titillated by a *Love Story*, a *Valley of the Dolls*, or a *Peyton Place* (which do nothing to color its mind, much less to raise or lower its standards).

The principle of search for life, liberty, and happiness is its main preoccupation; but this has become predominantly thing-oriented and is still mindful of the American dream. The two, dream and thing-orientation, go together peacefully.

The human dimension in America comes nearest to philosophizing at some moments of genuine pathos in Bonanza or Marcus Welby, M.D. Its laughter is raucous at the Johnny Carson Show but cosmic during the Flip Wilson or the Mary Tyler Moore Shows, for then it laughs heartily at itself. Its nearest approach to self-pride and self-criticism comes during the Miss America or the Junior Miss pageants. Its laudation of heroes and heroines takes place at ticker-tape parades, the Rose and Orange Bowl festivals, or at the film awards of Oscar and Emmy. Americans often inter the evil that men do with their bones. The good they did lives after them, in the soapsuds of a commercial or the metal alloy for airplanes.

America rarely ponders its past except when a folk singer like Johnny Cash raises its thoughts, and it does not overly reflect on the present or the future except when confronted with an all-American singer like Anita Bryant or when a passionate peasant like Eric Hoffer performs in front of it. It is big enough to breed, carry for a time, leaven, dissect, isolate, and finally assimilate or expel all sorts of subcultures, political, socio-cultural, and religious. Nothing appears within its broad spectrum that does not slightly ravage it but that it does not finally nail to the solid terra firma of its pragmatism: Rock, Panthers, Young Lords, Fascists, Street People, neo-Buddhism, pseudo-Zen, Old Catholics, New Catholics, clapboard cathedrals with their bishops and priestesses, the contradictions of the Liberal, the intransigence of a Carl McIntire and a Huey P. Newton, and the dreadful and destructive angelism of a Berrigan, a Timothy Leary, a Rennie Davis.

Never in the history of the West has such a large diverse population been so internationalized in its daily and personal thinking as the twentieth-century population of the United States. Vietnam, the Tonkin Gulf, Peking, Formosa, the Middle East, the other side of the moon, South Africa, Biafra, Russia, China, the Antarctic, Zambia, Rome, London are words and places and issues that easily enter conversation and easily supply reasons for happenings in the daily and personal lives of all Americans.

There are genuine upheavals working feverishly through this population and surfacing in city streets, in legislatures, in political parties, in the privacy of family life, and in the thought processes of the individual. These are indications that something radical and profound has changed or is changing in the human dimension of this people as a whole. In fact, America is engaged on a human experiment never before attempted in the history of the West, and in this sense, as said before, Americans are the guinea pigs of history. The object of the experiment is at present the remote hope of all nations in the West and of all others who are influenced by the West and by the United States in particular.

In America, it is safe to say, the human dimension today is centered around a *structuralist* view and treatment of the individual. More and more, the ordinary man in the street is acquiring the viewpoint that he is, as is his neighbor, a synthesis of parts: a bodily organism, a bundle of ego controls, a psychology. He has a personality, that is to say, a synthesis of emotions, thoughts, memories, instincts, experiences, and influences, a sum of various delicate parts, a structure of coded cells and interacting chemical substances. He is a very particular kind of animal; the pleasure areas of his brain must be kept activated so that his animal nervous system may function. His religion, his social institutions, his sex, his human and subhuman traits, his survival, his extinction—all stem from this structure.

This structuralism extends into the societal life of the ordinary man. In that life, he is identifiable and recognizable as a man because of an intricate structure of relations. His relations to governmental organs (Congress, Senate, political parties, for instance); to social life-supportive systems such as social security, labor unions, law-enforcement agencies, insurance, banks, job location, credit ratings. There are additional relations in the order of his convenience and luxury (clubs, vacations, hobbies, etc.).

In the past, we can find parallels to all these relations in the lives of men now dead and gone. But today the specific note of our latter-day structuralism is its self-sufficiency. It is a closed system of relations; the system as a whole is not referable to anything outside it, including religion and morality, which until now have been at the heart of man's concept of himself.

We can define an ordinary man quite adequately for the normal modern mind *solely* within this context of relationships. Such is the accepted human dimension. The John Doe of today is the object of a most complex and dedicated research. Scientists are at work endeavoring to explain and manipulate for his good each part of his physical organism. Others are probing his mind with a view to curing its aberrations and rendering it more efficacious than ever. No part of him, physical or mental, is neglected: his religious aspirations, warring instincts, all that used to be called his virtues and his vices. Nothing in the ambit of man's whole society can check this search for man as structure. The doors have opened in the dark room of his mind. Control by formula, by sacred ritual, by shared myth or individual dream is no longer possible. Western pragmatism and romanticism cannot check it. All the wisdom of the East cannot check it. The major religions are infected with it.

Before this human dimension became a common frame of reference, men were held fast by a great in-winding mystery. There was a total suspension of disbelief because people still had a sense of balance between the harsh reality of life and a very ancient dream inherited from the forests of man's first dawning. Life was to be lived, but the dream was to be pursued. With hope. With defiance of all obstacles. With innocence as long as it lasted. But even when innocence was lost, the spirit was never extinguished. Man was not merely a structure. He was a substance, the substance of a wild hope and a continuing dream. And so there was no theater of the absurd and no culture of despair. Today, with the hope gone, and cleansed of his dream, John Doe is a structure of problematic parts. He has many problems, mechanical ones, on which whole teams of sci-

entists and researchers are working. For the modern challenge is
not the exhilaration of an ancient aspiration or a poetic paradise
beckoning over the distant hill. It is a total explanation of John
J. Doe, of his deepest reactions, all his thought molds, and the
mechanisms of his social and individual behaviorisms.

Two hundred years ago, no one would have dreamed of describing the human dimension of John Doe in such a fashion.
Gee-whiz stories, spicy anecdotes, and stunning statistics were
current fare then, as they are today. But the human dimension
in which these existed was different. The thrust of human society was based on different motives. Even one hundred years ago,
men would have been surprised, just as today it would surprise
millions of men in Asia and Africa and millions of men in Europe to know the nature of the profound change in the human
dimension. Yet we know that somehow, somewhere during this
time, a change took place. It was not the result of any organized
plan, nor did it spring from any theory. It was ushered in by
millions of minor and major decisions formed by individuals
acting in order to cope with the circumstances of their individual
lives. The change is so great that today certainly and inevitably
all men living and all men about to live and to take their places
on this planet earth are destined to enter this particular frame
of human dimension. This is the thrust of man's modern society.

We do not regret that the wild horse was harnessed to a plow
or that one hundred million homes have been built on the land.
Sometimes we regret that the eagle was shot from our skies, or
that we cannot wander as little children in a poetic wilderness.
But this is a passing whim. Stephen Vincent Benét's vision is the
thesis of a squeamish soul. For the wind in our city burns across
the skyscrapers and the asphalt beds where American men and
women live and die. It moves no soil and whips no scurrying
tumbleweed. It raises dust. It shuffles polluted air. There is no
semblance of God in Rockefeller Plaza carved by superstitious
hands to confront the buses, the taxis, and the little Puerto
Rican Santas with pathetic bells at Christmas time. We can read
of prairies pounding with hoofs, and gaze at deserts stretching
lonesomely away to purple-black mountain ridges shawled in the
haze of wild romantic images, from the inside of an air-conditioned trailer or the family station wagon. But: we put down
the book to get another beer from the icebox, and we head
back "home" to the city. There is no voiceless mystery of love or
of anything in megalopolis. We do not emerge from it all as at
dawn from a dark and consoling dream. For we quested ghosts

and their shadows spoke to us. And we return to a kingdom of night where the mechanics of structure represent the fulfillment of all we drive at.

In our better moments, we have a nagging suspicion that our structuralism is not completely achieved. We have flown faster than the sun; our city traffic idles in the clogged streets. We have walked on the face of the moon; from our golden towers we watch little children starve. We have special desolations called ghettos, and rotting, sullen thousands in the Appalachias. Our country is, in part, the country of the damaged, the humiliated, the stunted, the lost. We must take all those stuttering and stammering surrogates of American man, the black, the Chicano, the Indian, the white trash, and lead them out of the avenues of despair. Not until we have uprooted the last night-torn hovel and replaced the last foul and dismal ghetto cellar corner will we lose our shame, will we cease to scorn this ground and this country of which we are simultaneously proud. We will structure, structure, structure . . .

Any society, in the U.S.S.R., in Europe, in Asia, in Africa, which aims ultimately at achieving the material prosperity and the technological state of the United States—and which of them does not?—is going inevitably and unavoidably to develop as American society has developed. The Chileans want TV's, refrigerators, dishwashers, automobiles, beauty salons, birth-control clinics, hospitals, big cities, modern turnpikes, a four-day week, state-subsidized schools and farms, pensions, and the lot. So do the Zambians, the Kenyans, the Tanzanians, the Ceylonese, and all the others. The Soviets want a perfectly organized and surveilled population, and the population wants all the "goodies," as do the French, the Italians, the Germans, the Spaniards, the Irish, the British—as all of them do. Americans are crude, it is said. But this is thought merely because Americans got there first. "Why must you Americans always be first?" was Zhukov's good-natured plaint to Eisenhower. But none of this is possible without the structuralism of the American thing.

4

Roncalli's Decision

In the fifties of this century, there was one salient truth concerning religion in general, Christianity in particular, and, closer to Roncalli, Roman Catholicism. Christianity in whole and in its various parts had not merely become detached from the civilization of the West; it stood outside that civilization. It was alien to it. Worse still, this civilization was still evolving, but no longer under the tutelage of Christianity in any effective way. All other sects of Christianity and the major religions of the world were in a like impasse. Humanly speaking, therefore, there seemed to be no hope for a renewal of religion. Roncalli had a clearly etched picture in his mind of the long association between Christianity and the civilization of the West.

Christianity had entered the Greco-Roman world of the Mediterranean just as the ideal of Man the Citizen was evolving into a reality. The John Doe of the Greco-Roman world, an Aristides in second-century Rome or an Ausonius in fourth-century Bordeaux, would hinge his whole identity in his participation in the commonwealth of Mediterranean man based on the rule of Roman law. On it was built the political unity, the Caesarism of Rome, the cultural character of social life, the religion of men, the economic interdependence of the member states and cities, and the civil equivalence of all Roman citizens, whatever their ethnic background. But this structure derived meaning only from a presumed ground or absolute: the domination of the gods, the example of mythical heroes, and the divinization of all things human by the power of the invisible world.

A quick end to this came with the disintegration of the Empire. Christianity had no substitute, no world outlook. It looked to the "other world." About seven hundred years later, between the twelfth and the seventeenth centuries, Western man again set up a febrile quest. This time it was for Man as Hero. John Doe of fifteenth- to sixteenth-century Florence was on a fresh venture. His world was hierarchized. He sought beauty around him (and power to install the beauty, and money to obtain the power), because all beautiful things formed a paradigm of the absolute beauty to which he was destined. He described himself in terms of three elements: body, soul, and city. One was mortal, lecherous, subject to disease and death. The other was immortal, beset by passions, saved by Jesus, guarded and guided by Holy Mother Church, cleansed by grace, finally admitted to heaven. The third was the forum of his greatness, of his heroic stature.

Again, he identified himself by a structure, but the structure had a meaning from without its own bounds. The invisible and the absolute of the Christian God provided that meaning. For all. For saints, for sinners, for heretics, for popes, for princes, for emperors, for crusaders, for painters, for sculptors, for poets, for farmers, for serfs, for soldiers, for guild members, for courtiers, for countries.

Man as hero never evolved fully. His evolution could only be pursued within an achieved unity. And the overall unity provided by the Church was dissolved. The Protestants in their haste adopted the principle of their own disintegration: every human conscience is its own judge and ultimate criterion. Under their liberal aegis and their weakening grasp of essential Christianity, there developed some of the instrumentalities in science and technology which gave birth to the structuralism on which Protestantism has choked and died as on a scaffold of its own making.

The Roman Catholics, in their fears, erected a fortified City of Power. They reduced religious fidelity to a mental adhesion. They tried in vain to inject a "Catholic humanism" into these dry structures. There developed, then, the religion of power, the ethics of power, and the humanism of power. Midway in the twentieth century, the inherent weakness of all this became apparent. While Catholic and Protestant were competing for power, the quest for Man as Hero had been given up; at the beginning of the eighteenth century, it was no longer. Searching for this role, man had found it necessary to know in a new way, by scientific research, by inductive reasoning, by practical demonstration. The structure of things, of man included, was what mattered. Forget the invisible absolute, the great beyond, the hidden God, or any ultimate cause. None of them is measurable, quantifiable, or qualitative. The human dimension was not understood as a structure. Christianity could not cope, any more than other ancient religions.

A lot of aery-faërie statements are made from time to time about the Orient, the land of Tsin, mystic India, and the rewards of the Eightfold Way of Lord Buddha. Westerners were told of their crudeness, their uncouth intelligence, their lust for blood, their stupid reliance on discoveries, their thirst for empire, for possessions, for all that glittered, for trade. Paul Valéry makes his ever-wise China Man revel: "I prefer to be ignorant of your disease of invention and your debauchery of confused ideas. I know something more powerful . . . Every man here feels that he is both son and father, among thousands and tens of thousands, and is aware of being held fast by the people around him and the dead below him and the people to come, like a brick in a brick wall. He holds. Every man here knows that he is nothing apart from this composite earth." If this was ever true outside Paul Valéry's mind, it is not true now.

Some tired Americans kneeling nude at sunrise in a preheated patio on Big Sur may think that they actually are entering that brick wall. Some battered New Yorkers may feel ashamed of our "disease of invention," as they listen breathlessly to an itinerant swami in straw pants and a bed sheet telling sibilantly about the harmony of om. The "young," the "kids," may piously speak of the simple life, the sins of modern society, and/or the ecstasy of Consciousness IV. The nude still need medical operations. Om is sometimes the only vocal sound possible in a dentist's chair, or when a mugger's bullet enters your thorax, or when you hit the jackpot at the OTB, or when we cannot afford that trip to Martinique. Bell-bottoms, drugs, rock music, sesame seeds, and coral beads hung on your pubic hair will not cope with your gonorrhea or excise that ruptured appendix. Mom and Dad must keep the weekly check coming and no "young radical" ever protested against those very green dollars in his royalties account. And Mao would summarily truss up Paul Valéry's smug China Man and pack him off in a truck to a pig commune in the Shantung uplands for re-education, while the Party structured the people with his little Red Book and with the little lies of personality cult that tot up to the Big Lie repeated endlessly before him by Adolf Hitler and Genghis Khan and Peter the Great and Doc Duvalier and Walther Ulbricht and Charlie Manson and every Big Brother who ever watched his little brothers lest they sin by thinking for themselves.

The sayings of the Lord Buddha lie starkly beside the modern mind much as a rigid pole beside a subtle maze. The "courtesy" of Confucius and the "self-control" of Shinto are fossilized bones. They will not simply fit in the narrow alleys and passes. They stick in the doorway. Buddha's words become dunghills of irrelevance. Confucianism is without heft and Shinto without beauty for the viscous, fluid mind which must subsist in the structurized maze to which all modern men are hurrying.

So it is also with the great religions today. Judaism and Islam are fossils, for they have no real hope of becoming anything religiously. But Judaism has pragmatically opted for something more viable. Judaism has become a mystical racism benign in its intent—to survive and to survive well. It has developed a super-ethnicity for dwelling within any other major ethnic group, and a supranational ethos hopefully compatible with any larger national ethos it may inhabit. That mystical racism has been concretized in the nationalism of modern Israel, within the compromises of Conservative and Reform Synagogues, and within the rigid and permanized struts of normative Judaism as preserved in fossil state by Orthodox Jewry. That mystic racism is perfectly compatible with modern structuralism. But Orthodox Judaism will be preserved like a vestigial jawbone in methylated spirits or a hard diamond in the closed, tranquil fibers of a rock.

Islam is not in a desperate plight, nor is Buddhism. The time for desperation was about four hundred years ago for Islam and about a thousand years ago for Buddhism. A desperate man still has hope, even if only a desperate hope. He has an option between continuance or interment. Islam's problem is how to be interred decently in a world where it cannot make sense and in a structuralism to which it cannot possibly adapt. It can only so transmute itself that it ceases to be Islam. No Moslem can admit that, any more than a Buddhist can admit the same concerning Buddhism. Both these religions posit, as an essential condition of their existence, a way of life and mode of thought about man and human things which is in no way adaptable to modern structuralism. Modern Pakistan is a case in point. Pakistan army authorities in May 1971 sought out and killed some hundreds of students and fourteen teachers at the University of Dacca (including the well-known Dr. G. C. Dev) because, as an army major said, "You hear of things unheard of in a Moslem society.

The new generation must be brought up according to strict Is-
lamic principles, with a return to the old ways." "Pakistan,"
mourned a Dacca student, "offers a fine setting for an epic poet,
but for engineers and practical people like myself it is sheer
hell."

Of course, both religions profess to make "adaptations." But
these should be called substitutes and ways totally alien to the
spirit and to the letter of both Islam and Buddhism. After Alexander the Great's invasion of India in the fourth century B.C., we
find a short-lived efflorescence of Buddha statues fitted with the
very Greek face of Alexander of Macedon. This was not an
"adaptation"; it was a craze which rapidly died out, and today
such statues are collectors' items adorning cabinets in Swiss private houses and Italian museums.

Any pope arriving at this juncture faced one of three possible
policy decisions. He could concentrate the energies of his administration on developing the Roman Church as she stood. More
effective hierarchic control; elaboration of Church missionizing
efforts; the establishment of more effective bastions of power
and influence in the fields of international politics, finance, and
social development. The policy thus initiated would be world-
oriented. The Church would stay with the world. It presumed
that spiritual hegemony could be achieved and reimposed by the
Chancellery, the vested interest, the concordat, the lobby, the
control of doctrine, and by social involvement. It amounted to a
more heavy-handed pursuit of Pacellism. And it may be called
the *holy-leaven decision,* for the main idea was that by being
with the world in this fashion, Rome could act as a spiritual or
holy leaven.

This approach was based on the assumption that Christianity,
and particularly Roman Catholicism, was still "inside" Western
civilization. But it was *not.* Besides, even the arch-conservative
mind had become more centripetal than ever. It recoiled in
horror from closer contact with the ever more "pagan" world
around it. Finally, there was no guarantee of success at all. The
whole proposal was fraught with expenditure of men, money,
energy, and of valuable time. Time was running out.

A second possible decision was simply to withdraw, to con-
serve, to develop, much as in a besieged city: tighten defenses;
intensify "inner" qualities; cut off, if necessary, rotten members;
face, eventually, even a sharp reduction in the number of perti-
nent members. Such a decision presumed, of course, that even-

tually the world would need Roman Catholicism. It was in essence a flight from the world. It depended on some catastrophic or apocalyptic development in the world and some correspondingly apocalyptic guidance from God. We may call this the *apocalypse decision.*

The objection to this arose from practical considerations. You cannot turn your back on the world in such a complete fashion. It would amount to an ecclesiastical and theological negativism. Besides, Christians outside the Catholic Church seemed to be drawing closer and closer to each other. There was a divine opening here. It could not be neglected.

A third possible decision concentrated more on Christianity than on the world. Was it not time to tackle dissident Christianity (that is, all those outside the Roman Church)? The various sects were undergoing the same alienation from the world of man. Needed would be a subtle flexibility in inter-Church relations, perhaps even a greater adaptability in the application of Church laws concerning the validity of Holy Orders, the sacrament of marriage, etc. Such a decision was oriented primarily toward Christian elements in the world. The idea was to collect together as many Christians as possible for mutual defense. This can be suitably called the *British Square decision.*

The objections to this were immediate. What new element in the situation would warrant any success for this course of action? Take the Roman Church, for instance: how far could she bend in order to make such an approach even credible to the principal sectors of non-Roman Christianity, and still maintain her integrity? Besides, this would be a sorry gathering of orphans, of fellows caught in the same misery. All parts of Christianity were outside and alien to Western civilization. They were all orphaned of this vital carrier culture. They all were experiencing the misery of increasing isolation. The Square itself merely guaranteed that all would die together. It had no access to survival.

John opted for none of the preceding decisions. His own decision was a highly personal one. John could not propose and foment a withdrawal. This meant giving up on the world and on non-Roman Christianity. That, in turn, meant giving up on love. On the other hand, John had been through the diplomatic sawmill. He had touched the limits of its potential. He was well acquainted with the worldly aspect of the papacy and the Vatican. He knew that in today's world there was no real competing on the plane of power with the existing centers of power. And finally, he was no apocalyptist. He did not believe either in sudden cataclysms or in burning hell-fire for all nonbelievers.

He had been rather a big success, especially in his latter years abroad in Turkey and Paris as well as at home in Venice. When all was said and done, what seemed to pull off the impossible, he had found, was almost always of a charismatic nature. It was either personal charisma of his own or somebody else's. It was charisma which arose spontaneously among a group of people or which was elicited from people by events exterior to them. But it was charisma. It resulted in an unexpected synergism. It made possible what was apparently impossible. The finer and rarer solutions it effected partook of an almost faery quality: the achievement of the undreamed of, the miraculous, of what could not happen in the ordinary condition of mortal man. It was a certain excess poured out over human relations, thereby lifting human actions from the mundane plane of self-seeking onto a plane where grand designs were possible, where two and two could quite feasibly add up to twenty; and where actual results went far beyond original intentions, transcending them, and purifying them.

His search for a decision, therefore, led him to seek the creation of some dispositive event. "If I can create with the materials in hand a situation, a forum, a configuration, of men and things apt and suitable for the spirit, then the charisma of the spirit will take." So went his thought. No imaginable event, he came to feel, could do this better than an ecumenical council. All Christians could eventually participate in it. Eventually, also, it would attract Moslems, Jews, Far East religionists, and all men of good will. Hence the Second Vatican Ecumenical Council. This was John's *charismatic decision*.

John made a desperate bid to achieve the apparently impossible: not to let his Church succumb to the circumambient structuralism, but to launch a new spirit, to cleanse its baptismal waters, so that it would be again a beacon of light on a high hill at the crossroads of the nations. His effort was in the nature of a true gamble. For he juggled with two explosive elements: the Holy Spirit and chaos. There is nothing so ungovernable as the Spirit. It vivifies. It destroys. The Spirit goes where it wills, does what it wills, is no man's slave, obeys no beck, is at no man's call, chooses its favorites, rejects any front-runner it so pleases, can evoke order from chaos, dismal failure from a brilliant beginning, and success from total disaster. Chaos reigns in disenchained minds unused to freedom, unshaped to the license of decision making, unfamiliar with their own conscience as the ultimate criterion of human behavior. That chaos veers giddily between two excesses: exultation and irresponsibility. But the abyss of ludicrous and grinning insanity always yawns beneath. It can parade with the apparent innocence of an unhurt child and simultaneously juggle with the unclean like a child playing unknowingly with its own excrement. John was a stubborn man, despite the milk-and-sugar-and-pasta character so often ascribed to him. He was stubborn to the point of death; and he was also a desperate man. He understood the crisis in the human dimension. He read all the signs correctly. He decided to gamble everything for the sake of everything. All or nothing.

He gambled. He lost. The Spirit did not will to blow his way. The chaos of exultation and irresponsibility was let loose. Today John's successor, Paul VI, is paying the price of that lost gamble in the gathering shadows of his last days on earth. He cannot govern the irresponsible. He cannot share the exultation. For in his Church they both share the grin of insanity, and their course is ludicrous. John had read the signs but jumped his signals. In his language, God had simply refused his solution. In ordinary parlance, he had made a huge historical miscalculation. Nothing is as unforgiving as history. But history has the ultimate pity: it buries human failures. In the domain of God's drama, every failure, as every success, is inserted permanently in the mosaic of self-sustaining existence.

The Council failed because there was no outpouring of charisma. There was no Event. At the onset of spring 1963, this was clear. Subsequent experience confirms that judgment. It failed because in no real sense was there an event such as John awaited: nothing overwhelming, overawing, all-absorbing seized Council members, Council participants, Council onlookers, or anybody. Foreign-government watchers stood up, as it were, stretched themselves after a tense wait: nothing, after all, profoundly affecting their nations and their problems was going to come forth. The anticipated movement never got off the ground. The great gamble failed. At the end of spring, John died. Within the next two years of the Council's life, a whole series of dynamisms were let loose both within the Roman Church and within Christianity. They had existed before Pacelli's time. John had guessed and measured their existence and brute power. He had sought to transform them. He failed. With his death, they went amuck, taking the forms of madness and of would-be wisdom among clergy and people. They unpoped Paul.

The agony of Paul VI can be understood in this context. He realizes that John's gamble had failed. It can even be argued that he never believed it would work. Paul knows that the jig is up. He knows that Christianity is alien to Western civilization. There is consequently a necessary delicacy in judging Paul. He is awaiting an "event" of another kind. The reins of history never really lay in his hands. He must busy himself with scolding the naughty, repeating traditional doctrine, wringing his hands over human mistakes which he cannot avert or correct, and trying to keep his Church within the vision and interest of the wide world. He can never become enthusiastic about ecumenism. He knows that ecumenism has no future. In other words, he is resourceless. His is a direful position.

He is relying, however, on history; not on the abstract science and knowledge we sometimes call history; but on history as unfolding drama whose plot has God as playwright. In this, Paul not only is faithful to the spirit of Christianity. Apart completely from the dictates of his faith, he is correct in assuming that history is more than a congeries of established facts. History cannot be summed up or understood by saying, "These are the facts." Nor is history ever merely or principally a matter of "I-was-there-and-let-me-tell-you-how-it-happened," as we learn from the diary of Samuel Pepys and the chronicles of Herodotus. For this reason, this study is not put forward as such an account. For every claimant witness, there are ten more to contradict each point made. History is by necessity interpretative. It always implies understanding and comprehension. An account of history is a statement of meaning, and not merely or principally an exact chronicling of events in a sequential pattern of autobiographical or partisan nature.

5

Visible and Invisible

Of the papacy, the pope, and the Vatican there traditionally have been three predominant images. We find these images sometimes combined together, sometimes entertained separately. Sometimes we find only one admitted as true, the others completely omitted, explicitly denied, or considerably watered down. Usually one's choice among these images decides what one thinks of the Roman Catholic Church as a whole. These images are briefly considered here, before we consider Pacelli, Roncalli, and Montini in their functions as popes. Thus the difficulty of studying the differing mentalities and policies of the three are in some measure reduced. For at first sight this seems to be a thankless and impossible task.

Vatican records, for one thing, are ordinarily rather inaccessible even years after a pope has died. Sometimes they are never opened. Second, it can be argued, we are too near Montini and Roncalli to be able to judge them; and Pacelli's image has been confused by the controversies that have surrounded his name. "It takes sixty summers to make a pope, sixty weeks to get used to him, sixty saints to love him, sixty years to understand him, and all eternity to forget him," lamented Lorenzo the Magnificent once to a papal envoy. Lorenzo's exaggeration and exasperation hold an underlying double truth. It is very difficult to be neutral in regard to the pope, his papacy, and the Vatican. "No man turns his back casually on Rome," remarks Duff Cooper apropos Talleyrand's efforts to do just that. On the other hand, both the casual observer and the professional watcher find it

47

difficult to fit together into a coherent pattern the variegated, contrary, and sometimes contradictory elements which the triad of papacy, pope, and Vatican presents. Usually, one relies on one's prejudices, for or against, to decide on a pattern. That is the degree of its objectivity. Involved in every such patterned judgment about the pope and the Vatican we find something of the following images.

The first is the *juridical image*. The papacy, pope, and Vatican are seen as making one complex authority: ruling, judging, governing, authorizing, validating, condemning, punishing, legalizing, forbidding, permitting. All else is explained as an appendage to this authority. It dictates what must be believed. It states what is forbidden and permitted. It decides who is right and who is wrong. It admits to heaven. It consigns to hell. It does all this because of its stated conviction: such power has been given it by none other than God himself. In a word: it is the supreme claimant authority.

Those who have no religious beliefs, or who entertain religious views diametrically opposite to the Roman Catholic Church, regard this complex authority as just another human and amazingly persistent institution provided with a marvelous myth and equipped with a paraphernalia to perpetuate that myth. Its head, the pope, is an authoritarian ruler. Its bureaucracy in Rome and abroad is just another such structure subserving this authoritarian institution and fulfilling in due measure both the Peter Principle and Parkinson's Laws. Its authority rests to a large degree on the perpetuation of superstition and myth. It trades in "the opium of the people." Its financial sinews as well as its political know-how and influence are a source of marveling, of jealousy, of emulation, and of attraction, for other human institutions and for individuals.

Those who share Roman Catholic beliefs have hitherto in their majority regarded this juridicism of the Church as a most consistent trait. Jesus gave it all power so that it could lead men to salvation and to heaven. Economic and political muscle is regarded as a necessary condition for the exercise of this important function.

The second image is the *heavenly image*. Papacy, pope, and Vatican are considered to be a visible and this-worldly replica of the paradise or heaven which all believers aim to enter. The pope is the Vicar of Jesus, of God. He takes the latter's place. Obeying him, you actually obey Jesus. Spurn him, hate him, disobey him, and you actually spurn, hate, and disobey Jesus. The

Vatican, the papacy, and the bishops of the Roman Catholic Church are, as it were, an extension of this Jesus personality incarnated in the pope. They, together with the pope, *"are* the Church; the others, the rank and file faithful, *belong* to the Church," to quote a present high-ranking member of the Vatican.

Further still, in part this conglomerate body is already in heaven. Actually, a real and existing part—those who died in faithful communion with the conglomerate—are either in heaven (the Church Triumphant) or at least well on their way to heaven while cleaning up a few outstanding debts to God in a place called purgatory (the Church Suffering). The part you see —pope, Vatican, bishops, and faithful—is the Church Militant. Belong to it, and you belong already to heaven. It is a replica on earth of heaven: its praise of God, its good works, its purity, its perennial and persistent existence. Heaven itself is a life of praise, of love, of purity, of perennial and persistent existence. Sufferings on earth are a replica of the Church Suffering, which is in purgatory.

This image is fully entertained only by some Roman Catholics. Non-Catholics sometimes catch a breath of it, sometimes even give it mental obeisance or a momentary place in their hearts. Many a Jewish or Protestant American serviceman listening to Pacelli in the mass audiences he granted to GI's after the Second World War had this vestigial experience. Today many a non-Catholic and nonbeliever has an emotion of yearning during a Vatican ceremonial, a sort of "there-is-something-beautiful-here" feeling. But something analogous is felt by many who are present at the Moslem pilgrimage to the Kaaba in Mecca, or by newlyweds who see Fujiyama at dawn in each other's company, or listen to Wagner's *Tristan und Isolde.*

The third image is the *nonsense image.* According to this, pope, papacy, and Vatican really make no sense in this day and age. It is not merely that they present us with a huge anachronism. Sometimes anachronisms make sense. But these do not make any sense at all. They are rank nonsense. Furthermore, as modern nonsense, they are either disgusting and hateful, or quaint and old-worldly, or delightful and rather decorative, or useful and redoubtable, or pitiable and regrettable, as any nonsense can be. But, in the final analysis, they are an egregious nonsense. Sometimes one or many of these reactions to that image closely resemble the attitude of modern man to the mummified glory of Tutankhamen, the reaction of technotronic man to the civilization of the Aztecs, the revulsion of Western man to surviving cannibalism, or the nostalgia one feels on reading Gray's *Elegy Written in a Country Churchyard.*

In this image, decorative and delightful are: papal ceremonies, Vatican museums and palaces, red-robed cardinals, Vatican Swiss Guards, and Vatican treasures. Disgusting and hateful are the superstitious practices: the hocus-pocus of Mass, of monk, of confession, of Mariolatry; the Machiavellianism and politicking of clerics; the trading in money and vested interests; the stubborn maintenance of anti-abortion, anti-contraception, anti-homosexuality, anti-Communist views and laws. Useful and redoubtable are: the diplomatic status of the Vatican; the moral stature of the pope; the rich wine and beer produced by abbeys and monasteries; the good done by leprosaria and clinics and relief works. Quaint and old-worldly are: holy water, pilgrimages, Madonna shrines, Nine Fridays, Forty Days, Seven Sundays, triduums and novenas, cloistered nuns, mellifluous Gregorian chant, resounding church bells, harvest blessings and blessings of the sea, the Christmas spirit. Pitiable and regrettable are: the Church's passing from the human scene, the cessation of its onetime glories, the weakening of its strength to an effete decay, its aspect as a venerable institution which is disappearing from the earth.

In all fair-mindedness, it must be said that none of these three images adequately describes what the triad of pope, papacy, and Vatican signifies or means. But the images are as much the results of a genuine bafflement and puzzlement as of the sincere love and distrustful dislike which the triad has continually inspired. Monsignor Casaroli, the Pope's envoy, is photographed in the Kremlin, Moscow, in March 1971, drinking a toast in the company of Soviet officials, to the Nuclear Non-Proliferation Treaty. He had just deposited with the Soviet government a copy of the Vatican's endorsement of that treaty. *Juridical image:* "Without that endorsement, the treaty lacks an essential element, God's blessing" (Roman-Catholic). "As a significant element in politics and finances, this Vatican endorsement is valued and valuable" (non-Roman-Catholic). *Heavenly image:* "This treaty is now ratified in heaven." *Nonsense image:* "Clerical politicking and inflated self-importance. They are still acting as if the Pope ruled Europe."

During the Nigerian civil war of 1970, the Vatican organized flights from the island of São Tomé to the Biafran mainland, bringing food and medical supplies. *Juridical image:* "The charity of Christ's Church has an obligation to care for those over whom God has given it authority, the hungry, the wounded, and the sick." *Heavenly image:* "Jesus again feeds the multitudes, again he has mercy on them, again he consoles the maimed and the ill, through his Vicar." *Nonsense image:* "A futile interference in a matter internal to Nigeria. Obviously, the Vatican is interested in the oil potential of Biafra. All help should be channeled through the United Nations Organization and its agencies."

The by now classic case of Pius XII and the Jewish Holocaust of World War II provides a prime target for this triad of images. It is established beyond all cavil, on the basis of documentary evidence and sworn testimony, that Pacelli and the Vatican did indeed know what was going on, that they did know in detail of Hitler's Final Solution, its grisly details, its extent, and its ultimate purpose. It is beyond any doubt whatever that Pacelli was urged to speak out as one of the few, perhaps the only voice of moral conscience, left free in Hitler's European fortress. Likewise, it is beyond all doubt that he did not because he personally decided not to speak.

Juridical image: "The Pope has no obligation to invade the area of authority proper to a foreign government, especially if such an action would seriously imperil freedom of movement— or even life itself—for the Pope and the Vatican" (pro-Pacelli). "The Pope is supposed to exercise a moral authority and to condemn any and every excess in human behavior" (anti-Pacelli). *Heavenly image:* "It is not life, but where we end up after death, which matters. God will amply repay in the next life the massacred Jews for their sufferings in this life. He may even have taken their sufferings as baptism of desire and so admit them to heaven. The important thing is: the Pope should survive." *Nonsense image:* "If the Pope had had any sense, he would have spoken out, because this would have lifted the Roman Catholic Church out of the Middle Ages and plonked it down right in the middle of the twentieth century. If he and the Vatican fail to act in such a crisis, what in the devil is their further use to mankind?"

The same images are applied holus-bolus to Pacelli, Roncalli, and Montini when they are considered against the backdrop of the contemporary world since World War II. Pacelli was either the "Pastor Angelicus"—an image of Jesus the Lover of Little Sheep and Pure Lambs, the "voice pleading for a peace based on justice" (did he not choose *pax cum justitia* as his motto?), or

the "moral beacon of our time," the "inspiring leader of Roman
Catholic millions," or the "image of neo-Roman imperialism," or
an "almost physical representation of God's solicitude for men."

Roncalli was "named John, a man sent by God, or 'a simple
peasant' searching for love"; he wanted "to update the Church,"
to "open windows on the world," to "undo the authoritarian grip
of the Vatican"; or he did not know what he was doing by un-
leashing the chaos of "individual thought and allowing masses
of people to participate in reforming" the Church.

Paul is a Hamlet, beset by doubts as to whether he should or
could exercise his authority; or he is a Christ-figure crucified
with the nails of liberalism and conservatism; or he is a mock-
rendering of more ancient and authentically powerful popes, but
he has had the misfortune to be elected when the papacy and the
Vatican are in their last throes. The images recur and recur,
bumbled, confused, amalgamated, combined, sharply con-
trasted, ever puzzling, ever baffling.

Trying to undo them, to distinguish them, to form an intelligible and objectively acceptable notion is like wandering in a
constructed maze of mirrors each of which distorts and multi-
plies a central labyrinth. It is the weekend nightmare of a Madison Avenue man. Each element has a thousand different forms.
There are steps within steps leading to more steps. There are
essences of essences within quintessences. Contraries unite.
Contradictions walk arm-in-arm. Blood is mixed with air, oil
with water, bread with earth, flowers with filth. Where one person sees polish, another sees only vanity. Where one finds a brilliant fire illuminating his life, another finds merely a picture of a
fire which does not warm his soul. It is one of the more finely
turned ironies of contemporary history that an institution professedly standing for truth and reality should be locked in such
an ancient undergrowth of pride, prejudice, and fanciful presen-
tation.

In order to approach an understanding of pope, papacy, and
the Vatican, one has to see beyond the exercise of authority. The
obvious anachronisms have to be ignored; the heavenly aspect
must be put in proper light. The character and motivation of all
three is predetermined by a built-in dualism. This dualism can
be formulated only in terms of activity, in fact of dual activities,
which characterize the triad. There is, on the one hand, the activity of an inner Dynamic and, on the other hand, the activity of
an external Mechanism. Together, they are the sources of this
basic dualism.

The first activity deals with the unmodified, spontaneous elements in man, those things in him which seem of infinite capacity and of dimensions imperceptible to his five senses: his love, fear, hate, compassion, and hope; his mysticism and poetry; his sense of awe; his instinct for home and for what is "his own"; his desire of perpetual and never ending light; his capacity for pleasure and achievement, to build taller than himself, to reach beyond all perceptible boundaries, to know outside and around all knowing, to be more than himself in order to be fully himself, to be one with millions of fellow men as his brothers and sisters, to be unique as emperor and pontiff of all he can encompass, to be able to laugh irresponsibly, to weep without shame, to love what loves him, to be stronger than all weakness yet weaker than a newborn baby in his security. This inner area, this fatal essence of man provides the Dynamic of pope, papacy, and Vatican, as in any human institution.

In this triad, the Dynamic has received a colorant. We cannot describe the latter simplistically as "Christianity," or even as "Roman Catholicism." For both these terms have long been infected with the dualism we are analyzing. The colorant is an ancient and hoary one. It is best summarized in the term the *Cross:* need of "salvation from sin"; a "redeemer god-man" of historical existence; a physical death on a cross in virtue of which "salvation" was "granted" by "God" to all men, regardless of their knowledge or their consent; and the consequent working out of this "salvation" during life on this earth, so as to "live forever" in "heaven." For this is the net meaning of the Cross according to Roman Catholicism.

This Dynamic, then, elaborates itself dynamically, oriented to what is "inside" man, to what he feels, thinks, aspires to. Its first step is recognition of what is awesome and sacred. From this awe it proceeds to think, to theologize. Theology is born. Instinct for the awesome and the sacred spills over on to men and things, making them likewise awesome and sacred, therefore "holy" in their eyes. Men's lives, and the things they live by and with, are "sanctified" from the inner Dynamic. This is its hagiography. It reaches even further, when theology and hagiography blindly pour out over man's life workshop: the bread and butter of his living, the stone and steel of his soaring ambition, the minting and the mania of his wealth, the beds of his birth and his pleasure as well as of his death. This inner Dynamic becomes utopian, sees all through the tinted glasses of an angel. Thus Angelism, as a last step, is reached.

The second element of the dualism, the Mechanism, addresses itself to every finite modified form of the Dynamism which unfailingly appears wherever we find the dwelling of man: his pain and his punishment by the impersonal forces of nature and at the hands of other men; his pleasure and reward within the City of Man; his profits and his losses; his machines that work and his inventions which solve problems; the territory he acquires and the woman he appropriates; the children he begets and the citizens he affects; the laws he makes and breaks and upholds; the stone and wood and water and air and chemicals and atoms he adapts for his survival, his victory, his pleasure, his poetry, his art, his music, his reverence and adoration; the days he spends in labor, and the nights he sleeps, and the years he lives, and the ground he is buried in.

This Mechanism is decked in a thousand colors and expressed in myriad forms. It incarnates itself step by step, as does the Dynamic. The Mechanism is outer-oriented, is directed toward the Crown, man's crown of achievement, of fullness, of completion, of satiety as man. Its first step is recognition of the profane —whatever is not sacred or awesome. There follow man's thought and devising, his unique, human, and intricate structuring of practical thought, by the force of his consciousness of himself, by his imagination, by his reflection and his analysis. This is his Rationalism. All and anything can be its object. Nothing is unthinkable. Even man himself can be the object of that Rationalism.

But the Rationalism never stops there. It is turned inevitably by man on man himself. Man becomes the subject of man's Mechanism. Instead of being the object of knowledge, man becomes the subject for experimentation, for capricious restructuring, for the whim of his sadism, the whip of his masochism, or the stare of his boredom. Thus arrives the Prostitution. The only obscene word which remains is the word "obscene." Pornography, as a term, loses any meaning. Might is right. Weak is bad. What you will is beautiful merely by willing. Only failure fails, and the only failure is death.

Once the Prostitution has been effected, it is one short step to the ultimate in the rule and the role of Mechanism: the triumph of unreason. Intelligence, in itself and for itself, expels and evacuates any love, any compassion, any reverence, any place for weakness or for what is lowly. Intelligence not only mans the mountaintops of human doing with its cold metallic calculations. It aims at the skies and at any god of loveliness, of hope, of trust, of perpetuity, whom man may have adored. Such is the Diabolism of man's mechanical urge.

In the human dimension, Dynamism and Mechanism develop as competing partners. One is never present without the other actively trying to interfere, to outstrip, to overtake. So it is with the triad of pope, papacy, and Vatican. The inner-direction of the Dynamism is inner because of the outer-direction of the Mechanism. To "go-in" or "be-in" means to "go-in" from some "outside," to "be-in" something which has an "outside." The Cross triumphs; and all its adherents are crowned in glory, are the victors, must dominate on earth as well as in heaven. Jesus wore a crown of thorns. "Lord, remember me when thou shalt enter into thy kingdom." Christ, the King.

What is sacred is seen and possessed as sacred in contrast to what is profane. "I bless this water in the name of the Father, of the Son, and the Holy Spirit." Billions of tons of water in seas and streams remain unblessed, profane. "You are now two in one flesh. Your marriage is a mystery, like Christ and his Church." The whores and lechers, the lovers and the mistresses are profane. The iron of Jesus' nails on his cross is sacred, but not the mine from which their metal was quarried. The priest's hands are holy, but not so the hands of the mother who gave him his hands. The Bread and the Wine of Communion are sacred, the Body and the Blood of Jesus, but not the wheatfield where once these grains ripened on yellowing heads, and not the vine where the grapes hung heavy. Bury your dead in consecrated ground, not in the earth simply. The Holy Places were in no danger of profanation as long as they were in Arab hands. Once the state of Israel took Jerusalem and the Holy Places, the Vatican was deeply concerned about their profanation. "The Holy Places must be internationalized," Paul VI declared in March 1971. Never a like word during the years of Arab possession of Jerusalem. Most Christians in the Near East are Arabs.

Theology proceeds only by rationalizing on its teachings, on revelations, holy books and historical events. It can rationalize its adherents into heaven, its enemies to hell. It can decree with absolute authority that mine workers in a Chilean company to which the Vatican has given a large portfolio should be provided with brothels—at company and therefore Vatican expense—in order to be better mine workers. It can justify a German priest praying for victory on the eve of an attack against French troops, whose chaplain, in turn, is praying God for a victory against the oncoming Germans. Once upon a time it had no more difficulty

in declaring all the unbaptized babies to be burning in hell-fire
than it has today in justifying Church wealth.

Hagiography contends with Prostitution. Léon Bloy can describe his mistress's breasts as two Sacraments because the
bodies of the saints are "temples of the Holy Spirit." And she is a
"saint." Christian, specifically Roman Catholic marriage, is supposed to "sanctify" and make "saints" of man and wife. A Catholic married to a Catholic and with children from the marriage
leaves them, divorces her in a civil court, marries a second wife
before a Justice of the Peace, produces new children by his second wife, leaves her in turn, returns to his first wife and children. He was living in sin. His children by the second wife were
illegitimate. His second wife was a concubine.

Young girls must be brought from India to Italy to be trained
in holiness and the religious life. They must pay for their passage and their keep. Keep them there, even if they wish to leave.
Hold them to their contract. The flesh is weak. Work them hard.
The hard-working friar traveling through early Mexico on missionary work during the Lenten fast consecrates an entire keg of
wine. He could then slake his thirst at will, never breaking the
Lenten fast. The wine is no longer wine but the Blood of Jesus.
The Kingdom of God must advance.

The innate Angelism of man is paralleled by his Diabolism,
which is always possible. This is the peak point of the inherent
dualism. Human activity becomes a fuzzy area where all distinctions disappear between the two. Every earthly utopia designed
by man on the social or the individual scale has somehow ended
in a terror or a degradation or both. Flower children become
street people and freaks. So it has been with Roman Catholicism
and Christianity. Angelism decries birth control and so spawns
starving, deformed, subhuman men and women. It relied on a
simple yes or no response to the question: "Do you believe in
Jesus?" and it produced the grinning horrors of ecclesiastical
torture chambers where the rack and whips were blessed by a
priest sprinkling holy water in the name of Jesus Savior.

It has extreme spasms, which are possible because of horrendous faith invertedly linked with a divinization of the profane.
There is the Black Mass celebrated by a naked priest reading
prayers and performing ritual backwards, using the pubis of a
naked virgin as his altar stone, and the act of deflowering the
virgin is his act of thanks for eating the Body and drinking the
Blood of Jesus which were validly consecrated by him. There is
the apparently angelic simplicity of those who advocate the

blowing up of "all arsenals and military installations," of bringing the "business of this government to a stop," for the sake of peace and love, in the name of Jesus.

But the Angelism of the proposal scarcely hides the gleam of Diabolism. There is the use of slander and calumny to destroy the enemies of the Church. An opponent of religion can be rendered helpless, if we reveal his past indiscretions or entrap him with wine, women, money, little boys, or the wrong political affiliation. There are the grotesqueries of ecclesiastical portfolios in armaments, the hate and evil-doing in Church rivalries, the refusal to visit the sick who are poor, the grinding of an ecclesiastical machinery which permits advancement only by currying favor, by biting the hand that once fed, by subtle destruction of the worth and reputation of one's rivals. Man's Dynamism can reach Angelism rapidly, almost without effort, and then start off by making its food the manna of angels and thinking celestial things. At times it seems, however, to be but one side of a coin. The other is the Diabolism inherently possible to all men, no matter how they start. Their Angelism can start in the high animation of sheer altruism and end in search of a suitable prey. Then, like the jackal, it always begins at the anus of human misery.

Only in the interplay between Dynamism and Mechanism can we piece together the puzzle that adheres to the external sight and trappings of pope, papacy, and Vatican. The firm believer in the tenets of Catholicism will choose other terms and speak, probably, of the "spiritual" versus the "temporal," of "original sin," of the highly personal "Devil" (Satan), and so forth. But for a large generality these terms either have lost all meaning or are not syndynamic with their counterparts on Catholic or Christian lips. Many Catholics and Christians still mouth them, but will fearfully refuse the painful task of laborious thought in order to make them more than shibboleths and their use more than lip-service.

In considering the policies and mentalities of both Pacelli and Montini as popes, we must remember the inherent dualism. For their policies and mentalities are to be seen as structured on the basis of this dualism. Only in Roncalli's case must we think otherwise: this is the difficulty one encounters in assessing him. He decided on a course of action which, he hoped, would not end in the excess of Angelism or fall into the sin of Diabolism. He sought to undo an ancient system. That in this he failed is irrelevant to understanding his effort, but it does explain Montini's inescapable dilemma. He and his Church structure are caught in a historical trap-gate of change; and for once there appears to be no immediate solution. One is reminded of what Roncalli remarked to Pacelli and Montini at their May morning meeting in 1954: "Events have overtaken all of us."

6

The History Meaning-Box

Today almost anyone who is asked to comment on America of the sixties and early seventies will answer unequivocally that some change is taking place. Some would prefer, perhaps, to speak of "changes" rather than of "a change." But whether it is "change" or "changes," most people agree that what is happening is of a profound nature. Questioned further, they will point out that "nothing seems to be working as it should." "Working" here is used to mean fulfilling the purpose for which something was established.

Therefore, transport, road, rail, and subway do not work. The judicial system does not work. The prison system does not work. The telephone system does not work. Control of drugs and pollution (air and ear) does not work. The sewage-disposal system does not work. Congress does not work. The F.B.I. does not work. The C.I.A. does not work. The Presidency does not work. State and local government systems do not work. Our system of proportional representation does not work. The Electoral College does not work. Public education does not work. College structure and education do not work. The labor-union and mediation system does not work. Sanitation does not work. Our cities do not work. Housing does not work. The economy does not work. Our foreign policy does not work. Farm policies do not work. The merchant marine does not work. Marriage does not work. Heterosexuality does not work, but neither does homosexuality. The nuclear family does not work. Parenthood does not work. Even our rodeos and ball players do not work. Nothing, in fact, seems to work, to achieve at least a satisfactory minimum of its intended purpose. The striking fact is that all such statements, taken singly, seem to be indubitably true, at least to some impressive extent.

Others will go further and attempt to analyze cause in a deeper fashion. Here personal prejudices and desires, ethnic bias, religious stands, political leanings, economic status, and cultural presuppositions dictate the choice. For some, Americans have lost the frontier spirit. For others, Americans have become corrupted with imperialism and wealth. For others still, Americans have been the victims of the most insidious plot and subversive infiltration in the whole of history. Analyses vary: religion is dead; or, we have no "tragic sense of life"; or, "we have entered the long night of an attempt for psychic survival"; or, the United States is being subverted by a Communist plot; or, our politicians are corrupt; or, the American system is decadent; or, the American Constitution is out of date. And so it goes on. All answers and analyses wind up as historical commentary: the change or changes are historical.

Whatever the answer and the analysis, and apart from their unmitigated pessimism, there is one trait in common: people arrive at conclusions by accumulating facts and allowing these facts to structure themselves according to the bias and character of their majority. Since the facts are of a nihilistic bias and a despairing character, the answers and analyses are correspondingly nihilistic and despairing.

Thus all such answers and analyses must be described as structural; i.e., they emerge from a structural argument of facts in themselves. The answers and analyses are structuralist. Such interpretation of contemporary history is structuralist.

Today the most notable and widely shared structuralist version of historical change in contemporary history concerns the decade of the sixties which we have just left. That decade was, in the popular mind and for a rather large body of vocal and highly articulate writers and commentators, an American psychodrama in three acts which we could suitably entitle *Long Evening's Journey into Night*.

Act I, *Twilight Promise*, began with the election of John F. Kennedy. It was the advent of hope, of youth, of grace, of feminine beauty in the White House, of a New Team in the Administration. All in all, it was like a shout of joy and exhilaration. All this in the hushed aftermath of the Eisenhower era, the cottonball era, when McCarthyism lacerated the finest, the most brilliant, and the most interesting minds, and when all initiative was swallowed up and lost in one long, rambling, senseless sentence, without subject, verb, or object, which never reached a definite period. Deceptively, the new era looked like dawn, but it was merely a short twilight climaxed with a horrendous assassination. America had already committed itself to Vietnam. The symbol of it all was buried in sorrow.

Act II was *The Great Trek*. The King and Messiah of Youth and Hope was in Camelot with his court. All set out trekking for Camelot: the hippie, the black, the college youth, the Puerto Rican, the Chicano, the Indian. These were the days of giants. The Civil Rights Act came in 1964. President Lyndon B. Johnson proclaimed the goals of the Great Society. These were the days of the Freedom Riders, the Martyrs of the South, the Great March to Selma. Flower children multiplied. Youth communes appeared. Eugene McCarthy rode momentarily to victory in New Hampshire. Robert Kennedy campaigned for the Presidency, endeavoring to turn the country around on the basis of the black and the youth vote. Poverty programs multiplied. The cities of the North filled up with immigrants and welfare rolls swelled.

Act II had a double climax, a double assassination: Robert Kennedy by the hand of Sirhan Sirhan, and Martin Luther King, Jr., by the hand of James Earl Ray. The Priest of Renewal and the Prophet of Hope had been done away with. Both assassins still appear to most people as figures wisping onto the plane of reality from some dark, hitherto unsuspected underside of America. It was the height of American involvement in Vietnam: over 500,-000 men committed to the field, an average of 500 dead each month. The long night had begun and with it the struggle for psychic survival. The evil of American imperialism and moral rottenness had stuck its head out of the mist.

Act III, *The Long Night,* is still with us. Richard Nixon was elected President. The campuses flared. The S.D.S. rampaged, plotted, bombed. The Black Panthers armed themselves. The Young Lords armed themselves. There were shootings, bombings, raids, mock trials. Close surveillance by governmental agencies was instituted. A "no-knock" law was enacted. The stock market dipped. Unemployment soared. There were sit-ins, teach-ins, pray-ins, shout-ins, busts, trashings. Guns were turned on students at Kent State and Jackson, Mississippi, universities. The drug culture boomed. High-school children rioted. The Gay People paraded. Women's lib paraded. Revolutionaries went on the run. They exiled themselves: Cleaver, Williams, Carmichael,

Dohrn, Leary. Hippies gave way to street people and freaks. Cambodia was invaded. Laos was invaded. Vice-President Agnew took on the news media. The Mylai massacre came to light. Over the whole of America an iron clamp descended, choking the spirit, threatening survival. Over the scene hung the threat of pollution, of tight money, of increasing crime, of crumbling social institutions. Act III is still on.

Thus, the psychodrama is limned by the accumulation of facts, all bearing the same tag: disruption, breakdown, violence, government interference, death of human rights, the fading out of any American ideal. Americans, who had walked on the face of the moon and flown faster than the sun, were turning their land into a grotesque slum and a desolation of human bondage.

A similar process is in almost exclusive vogue among Roman Catholics and those involved in any active way with the Roman Catholic Church as a preponderant part of world Christianity. Things simply do not work. The school system does not work. Marriage laws, anti-abortion laws, anti-contraception laws, do not work. Celibacy does not work. The traditional relationships of bishop to parish priest and of parish priest to his assistants do not work. The traditional system of nuns and women's religious orders (way of life, clothes, occupations, rules, housing, etc.) does not work. Nor does the traditional system of men's religious orders: monastic poverty does not work; obedience to the religious superior does not work; community life does not work; clerical clothes do not work. Local Church finances do not work. The hierarchic system does not work. Church rituals do not work. Church "holidays" do not work. The Vatican way of ruling the Church does not work. The pope's office and function do not work. His infallibility does not work. Traditional beliefs do not work. The list could be multiplied.

Some go further in order to deepen their assessment of what causes all this. The Church is "out of date." Roman Church "imperialism" is bankrupt. Religion itself is effete and past its day. People had their eyes opened by the Second Vatican Council and they no longer want any of the traditional partisanship, prejudice, and bigotry. The conservatives in the Church are blocking progress. The Church is paying the penalty for mistakes in past centuries, its dictatorial behavior, its alliance with political power, financial wealth, social prestige, and imperialistic and colonial ventures.

Science and technology have evacuated religion. Celibacy and monastic vows have no place in a post-industrial and technotronic society. The Roman Catholic people, like the members of greater Christianity, wish their Church to join the struggle for human dignity and human rights, and to stop wasting its time in "churchy" matter.

˙ There has emerged from all this a normally accepted structure of thought based on a structuralist interpretation. It is again a psychodrama conceived as a ninth crusade or as the twentieth-century *achievement of Luther's sixteenth-century Reform.* Act I, *The Good News,* was the advent of Pope John XXIII and the proclamation of the Second Vatican Council. John appeared as a smiling face, the reconciliator, the father, he who understood men, in contrast to the hieratic, untouchable figure of Pius XII with his too long reign of suppression, of ecclesiastical jingoism, of centralist control, of authoritarian religion, and the fearful ipse dixit of his attitude to all and sundry. Act I was a period of unlimited hope, of limitless expectation.

Act II, *The Magna Charta,* began with the last session of the Council and the proclamation of the Council's reforms and decrees. All was new or going to be new, not simply renewed: new prayers at Mass, new actions and modes of worship, new freedom to think, to write, to teach. New relations with Jews, with Moslems, with atheists, with Protestants, with Eastern Orthodoxy, with all Christians and non-Christians. A new everything. A full freedom. Pope Paul went on his travels.

Act III, *All Together,* began imperceptibly and is still in progress. It contains the real climax of the drama: all together, all must strive to liberate Christianity and Roman Catholics from the grip of traditionalists and their traditionalism. Priests rebelled, caucused, organized themselves. The clerical habit was dropped. Nuns rebelled. Whole convents of nuns walked out and laicized themselves in order to be more relevant. Up around Morningside Heights, in middle and lower Harlem, New York, groups of young religious men and women took residence in apartments in small groups, signing their very own checkbooks this time, living a more authentic life. Ordinary men and women of the Church rebelled against priests, against bishops. Bishops refused to comply with the Vatican. One cardinal proposed a new General Council off his own bat. A synod and a counter-synod were held in Rome. Catholic professors rebelled with Catholic students against episcopal orders. Married priests and nuns went on the air and television. New Mass rites, new Easter rites, new baptism rites, with no blessing or authority from the Church, were introduced. Ecumenical meetings and agreements abounded. Cardinals, bishops, and priests preached Jewish-Catholic sermons. Rabbis gracefully accepted tributes to the Prophets, but disliked the mention of that Man who once belonged. Priests ran for Congress, organized strikes, went around with bodyguards, participated in guerrilla armies, raided government offices, were put on the wanted list of the F.B.I., were indicted on conspiracy charges. The whole drama has been one of making religion meaningful, up to date, and relevant to our time.

As in the first example of modern America, the answers and the analyses are established within a structure of accumulated facts. The facts are assembled, and by the gravamen of their very character tumble and fall naturally into their places, thus forming what is, indeed, a truly horrendous picture, pessimistic in character, nihilistic in outlook, negative in its conclusions. Again, these answers and analyses and conclusions are structuralist. There can be no cavil or doubt: the facts do automatically structure themselves into a pessimistic and negative framework of thought and conclusion. There emerges thus an interpretation of current history which is structuralist.

Indeed, most attentive commentators will agree that we are witnessing historic change or historic changes. But it is equally certain that, in a majority of cases, these historic changes are assembled in a structuralist fashion and are, therefore, interpreted structurally. The structuralism of religious commentators is all the more striking because in most instances they start from a non-structuralist point of view. They possess some form of religious ideology and admit to a corps of beliefs which together go beyond any mere structure and reach into a region of intuition and total perception. This totality of perception, however, is, as it were, anchored in the mid-air of their understanding as an admitted presupposition. Beneath it, on the ground of statistics and inductive reason, their analyses and conclusions are assembled and structured. It can happen that the structured view thus formed finally obfuscates their vision and perception of that original totality of belief. In this case, they usually walk on that solid ground carrying the tab of "unbeliever," "atheist," "agnostic," "ex-Catholic," "lapsed Jew," "enlightened Baptist," "progressive Lutheran," "former Protestant," or whatever.

There is obviously an implied view of history and of change in all the above methods of analyzing, assembling, and describing the elements of change which gyrate in front of our eyes today.

It is this implicit view of historical change which must be examined here. For, without such an examination and without an understanding of that implicit view, there is no understanding possible of how Pacelli failed, how Roncalli hoped and failed, and how Montini is trapped.

Underlying both these interpretations of contemporary history and historical change, there is a conception of history which, we find, did not exist a hundred years ago in any popular vogue. We find no trace of it, for instance, in the writings of a popular essayist and historical commentator like Thomas Carlyle, nor do we find it at all in the writings of Edward Gibbon, who lived in the previous century. Carlyle gives a careful exposition, in his well-known "The Signs of the Times" article, of the prevalent viewpoint: changes come and go, but the solid things remain, to be transmitted with care, and to be transmuted into better things of the same kind; the eternal verities are living in each phase of the transmutation. He refused to structure the future or the past: "Our grand business undoubtedly is, not to see what lies dimly at a distance, but to *do* what lies clearly at hand." Edward Gibbon sees all Roman history as leading up to the glory of the Enlightenment and the future age of human happiness.

The minds of people today are different. There is no question of a conception with any pictorial or graphic character. It is rather a mental mode of marshaling single historical events according to the statistical and individual quality of each. It is a ready-made model of meaning: provided single historical events are fitted within it, they have a meaning. We will *know* what *really* is happening. Outside its framework, there is no real knowing. There is no landscape, no contour map. There is rather a box, the history meaning-box. Its dimensions are predetermined, and therefore the extent and the meaning of its contents are predetermined by its six walls. The history meaning-box thus presents the full and only dimension within which sustained historical events and historical change can be understood.

The history meaning-box was the mental child of an aberrant genius called Karl Marx (1818–83), whose *Das Kapital* and other written works dictated the way of life for well over one-third of the human race in the late twentieth century: 800 million Chinese, 230 million Russians, and 100 million other Europeans. Westerners should always remember, in the middle of their discomfort with Russian and Chinese Communism, what Marx wrote to Engels the night he finished the last page of *Das*

Kapital: "I hope the bourgeoisie will remember my carbuncles all the rest of their lives." Marx suffered from almost every ailment, including suppurating carbuncles.

Marx changed modern man's appreciation of history. He launched a concept of total earth-and-man history which has titillated the human mind ever since. The material from which he constructed the history meaning-box was his concept of the inevitable. Human history on the planet earth was an inevitable system resulting from the inevitable iron-clad laws expressed in economic forces. In Marx's theory, which was greatly influenced by Hegel's philosophy, capitalism was doomed to self-destruction; but socialism, dictatorship by the people, and the withering away of the state—as such, these were inevitable. Marx interpreted all of history in this sense. For the first time, then, there was born a concept of universal earth-and-man history as a closed system working by logical and inevitable laws which could not be contravened. The history meaning-box came into being.

It matters little to the present context that Marxian economics were exploded and that Marxian ignorance of history has been fully decried. The total concept of a closed human history came into being and it passed into the common parlance of nineteenth- and twentieth-century thought. In that concept, historical change is recognized by the accumulation of events and their arrangement in a structure dictated by their nature. Events shuttle back and forth, are stable and are mobile, move in and out of appointed places. But all this takes place under the sign of the hammer and anvil of inevitable history. For each event bears the thumbprint of blindly working and systematic laws. It is by such a statistically based count that the American and the Roman Catholic psychodramas are structured and therefore "understood."

One consequence of the general feeling today that our world is involved in some profound process of change is that writers have started to describe the near future. Hardly a month goes by without some publication, a magazine article, or a book in which an author outlines what kind of future lies around the corner either for America alone or for America and the great world around it. Some of these futuristic sketches are, self-admittedly, gropings rather than firm assertions. Some of them are put forward as naked prophecies with as much self-assurance as we find in the threats of an Isaiah and the ingenious confidences of Dr. Nostradamus; they are an offshoot of science fiction. A vast majority are gloomy and pessimistic: civilization is a phoenix about to consume itself in its own fire, so that its double can rise from its ashes. A small minority are optimistic, even utopian: the future is a struggling chick breaking this rotten shell of our present civilization in order to emerge fresh, new, and young again.

Most of these futuristic writings have one trait in common: in the preferred configuration of the future, man is fundamentally the same. A little more mechanized; a little bit more humane, or vastly more inhumane than he is today; a user of a new gobbledygook; somewhat more subject to "scientific conditioning," but fundamentally the same—even if he is enslaved or obliterated in a world of robots, overcome by alien "things" from deep outer space, or mutated into a "superman" type of genetic fiddling, deep brain surgery, and biochemical marvels.

In order to examine and assess them, it is necessary to consider first the trap-gate of history, as illustrated in two distinct periods during the last nineteen hundred years of Western society. One period lies between the second and the sixth centuries; the other between the twelfth and the eighteenth centuries, of this era.

In both periods, we find the same process. A society attains a very specific human dimension, a condition of efflorescence, in economic conditions, in the rule of law and the civic order, and in the related fields of art, literature, and education. A new force or series of forces enter from the outside animated by a motivation which is alien to that society. For one reason or another, the society fails either to expel or to annihilate these forces.

There follows a protracted period during which the new forces are seemingly assimilated. At the end of that period, however, a double change is noticeable: the society is changed because a new human dimension has emerged in it; and the original forces have also been changed by becoming part of that new dimension. That new dimension is irreconcilable with the original human dimension of the society. Neither in the society nor in the alien forces, as they fuse, do we find that the participants have any clear concept of how they will end up. Yet, as far as we can judge, they are on the highroad to that new dimension.

We call that protracted period the trap-gate of history. For, once the society and the alien forces have entered it, there is no turning back. They have entered a powerful stream of change through a narrow bottleneck; as in the case of the salmon jumping the trap-gate, there is no returning. In a certain, real sense, they are doomed to extinction, as they were up to that point. And nothing they do can obviate this consequence. At the end, both are irradicably changed.

The only area open to speculation in this process is the beginning of the trap-gate period. Some profound change has already taken place when both engage in it. When does it take place? What do both renounce? What subtle changes were unconsciously adopted, and when, in an adaptation which seemingly locked them both on what at its end is seen as inevitable and unalterable? In both our sample periods, we find that people gave answers. Christians shouted exultantly about the "victory of Christ." The humanists and rationalists of the sixteenth and seventeenth centuries extolled the spirit of freedom. But these answers were always colored by ideological—religious or philosophical—motives. Perhaps answers to such questions are not to be formulated with accepted human concepts and according to current categories. For both categories and concepts are necessarily colored by specific motives.

Part II

THE TRAP-GATE OF HISTORY

7

Of the Roman Citizen

Toward the end of the first century, Christians in the Roman world numbered, according to conservative calculations, not more than 4,000 to 7,000 in the Near East, about 8,000 to 10,000 in Greece and Italy, and another 2,000 to 4,000 throughout the rest of the Empire. All told, a maximum of about 20,000. They lived mainly in the big cities: Antioch, Damascus, Jerusalem, Alexandria, Ephesus, Athens, Corinth, Thebes, Rome, Marseilles. We know of no important figure in sustained public service at that time who was Christian. From what we know of their beliefs, they were in opposition to the established order of the Empire. Their religion was Semitic in origin, Jewish in its terminology and concepts, and puzzlingly deficient to its contemporaries in the accepted marks of a religion: no statues, no sacrifices, no temples, no priests. Christians laid a funny emphasis on virginity, on chastity, on pacifism. They refused to fight in Roman armies, to participate in sacrifices offered to the Roman gods, to take part in public rituals (parades and processions, games, cultic celebrations, temple mysteries), all of which involved the cult of Greek and Roman religions. A substantial number lived in daily anticipation of a final cataclysmic end to the world and a second coming of Jesus. As a body, Christians therefore had no political ideal, no social manifesto, no pragmatic solutions for any of the current problems of their day. They did not belong. Deliberately.

They organized themselves in communities guided and governed by overseers. To a large extent, they shared their money and goods. They shunned the Roman educational system, derided the stories of the gods and goddesses, avoided intermarriage with non-Christians, provided for their aged, their widows, and their orphans, met in private for their ceremonies, and buried their dead rather secretly. Communities kept in touch through itinerant preachers and by letter. Socially, they belonged to the general working proletariat. More scorned by their contemporaries than were the medieval Jews in their ghettos, more alien to the Establishment of their day than are the Tupamaros of Argentina to theirs today, more bloodied by their society than were the Irish under Queen Anne; hated by Jews, despised by Greeks, condemned by Romans, jeered and mocked and smeared in the popular mind as child-killers, donkey-worshippers, lechers, cowards, ever ready scapegoats for public ire and disappointment; suspected and misunderstood by all—they were the rag-and-bone men of Roman society, tent-makers, laborers, manure-lifters, dockhands, seamstresses, slaves of all kinds, dwellers on a semi-outlaw fringe of an alien culture, living in the hope of a better world soon, very soon. They were truly the parasites of their time. They had no intention of joining the Greco-Roman world. Soon, very soon, it would all be over. These were the Christians of the first century: an alien and insignificant force just barely subsisting in the solid monolith of the Empire.

At the end of the first century, the Roman Empire had reached its final limits. In Western Europe, it possessed the present territories occupied by England, France, Spain, Portugal, and parts of Switzerland and Belgium. In Central and Eastern Europe, it included all territory west and south of the Rhine-Danube line, in addition to Greece and Turkey. In Africa and in the Near East, its boundaries corresponded to the edges of the Sahara and the Arabian desert. A strip of coastal territory from the Nile to the Atlantic lay in Roman hands. The territories of modern Syria, Lebanon, Israel, and Lower Egypt were within the Empire. These frontiers were to change but little in three centuries. The center of this empire was Rome, with a population of close to one million. At its head was an emperor.

Of this empire, only the peoples of the Italian peninsula had so far been formed into a federation of allies with Rome and enjoyed the privileges of Roman citizenship. All other territories were exploited as subjects and vassals. Tribute and products flowed to Rome: taxes in money and kind, wheat from Africa, fish from the Baltic, iron ore from Spanish mines, honey and olives from Greece, ostrich feathers from Tripoli, perfumes and spices from India, gold, silver, and lead from Sicily and Asia Minor, slaves from every land. The Romans were the second European people after the Greeks to have African blacks as slaves.

Once an all-powerful central nation has achieved economic and military control of divergent nations and races, it has but three choices. It can impose a devastating peace by maintaining a threat of annihilation. All activity is overshadowed by its doomsday machine, its swift and cruel knockout blow. As one Roman historian makes a conquered Gaul speak cynically (and doubtless wrongly) about the peace imposed by Romans: "They create a solitude [by war] and they call that peace." It can, alternatively, aim at an empire of slaves. All subjugated peoples become helots. This means policing the daily life of millions. It leads to sadism on an international scale, and the worst excesses of man's inhumanity to man. By the very fact of being subjugated. This is the Herrenvolk policy which Hitler adopted. The other choice is to set to work to transform the economic-military empire into a commonwealth. This is what the second-century Romans sought to achieve. Partially, it succeeded. It failed ultimately.

Some of the elements of change were introduced under the regimes of Vespasian (A.D. 69–79) and of Trajan (A.D. 98–117). These and other changes always had solidly pragmatic reasons behind them, but they all served one underlying need. By this time the Romans had succeeded in establishing economic interdependence throughout the Empire. They had eliminated any effective strife between little nation-states. That parochialism was finished. The Romans were too wise to impose an international peace by means of utter slavery or devastation. But they had not developed a political framework based on law suitable for this body, which was already unified economically and politically. They had developed no consensus, no universal principles of concord acceptable and adapted to the divergent races of the Empire. In the second century, they attempted to transform their military and economic empire into a commonwealth of Mediterranean man.

The consensus or concord which the Romans sought to spread throughout the Empire was inspired by the Greek ideal. It had emerged in fifth-century B.C. Greece. Rome prolonged its effective existence for four centuries of the Christian era. It was an ideal of human perfection, a balance of just proportions, through the use of reason, the practice of law, and the expression of human beauty completely satisfying and gently convincing in the peaceful harmony of ordered parts and in their related symmetries. At its center was man. Even the gods and goddesses were molded in man's image. According to this Greek ideal, man's earthly dwelling was a world of light, of confidence, of order, and of beauty. The Roman ideal was a commonwealth of men living in such an order of things.

The political structure of the Empire was transformed. A vast Roman civil service was established, drawing personnel from the provinces. Throughout the Empire, the Romans encouraged the locals to organize themselves: first as a *civitas*, a township; then, in a second stage, into a *municipium*, or municipality or town; then into a *colonia*, or full-fledged city. Throughout, Roman structures appeared which embodied the ideal: theaters, temples, statues, baths, marketplaces, courtrooms, schools, stadiums, monumental arches, aqueducts, viaducts, bridges, roads. Roman customs were inherent to all these: festivals, processions, games, religious sacrifices, literary and artistic endeavors, military service. From the Atlantic to the edge of the Sahara, from the Black Sea to Sharm-el-Sheikh and the Valley of the Nile, this writ of Roman man ran.

Men's lives in their daily details—birth, marriage, death, work, clothes, food, money, art, honors—were related intimately to the organization and its ideal. The Emperor at Rome received a new cult. A pattern of culture arose that assigned a place to each man, a status to every individual. Curiously but logically, human inventiveness diminished, grew enfeebled, and died. Latin literary production all but ended. Ancient standards of painting, sculpture, mosaic, were preserved and continued to be excellent. But little was discovered. Science and technology did not advance. Mathematics, astronomy, medicine, cartography, limped. Only in the science of law and jurisprudence were real advances made.

The Christians of the second century were a ragged lot. The century could have marked their end; the original site of their birth, Jerusalem, was destroyed in A.D. 135, plowed with salt, and a new city, Aelia Capitolina, built in its place. The founding community of Christian Jews (or Jewish Christians) was dispersed. Israel itself was entombed as a socio-political reality for the next 1,813 years. Judaism, the springboard of Jewish beliefs, was dispersed and dissipated. Jewish communities throughout the Mediterranean developed a professional hate and opposition to Christians. The latter were traitors, plagiarists, proselytizers, and apostates. In addition, the Christians refused to fit into the pattern of *Romanitas*. They refused the principles of Roman concord. We have a copy of one emperor's letter to his governor in Bithynia-Pontus. The year was 112. His instructions were crisp and clear: either they would bow to the gods, or they would be eliminated. It was as simple as that.

We have the names of some of the most prominent Christians executed. They were pitifully insignificant for the Roman world, nobodies and incompetents in that world's teeming urban life. Justin and Ignatius in Rome (about 110) and Justin in Rome (about 165); Polycarp at Smyrna (about 167). We know about other Christian nobodies: fifty of them were executed at Lyons in about 177. We have some of their letters, most unliterary, most inspiring. We have remnants of some of their writings. We have some of their funerary remains. Pathetically trusting.

Socially, Christians advanced little. Religiously, they remained parochial. Philosophically, they stayed outside the mainstream of the Empire. They were, in short, a parochial irrelevancy—inbred, intransigent, and too insignificant to attract what would have stemmed their movement: overwhelming doom at the hands of Imperial power. They were a flea bite on the rump of the Empire. They lived on.

In the third century, great changes and great strains overtook the Empire. A plague raged from 250 to 265. The Empire was racked by struggles for the Imperial throne. The first dreadful invasions by outside peoples took place. The Alamanni attacked on the Rhine and reached Milan in 256. The Goths harried Asia and the Aegean and Eastern Europe in 268. The Persians attacked in the Near East. The Empire was shaken by struggles for the Imperial throne, which finally became the prize of successful generals. Between 192 and 284, there were eighteen emperors: only two, Claudius and Septimius Severus, died in their beds; two were killed in battle against Rome's enemies; fourteen were executed, assassinated, or murdered by their own people.

The internationalization of the Roman ideal reached its peak. The very post of emperor was internationalized. He was no longer necessarily a Roman. In A.D. 222–235, for instance, Alexander Severus, a Syrian, aided by his Syrian mother and grandmother, was Emperor. He was followed by a Thracian, Maximinus. Some years later Philip, an Arab, became Emperor.

The Emperors began to base their power on divine right. The divine right of kings was an old idea in the ancient Near East. The Roman Emperors now adopted it at the cost of that other source of Imperial authority, the Senate. The Emperor Aurelian innovated the cult of the Sun God as the protector of the Emperor. This cult started in earnest under the Emperor Decius (249–251). Emperor worship now became a test of loyalty in Rome. The Christians refused.

The government of the Empire grew very complicated. Tradesmen—shippers, bakers, cobblers, metal smiths, farmers, miners, weavers, and others—were organized into definite corporations under Imperial direction. An album or list of prominent citizens (*curiales*) of every town in the Empire was kept in Rome. To these citizens the Emperor entrusted local administrative positions: tax-gathering, judicial processes, road-building, army recruitment, organization of festivals, food-provisioning, etc.

It was in the third century that the Roman world seemed to have sensed for the first time that something alien had been lodged in its midst. But it did not accurately pinpoint its identity, and its reactions were not violent enough. The Emperor, Philip the Arabian, was succeeded in 249 by Decius. And Decius was frightened by several things. Rome had just celebrated her thousandth birthday in 248 with the famous Games (*ludi saeculares*). Yet the Roman ideal was threatened: by the barbarians in the north and the east; by strange social groups throughout the Empire.

Between A.D. 180 and 250, Christians had changed. Most of them had decided that their world was not coming to a sudden end. They had settled down to acquire an education and to enter public and civic life. They studied Greek and Roman classics. They adapted pagan oratory to Christian needs, the pagan novel to the lives of their saints and holy men, the new technique of domes and pendentive roofs to their needs for a general meeting place, Roman sculpture in successive planes to depict the crowd scenes of the Christian Bible, Greek and Roman philosophy to the truths of a Semitic faith. Large, well-heeled congregations sprang up in Rome, Athens, Corinth, Carthage, Alexandria, and throughout the Empire. Christians wrote and published books. They founded schools. They held public positions of minor importance. They made some converts in high places. They produced a few great names: Tertullian, Origen, Irenaeus. They organized their people. They worshipped in public. They argued in public. The general mass of Christians still belonged to the vast proletariat.

But Decius and those like him did not separate the Christian threat from other threats: the threat of the barbarians, the threat from alien religions and cultural ideas emanating from the Eastern provinces of the Empire. When Decius was killed, Rome made a fatal compromise: his successors Valerian and Gallienus dropped the persecution. Instead, Gallienus attempted to revive all those activities which had given expression to the ancient ideal: art, philosophy, literary activity. It was a fatal move, because it was based on an error. Something had already taken place during the second century among the heterogeneous masses of the Empire. The Empire had offered them an image of Mediterranean man based on the ancient ideal. But the Empire had not been able to harness this idea to the common mentality, for the idea as it stood was suited only to a privileged class. The Greco-Roman ideal as such could not appeal to the masses; it had never been the ideal of the masses. It was too esoteric; it suited only a moneyed, privileged, ruling class. The Christian story was so simple, and it stressed the innate personal value of every man, regardless of his origin, his race, his color, his trade, his family. Gallienus' protégé, a Greek named Plotinus, even formulated a unitary philosophy. But it had no appeal for the masses.

Now Rome, its Emperor and ruling class, its vast urban masses and its provinces, had entered a new stream. The trap-gate had been sprung. There was no turning back.

It was all decided in the fourth century and concluded in the fifth and sixth centuries. But it overtook the Roman world by stealth. At the outset of the reign of that all-powerful genius Diocletian (284–305), any Roman official or noble would have laughed his head off at the idea that within thirty years (by A.D. 313) Christianity would be officially tolerated; that within seventy-two years (by A.D. 356), sacrifices to the Roman gods and Roman temples of the gods would be officially banned under pain of death; that within one hundred and six years (A.D. 390), a Roman emperor (Theodosius) would be forced by a Christian bishop (Ambrose of Milan) to do penance for having massacred seven thousand citizens of Thessalonica; and that two years after (A.D. 392), Christianity would be the official religion of the Empire. It was a ludicrous idea. Yet this is what happened.

8

Of Mediterranean Man

In A.D. 250, a man could walk from the borders of present-day Iraq to the shores of Spain washed by the Atlantic Ocean, and from London in England to Belgium and down to Tripoli in North Africa: throughout, he would have found the Greco-Roman culture and civilization, the "pagan" culture and civilization, as it has been called. In 350, the same man would have found a different condition of things: there was one totally Christian state. By 370, the twin kingdoms of the Georgians, Lazica and Iberia (both now in the U.S.S.R.), were virtually Christianized. Armenia became the first Christian state as of A.D. 303. The Imperial capital of the eastern Roman Empire, Constantinople, was dedicated as a Christian city on May 11, 330, by the Emperor Constantine. Syria, Lebanon, Palestine, Egypt, and all the countries of the North African Maghreb have a substantial Christian population and are already filling with churches, monasteries of men and women, schools, bishoprics, cemeteries.

What happened? Certainly, no sudden change. No cataclysmic overnight event. The whole process was like a gradual change of blood, an unconscious, almost subterranean, draining off of the old vitality as a new vitality entered the great body politic of the Empire. It seldom occurred in high places. There was no fanfare. It rarely disturbed official minds and provoked halfhearted adverse reactions only sporadically. The change was at the grass roots of the socio-political and economico-cultural life of the ordinary citizens.

Because the persecutions of the second and third centuries

were not thorough, Christians became known to their fellow men as hard-working and trustworthy citizens. They even produced some scholars. In public and in private, the ordinary man in the streets of Rome or Marseilles found that his Christian neighbors lived by a philosophy of life far more adapted to his proletarian life than were the abstract, absolutist concepts and intellectual fatuities of the Neoplatonists. The representatives of the Greco-Roman tradition had gathered around Neoplatonism and evolved a set of loosely defined values which were incomprehensible to the great masses and as inapplicable to their daily grind for sustenance as to their personal and communal aspirations.

The grass-roots change went deeper still. When the majority of the citizens in a town or division of a big city were Christians, the old Roman pagan festivals either were not observed or were subtly adapted. The Christians had not had a specifically Christian cyclical cult for the year. They adroitly substituted the celebration of the birth of Jesus for the December rites, and his crucifixion and resurrection for the ancient spring rites. In place of holy days in honor of this god or that hero, holy days were celebrated to commemorate Christian saints and martyrs. In Christian schools, where the Greco-Roman classics were now taught, a Christian interpretation was put on their content: Virgil prophesied the Virgin and the Child in his Second Ecologue; Orpheus rescuing Eurydice from Hades was Jesus snatching souls from Satan's hell; Troy fell because the god of Jesus deserted it. It was all relatively simple.

Political and Imperial pressures helped further. Constantine and his successors found that in many localities Christian officials, overseers, and bishops were the most trustworthy candidates for political office. They became the Imperial *curiales,* magistrates, judges, representatives of the Emperor. He conferred all-important judicial powers on the bishops. He exempted the clergy from the onerous *munera,* or obligations (service in the army, for example). Next he appointed them to governorships. More radically still, he put the cross as Imperial sign on his coins. His statues depicted him with some Christian symbol or gazing upwards at the Christian God in his heaven. The Empire was now under the protection of the God of Christians. Under pressure from Christian bishops, the Emperor Gratian (375–383) renounced the old Roman title of Pontifex maximus, or pagan high priest. The natural holder was the Bishop of Rome. Gratian withdrew all financial support from the old pagan cults in Rome.

Christians now change. They will not be compelled to perform non-Christian acts by accepting public office; temporarily, they will not demand Christian acts from the "pagans." Time is on their side, and they can afford to wait. Christians now see their way to fight in Roman armies. The Emperor's victory is their god's victory. Pagans still outnumber them. Actually, the term "pagan" is first encountered in the late fourth century. The state religion of Rome has become an empty ceremonial. The Olympic Games, begun in 776 B.C., were held for the last time in A.D. 394. The Delphic Oracle's last recorded message is suffused with the pathos and helpless resignation of a surely decaying thing. To the Emperor Julian, the message came: "The temple is overgrown with moss . . . The sacred tripod is rusting . . . The holy caves have collapsed . . . The voice of Apollo is silent forever." It was the year 360. Christianity already has a Jerome in the East, an Augustine in Africa, an Ambrose in Italy.

By the end of the fourth century, the takeover was complete. The ordinary vocabulary of civic and political activity was assumed by Church officials. Thus, men continued to use the same important words and terms but their significance now emanated from their Christian signification. *Sacramentum,* originally the sacred oath governing the fellowship of Roman armies, became the sacrament of Holy Communion. *Leitourgia,* originally the public service of emperor and pagan cult, came to mean all and every Christian ritual. Christian officials were called the *kleros* and their official meeting place the *ekklesia,* their principal local leaders *episkopoi.* All three terms were taken from the political and civic life of the time. The bulk of the ordinary Christian people came to be called the *laos.* Prior to and for some time concomitantly with Christianity, *ekklesia* was the general assembly of citizens transacting political laws; the *laos* (laity) were the people as distinct from governing authority; *kleros* signified a specially alloted civic or political duty. *Episkopoi* originally were executive officers in municipal affairs. Thus insensibly, the thought molds of civic and political life fell within a Christian context. The ancient Roman image of the Mediterranean commonwealth man was subtly changed into the Christian man.

Changes in more important terms and in the understanding of the reality they signified were also effected. Simple but key words were attached to key concepts of Christianity. *Soter* was assigned solely to Jesus as savior of men from sin. *Pneuma* was assigned as the title of the third person of the Christian Trinity.

A word like *aedificatio*, taken from the construction and building trades, now meant "building up Christian virtue." *Askesis*, originally the rigorous training of athletes for the arena, was taken to mean the training of and domination of one's spiritual energies and soul-muscle. *Ordines*, originally the privileged classes of Roman society, now pertained solely to the privileged classes of the Church: nuns, monks, and priests.

Persona, originally a mask worn by an actor, and then used to denote a character in a play, was used to describe one of the two fundamental Christian contributions to ancient thought. No ancient language has a word corresponding to our word *person*. The concept was alien both to Greco-Roman and to Semitic thought. Neither the Jewish Bible nor Greek philosophy nor Roman law ever conceived of a human being as a person in our modern sense. Judaism early adopted the Christian idea, as did the Roman lawgivers of the fifth and sixth centuries.

The second fundamentally and peculiarly Christian contribution was the transmutation of the Roman word *familia*. In its Christian sense, it meant the nuclear family as we understand the term today: a man, his wife, and their children. Again, neither in Greco-Roman nor in Christian Jewish thought was there ever a word for or a clear concept of the nuclear family. This was a Christian concept and it brought the Roman term *familia* to mean just that.

Christianity gets a further boost from the barbarian invaders of the Empire. Both the Goths and the Visigoths are converted en masse to Christianity about the middle of the fourth century. It matters little that their Christianity is Arian Christianity, a heretical form.

In fact, Constantine's Christian entourage and political support were so precious to him that he depended on the ecclesiastical unity of the Christian Church for the unity of the Empire. That ecclesiastical unity he went far to ensure. Christianity was riven by the Arian heresy. Constantine summoned a meeting of Christian bishops at Nicaea, in Bithynia, where orthodox Christianity was hammered out in concrete formularies beneath the pointed shadows of Imperial lances. Constantine helped to enforce the anti-Arian decisions of that council. Pope Leo the Great (440–461) persuaded the Emperor Valentinian to give all papal decisions the force of Imperial law.

The Emperor Justinian (527–565) finally crushed the old Greco-Roman paganism by a series of edicts. He was merely ending a chapter of history. Throughout the Empire, east and west, a new image of man had taken hold. A new ideal was rife in men's minds.

The quest for citizenship in a Greco-Roman commonwealth of citizens was not killed at one fell blow. Nor did it simply fall foul of "barbarian" hordes. Many of the new peoples admired the *Romanitas* of the Empire. They adopted Roman laws and customs. But that *Romanitas* and the ideal of citizenship had been an actuality only for an elite. That elite was swept away. It was the victim of irresistible circumstances. The original quest was founded on a political unity. And that political unity sprang from an economic interdependence established in the Roman *oikoumene*. Political unity disappeared and, without it, economic unity melted.

In the third century, under Diocletian, the Empire had been split into the Eastern and the Western Empire. Except for a brief period (324–337) under Constantine, they drifted further and further apart. The Western Empire fell increasingly under the Germanic peoples. By A.D. 480, it had ceased to exist. It was parceled out among Ostrogoths, Vandals, Visigoths, Suevic invaders, Basques, Burgundians, Franks, Alamanni, Frisians, Saxons, Thuringians, Lombards, Rugians, and Gepids. The intellectual and artistic and socio-cultural life of the West lost all its vigor. Churchmen had no literary, intellectual, much less artistic tradition of their own. There persisted into the sixth century and the beginning of the seventh no literary and artistic culture. Only, as one writer put it, a literacy persisted. But the wells of creativity were stopped, because there was no longer any socio-political unity based on a guaranteed economic security. Then literacy ceased. From the middle of the seventh century until well into the eleventh century, reading and writing were rare accomplishments. The extinction of the Greco-Roman tradition was complete by the middle of the seventh century: Islam sealed off Africa and the Near East. The West was cut off from the original source of its new inspiration in Christianity. Western man, in his quest for citizenship of this world, had ceased to exist.

9

Of Man as Un-Man

A lot of nonsense has been talked and written about the Dark Ages, as if the Christian Church enthralled for its own nefarious ends the minds of Western society in the darkness of superstition and myth. This, of course, is patent prejudice based on ignorance. What happened was simple. The economic and political unity of the Empire was swept away and with it the entire support and groundwork for classical culture. There were small kingdoms, petty rivalries, invasions, unsettling changes, continual warring, populations on the move, throughout the huge vacuum left by the Roman Empire. As a consequence, there no longer was any of the ancient quest. The ideal of human existence ceased to be man as citizen of a commonwealth.

Instead, the Church supplied the only image it possessed: man as a redeemed being, man as one whose existence on earth was only intended to prepare him for "eternal life in heaven." The only institutionalized and international force in Western Europe was the Christian Church: its bishops, priests, convents, monasteries, schools, missionaries, laws, rite, principles; its lingua franca, Latin; and the constant intercommunication between its members in Ireland, Yugoslavia, Palestine, Italy, Germany, Armenia, Algeria, Spain, Egypt, Ethiopia, and Iraq.

That "other-worldly" outlook of the Christian Church was all-powerful and pervasive. Man ceased to be the object of art. Art became abstract decoration: circles, curves, triangles, squares, convoluted colors, mingled with animal and bird forms. When we do find man depicted, it is either in stylized form (a "Christ,"

an "Apostle," a "Virgin," a "Saint") or in some freakish representation such as the image of man in the Echternacht Gospels. The
hands and feet are reduced to curving lines; the hair is a stiff
and unsightly arc; the body is an irregular square; the eyes
squinting triangularly heavenwards; the whole is an abstract
picture of a mummy.

Even with Charlemagne's empire and his effort at literary and
artistic revival, nothing changed. It is all symbolized by the
Cross of Lothair from the tenth century. On one side, there is a
delicate cameo of Augustus the Emperor embedded in gems and
gold filigree, surely a vainly revivalist gesture. On the reverse,
there is a flat drawing of the crucifixion on a silver surface.
Earthly power and heavenly salvation. Earthly king and heavenly God. Earthly protector and heavenly Saviour. These were
the two polarities of man as un-man. Man was still passionate,
still vigorous, but primitive and balancing over the abyss between them. The great need was to survive. The great motive
force was a Christian one: get to the other side. Heaven. Western man's society was molded by the need to survive. There was
no search for man himself, no search for intellectual light, no
search for new fresh forms to tell man's story.

Suddenly in the twelfth century there is an outpouring of
energy. Man seems to be in search of man. Throughout all sectors of Western European society and life there flows an irrepressible force, turning, twisting, weaving. It issued in the rage
of philosophy and theology, the rise of schools and scholasti-
cism, social organization, voyages, discoveries. It was, at its
height in the thirteenth century, a world of restless curiosity
within a world of system and order. It was marked by a parade
of emperors, bishops, popes, princes, saints, heretics, scholars,
and sailors. It is not a world of free and active men. We find this
new force vividly expressed in the Cluniac style with its sharp
edges, cutting lines, twisting and turning the plastic drapery, the
power of its chiseled draperies ever restless, never ending
finally, but disappearing into further folds of stone. It was in the
nature of an awakening. But Western man was not yet fully
awake.

His art, Romanesque, started off as dead and dull, a monumental sculpture based on a fusion of northern rhythms and
Oriental motives effected on the carcass of Greco-Roman art, as
Kenneth Clark remarks. Then it became an exercise in a self-
delighting daring. There were no studies of man by man for
man. Man was, as yet, an earthling, weighed down by mortality.

He was expectant of divine salvation. He was alien to his world. He was beset by bizarre and terrifying monsters. These he depicted: unclean apes with forked tails, fish with goats' heads, reptilian birds with hominid faces, centaurs and tailed quadrupeds.

Medieval man was as conscious of reality as any modern is. But his world was an ordered harmony of symbolic objects. Everything from stones to archangels symbolized an ideal order, a trans-sense order, an existence that could not be seen, heard, measured, tasted, smelled. Even one hundred years later and near the beginning of the Renaissance, Dante would still echo this view. His poetry is riven with a sense of the unearthly. Human light is a pale image of heavenly radiance. Human happiness mirrors the disembodied bliss of God. "As when" is an expression used by him again and again, prefixed to a description of sunlight on leaves, music over mountaintops, or the movement of the seas. The message was clear: everything human served only to make the trans-human comprehensible. The statuary reflected a new look. In place of the soul-less and arrogant faces of Greek gods and powerful Roman emperors, there appeared a new spirituality of face line, a selfless pride in being human, and an aura of detachment compared to which the frozen antics of a many-armed Buddha were faceless mouthings of human emptiness.

Then a lightness and a feeling of divine reason entered, bringing with it a more ennobling idea of man and his earthly home. It was the voice of Peter Abelard demanding to understand so that he might believe. It was Thomas of Aquin subjecting all known things to man's reasoned logic. It was Abbot Suger of Cluny arguing that "man may rise to the contemplation of the divine through the senses." Man's world was hierarchized for man's ascent to the absolute. Behind it all lay the growing conviction that only through the beauty perceived by our senses could we come to understand absolute beauty. This new conviction of man's innate potential to reach the divine expressed itself in Gothic architecture.

No longer was man's spirit expressed by the hooded dome and heavy structure weighing man down on the ground. Gothic art and architecture achieved what had not been achieved since Greco-Roman times, a sensuous and emotional impact. Not merely did it present man with an object of contemplation and admiration, thus lifting his mind to metaphysical things; it set up vibrations in man's air. It lifted man himself by means of its pointed shafts, clusters, and columns streaking into vaults and arches uninterruptedly and straight up to the sky of God's dwelling. It gave man himself a weightless feeling in his spirit. Man was about to search for himself as hero of creation.

There developed, then, the mentality of Western civilization as it has been known up to the twentieth century. The traits of that mentality have been diminishing in force. Some have effectively disappeared from Western society. As a total thing, that mentality belongs to a bygone world as dead and as unseeable as the turned face of the moon. Man's intellectual energy and its emotional basis, his feeling of compassion for other men; his sense of unity in mankind; his consciousness of man's congenital power, not merely to overcome by overpowering physique but to conquer by the power of gentleness, the strength of patience, and the irresistible power of beauty; his conviction that man can move, change, not merely modify, his environment; his ideal of woman and of courtly love; his romanticism.

10

Of Man as Hero

In the fifteenth century, new things appeared, new knowledge was acquired, new trends seized man in Western society. For one thing, Greek and Roman manuscripts came into circulation. Cosimo de' Medici built the Library of San Marco to house them. The old individualism of classical Greece and the heroic ambitions of the Roman ethos came into view. For another, America was discovered. It meant not merely expansion into a new *Lebensraum*. It induced a new dynamism into politics and economics. It shattered the persistent Christian idea that all men by that time had heard the Gospel of Jesus. For centuries, in those faraway lands, millions of men had lived and died without ever hearing of Christianity. What did this mean? The human mind exploded. The year 1500 was the pivotal date.

Before that time there was no alliance between Greco-Roman antiquity and Christian Europe. Man was not exalted as man or as citizen of his world. He was, in Aquinas's pregnant two-word expression, *in via,* a traveler, a pilgrim, staying overnight in a battered caravansary. Around Western man lay uncharted seas, unknown skies, hostile infidels to the south and southeast, alien kingdoms to the east and north. Beyond those boundaries were strange and terrifying lands inhabited by two-headed cannibals, full of living bestiaries, mysterious societies in China, Japan, and Arabia. At best, man's universe was an abacus reflecting a measurable harmony. At worst, man's universe was a place of exile. Mostly, man was crushed by the weight of his destiny. At best, he could fly away and forget himself in the absolute. Francis of Assisi (1181–1226) epitomized this denudation of the self, the renunciation of all.

The individual is discovered in Florence. In the fifteenth century a realistic aim appears simultaneously in the Netherlands and in Italy. Masaccio of Florence (1401–28) and van Eyck of Bruges (1390–1440) penetrated the surface of a scene in order to endow it with a sense of spatiality, of recession in distance, and of three dimensions. This realism, this humanism, attained both a glory and a pessimism, as we see in Giorgione's *Triumph of Death* and in Michelangelo's *Last Judgment*. Yet both glory and pessimism lay within the framework of gods and heroes. Giotto at the opening of the fifteenth century breaks with the tradition of flat linear style. He painted solid objects in space. Realistic portraiture starts. Van Eyck develops perspective and a sensitivity to atmosphere. Buildings appear that elevate and celebrate the light of human intelligence, not merely divine harmony.

The divine is humanized. The human is divinized. Painters depicted the ancient "invisible" truths such as the Trinity and Unity of God, the Godhead, hell, heaven, within a melodious tracery of human perfection in form and in scarcely felt movement. Divinity was clad in aery color. Angels' wings melted into aureoles of gold and interlocking rose petals. They invested human gestures of the Virgin, of Jesus, of the saints, with a trance-like movement, a breathless stillness, clothing their bodies in translucent flesh and robes, surrounding them with an aura of light through human space but without a human shadow. In Botticelli's *Birth of Spring*, Venus is given the figure of the Virgin. Michelangelo's *Paul*, blinded on the road to Damascus, cries to us of all human pain as well as of all human anguish in the spirit.

The Platonic idea of love is meshed with the medieval concept of chivalry and courtly love, to produce the new ideal of the gentleman, *il cortegiano*, of Castiglione. But now, instead of undying devotion, man as the gentleman seeks fame as the reward for his gifts. Furthermore, his world must be adjusted to the scale of his reasonable necessity. It was but a step to conclude that each individual must be helped to a greater consciousness of his faculties and powers, so as to attain his natural balance between physique, on the one hand, and intellectual powers, on the other. It was all summed up in Federigo Montefeltro's phrase: *"essere humano."* To be human. Humanism was born. When Gianozzo Manetti wrote his book, *The Dignity and the Ex-*

cellence of Man, nothing could reverse the tide. The age of man as hero and as giant had begun.

Almost one thousand years before the Renaissance, Protagoras had stated almost as a theorem: "Man is the measure of all things." In the twelfth century, John of Salisbury expressed contemporary man's view of all man's imitative gropings as inspired solely by a cultural parrotism: "We are dwarfs standing on the shoulders of giants." Now in the fifteenth century, Leon Battista Alberti writes of man: "To you is given a body more graceful than other animals, to you power for apt and various movements, to you most sharp and delicate senses, to you wit, reason, memory, like an immortal God." What had happened? We do not know the exact instrumentalities which produced it. In retrospect we can merely follow the parade of great men and note the quick leapfrogging succession of events.

Today those heroes and giants stand before our memories as in a rich, inaccessible tapestry hung against the lightsome sky of the Renaissance. We can contemplate their paintings, sculptures, woodcuts, buildings, mosaics; we can read their books and decisions; we can reflect on the lands they discovered, the seas they traveled, the empires and kingdoms they founded, expanded, and swayed, and on the battles they fought. They helped to make our modern world. None of them intended to make such a world as we live in. Between us and them, over and above the abyss of centuries and swift-rushing time, there stretches a veil of unknowing and, from our modern side of the picture, an inadequacy of mind. We are inclined to make lists of dates and of names, totals of particular acts and declarations, and to structure these into our sole understanding.

Thomas More writing of the earthly Utopia; Michelangelo depicting for the first time the heroic character of Greece and Rome but with a force of spirit unknown to the ancients; Bernini creating the complex of St. Peter's Basilica and the Square; John of the Cross and Teresa of Avila initiating a new strain in Christian mysticism and in the religion of the West; Dürer perfecting his woodcuts; Montaigne wielding a new weapon, the essay; Palestrina sending his new music floating through cathedrals and churches; Carlo Borromeo instituting a new tradition in religious austerity; Ignatius of Loyola, Huss, Wycliffe, Luther, Melanchthon, Calvin, breaking up the unity of the churches and endeavoring to forge new unities.

These are only a few of the names and the barest mention of their achievements. The mistake would be to think that any of them or of the vast procession of great men at that time did not think and move within the same world of ideas. They were, in a relative fashion and with individual idiosyncrasies, heroes and giants living out the new idea of man as hero and giant in a created world. They differed, as it were, in details. But, as always, it was details that counted. It was the national feeling of dislike for foreigners which arose in Germany and England. It was the rise of a solid middle class and the beginnings of what we know as capitalist economy. It was the crass condition of the Christian churches everywhere from the papacy down to the smallest benefice: vested interest, political alliances, great landed wealth, a contempt for the ordinary people. It was the beginning of the colonialist struggle: England, France, Spain, Portugal (and then Holland and Germany), fighting about new and rich overseas possessions. The quest of man as hero and giant in his world laid out before his eyes a new panoply of facts and objects, thus provoking man's curiosity and evoking from him a new method of knowing and assessing his very ancient world. For the way of knowledge taught him by tradition was woefully inadequate.

It is here that we sense the trap-gate beginning to close on the stream of man's development. A central figure is Francis Bacon (1561–1626). For his achievement and his contribution constitute a cameo miniature of what was happening to man in quest of his heroic and giant stature.

Bacon's aim was worthy of any late medieval man who sensed the dawning greatness in the Renaissance: "To endow the condition and the life of man with new powers or works . . . To extend more widely the limits of the power and greatness of man." The object of all this? The exclusion of the higher aims of life hitherto entertained by man? The wiping out of the divine image throughout the universe? The cessation of all traditional contemplation of wisdom in man's universe? Not at all. Bacon would have vomited his disgust in poised, epigrammatic barbs of scorn at such statements. Bacon's purpose was precisely to raise man's mind "above the confusion of things, where he may have the prospect of the order of nature and the error of man." Truth and utility are aspects of the same glorious ultimate. "Works themselves are of greater value as pledges of truth than as contributing to the comforts of life." "Works," for Bacon, consisted of what we would call scientific discovery and demonstration.

Man's method of knowing had been fixed by the philosophic method developed in the Middle Ages. It was built on certain fundamental assumptions. One of these was naïve: if you know the nature of human reason in itself, you will discover the nature of your world solely thereby. One was foolish: make some observations of natural processes and then you can reason to a wide measure of truth. One was ignorant: if you make a discovery, you have demonstrated its truth. One was fatal for progress: only those versed in theology and ecclesiastical philosophy can judge the truth of any scientific discovery and activity.

The insufferable naïveté and pathetic insufficiency of these presuppositions had been perceived by Roger Bacon (1214–94, and apparently no relation of Francis Bacon), philosopher and lecturer at Paris and Oxford, and a Franciscan friar. He wrote to the then Pope, Clement IV, proposing that the Church establish a team of savants and scientists who would work solely on the natural sciences: languages, mathematics, optics, alchemy, astronomy, botany, zoology, geology, geography. He proposed, in short, an institute of research and study along experimental lines. He employed both scorn and contempt against his enemies. He was, surely, the victim of a great credulity and subject to many of the same superstitions as the men of his age. But he did see what lacked. His plea was not fulfilled. Clement died in November 1268. Bacon was thrown in prison by his Franciscan brothers-in-Christ, who were appalled at his daring. He died in 1294. When his namesake, Francis Bacon, three hundred years later made his proposals, there was no choice for the Church or the ecclesiastical mind. The affair was out of their hands.

11

Of Man as Structure

Francis Bacon supplied the framework of the new knowledge: all the observable facts of man's universe. He defined the instruments of that knowledge: man's senses to collect the facts, man's memory to store those facts, man's imagination and reason to inquire into them. Man, the new man, man as he was to be exalted for the next two hundred years and depressed for the following two hundred and forty years to the end of the twentieth century, was defined by Bacon: "the servant and interpreter of nature, who can act and understand no further than he has observed, either in operation or in contemplation, of the method and the order of nature." Bacon, who had started off with fundamentally and explicitly the same aim as theocentric medieval man, had locked himself and his successors into a new way of considering man which would obviate and finally eliminate man as hero and giant. That quest was all but over. The trap-gate had shut. In retrospect, it is ironic to note Bacon's ostensible purpose, as he wrote in his *Instauratio:* to restore man to that command over nature which he lost by the Fall of Adam in the Garden of Paradise. Bacon even projected a political machinery and a state guidance in order to effect this.

Bacon had, in his own words, "rung the bell which called the wits together." Baconian principles were applied by Locke to psychological speculation. The French Encyclopedists of the eighteenth century derived their new division of the sciences from him. A galaxy of like-minded scholars surrounded and followed him: Galileo (1564–1642), Kepler (1571–1630), Stevin

(1548–1620), Descartes (1596–1650), Harvey (1578–1657), Newton (1642–1727). Then the Century of Lights dawned. At the dawn of the eighteenth century, something shook the various parts of the human race out of a timeless slumber, as if a sudden illumination had been granted to sightless eyes and new passions kindled in cold souls. Everywhere and in practically all departments of human activity, the fixed familiar surface of things cracked apart as new ideas and forces, new knowledge and fresh precisions flooded up to quicken the world.

Celsius determined that 100° was the boiling point of water. Lavoisier formulated the law of the conservation of matter. Thomas Savery constructed the first steam engine. Diderot accomplished his encyclopedic conspectus of all human knowledge. Daviel operated on the cataract. Marggraf produced sugar from beetroots. Bering charted Siberia. Cooke completed his South Sea voyages. Euler published his treatise on differential calculus. Lomonosov founded Russian belles-lettres. Haydn filled Europe with his chants, quatuors, symphonies, and oratorios suffused with profound beliefs. Handel's *Messiah* was presented in London. Adam Smith categorized the capitalist system. Hume sharpened men's ideas on human perception. Kant published his long-awaited *Kritik der Reinen Vernunft*. The illumination is perceptible even in the Far East. Tai Chen (1723–77) abandoned rationalistic neo-Confucianism and developed objective, inductive, critical methods of inquiry. Takeda Izumo produced the first popular Japanese drama, *The Village School*. The Bharat Candra appeared in Bengali verse. Pigalle carved his statue of Mercury. A Peruvian mulatto, Rosales, rebuilt the lovely cathedral of Lima. Man everywhere plunged into a new fever of thought.

For over a thousand years, European man had lived in the hegemony of a unitary faith and learned under the tutelage of Mediterranean Christianity. Now he broke away from his long indenture to the finely shaped rigidities of dogmatic Christianity. Men always live violently in Renaissances. They agonize in Reformations. In monolithic empires and ideologies, they breed and brood for revolution. But once exposed to the light of felt freedom, man exults anew, revives his courage; his mind burns with fresh hope, fertile inventiveness, unreflecting daring. So it was in this Century of Lights. It is called the Enlightenment because, according to its participants and their admirers, it was in this age that man opened his eyes to himself and to his world. Man certainly did this. The abrogation of man the giant and the hero was almost over. It was not merely that it had depended on

postulates of another world, of a god-given law, and of a final
other-worldly destiny for man. It was principally that the importance, the beauty, and the value of man as man were transferred
abruptly to the plane of inductive science and of sense data. The
rest was logical consequence and result.

Politically and religiously, the West changed its entire face.
Religiously, Europe was practically split in half, the northern
half predominantly Protestant, the south predominantly Roman
Catholic. In the Roman Catholic Church, there was established
a fortification and a world-wide defense system to withstand
the long siege. All the great agencies and ministries of Roman
Catholicism as we know it today received definitive form. There
developed, in Germany, Switzerland, Holland, and England
notably, the deeply entrenched Protestant ascendancy, fomenting in its midst the science and the technology that made
possible all modern science and technology. It was primarily in
this part of Western society that the search for man as a structure flourished and progressed. But the internal morality both
of Catholicism and of Protestantism suffered. "In trying to make
themselves angels, men transform themselves into beasts,"
wrote Montaigne about the Protestants of his day. This can also
be said of the Catholics. For they both developed Angelism and,
as an inevitable companion, bestiality.

In the development of European painting and art we find a telling illustration of the transformation in the quest of man. The
realism and the humanism of the Renaissance changed in the
seventeenth century. Artists now sought to paint consistently
the world around them in greater detail. No longer was there a
question of bathing all human landscapes and human beings in
godly or heroic light. Every object and any action of man, together with the landscapes of his life, were clad in the play of
human light: the sun, a lamp, a flash of lightning, the glare of
war, the gleam of discoveries, the sheen of love, the brightness
of peace. The same spirit of truthfulness which animated Baconian thought and the numerous followers in the field of natural
science and knowledge was also the inspiring motive of painting and art down to the rise of Impressionism. The political
cousin of this "truthfulness" may be seen as the inspiration of
the two great eighteenth-century revolutions. The American Revolution of 1776 gave birth to the first anti-colonialist state in human history. The French Revolution marked the first time in the
history of the West that the brute force of the people's masses

overcame every ancient structure on which their society had been built: dynasty, church, society classes, traditions.

The entire quest after man, in his structure and in the structure of his world, was marked over and leavened by a movement that is called Romanticism. Romanticism, in its full ambit, seems to have functioned as a "delicious counterpoint" to the stark and unbeautiful lines on which man was being sought and thought of. Normally, the term is applied to poets and painters, to a Byron and to a Goya. But Romanticism had a wider vogue. It dominated the minds of men until well into the second half of the nineteenth century. It found political expression in the romanticizing French Revolutionaries renaming days, weeks, months, and years, as well as in their political slogans and their naïve world outlook. It found philosophical expression in the smile of reason vaunted by Voltaire and in the noble savage of Jean-Jacques Rousseau. Voltaire and Rousseau blamed religion and specifically Christianity for all Europe's ills. The former decided that reason would save Europe. The latter exalted the natural virtue of man unspoiled by priest, rabbi, church, law, altar, incense, and prescribed prayers. Both believed that the goodness of natural man was superior to the superficial goodness of man sophisticated by a Church-taught society.

Romanticism found a permanent political expression in the thought of Thomas Jefferson and in the American Declaration of Independence. All men were born equal and had a right to pursue life, liberty, and happiness. No motivation was sought from any religious source. It was incidental that Jefferson and the founders of the Republic believed in God. Man, as man, was the source of all that man had and could have. In sum, Romanticism was part poetry, part politics, part artistic expression, part philosophy, and part life-style. It never became a vital determining force in the socio-political life of Europe or the Americas. That was dominated and determined first by the overriding political fortunes of the great colonial powers. Then, subsequent to two world wars, the rise of political Marxism in Europe and China, and the overall advance of technology, it was based on the structuralism of a latter-day comity of nations held together and at bay by a nuclear deterrent. Neither did Romanticism dictate a societal life-style on any grand scale.

"I wish that I could derive all phenomena of nature by some kind of reason from mechanical principles; for I have many reasons to suspect that they all depend upon certain forces by which the particles of bodies are either mutually attracted and cohere in regular figures or are repelled and recede from each other." So wrote Newton in 1687. To back up his statement, he pointed to the law of physical movement, which seemed wholly unrelated to any spiritual order. The basic principle behind his thought was that all phenomena in man's world were determinate. Before Newton, the states of man's body had been included under this principle. In the late eighteenth century and during the nineteenth century, the principle of determinism was applied to man's mental states. The germ of psychological determinism was proposed by Marx in *Zur Kritik der politischen Ökonomie* (1859); and biological determinism was inherent in Darwin's *Origin of the Species* (1859). The way was open for Freud, who first proposed an entire inner structure of man, and for the social determinism of Engels and Marx in *Das Kapital*.

Man as a structure emerged from this trap-gate of history. The medievalists had classified man structurally, of course: soul, passions, senses, mind, body, will. And they had structured his world: heaven, earth, hell. And they had structured the time of man: his nothingness and his creation, the years, days, and hours of his mortality as he balanced for a fleeting instant (*nunc fluens*) on the merest tip of God's static and majestic eternity (*nunc stans*). But all their structuring took place on a presumed ground or absolute of reality. That reality was not measurable, because for them it had no physical dimensions. None of the five senses and no instrument aiding the five senses could "reach" it, could know it. There was no knowing it by physical means. It could be known, but that was another knowledge and another mode of knowing. It was reality, because reality, by definition, gave meaning to all things in man's life. By it, man understood all things. He was an essentialist, therefore, because he regarded this ground or essence as the source of human meaning and value. The human dimension for the medieval and Renaissance Westerner was, indeed, a complex structure. But a substantial ground of reality gave the structure its meaning.

Modern man found that by seeking the structure of any object in his world he could advance his material well-being to some degree, great or small. He has applied this to stones, earth, plants, metals, air, clouds, the planets, food, animals, to man's body with its health and its sickness, to man's mental states and condition, and to man's society. This must be said: any advance in medicine, in economics, in the material conditions of societal living has come from the modern method of experimentation, of statistical observation, of inductive reasoning, of scientific demonstration of practical application. No metaphysical system determined the circulation of the blood. No ethico-moral commandment can bring a spaceship safely back to earth from the moon. No church blessing can be used to cure a split palate. Alexander Fleming did not isolate penicillin because he was an Aristotelian. No theological doctrine provides the key for pollution control, fire-fighting, a breech birth, or an impacted wisdom tooth.

Part of Western man's heritage is the conviction that he should seek such knowledge. Progress is measured today by the acquisition of such knowledge. According as man's technology has developed, modern man's life has become more complicated. His basics for survival (air, water, food, fuel, safety, clothes) depend on complicated systems of mechanical and electronic machinery. His means of living (cities, transport, communications, defense, production) and, consequently, his government have become complicated. Everywhere in all departments of his life, man structures: he seeks out the facts; he structures them according to a pattern which has a functional use toward his objectives and which the facts dictate in their mutual interrelationship. But because of this Western development, there has arisen a peculiarity which is called structuralism, or the structuralist mentality.

The peculiarity does not lie in the mass of detail or in the use of machines and electronics, in bureaucratic structures, the technotronic revolution, or the post-industrial character of a society such as we find in the United States. These are man's latest efforts to cope with new advances in his way of living, with his telescoped space and time, with his burgeoning population, with new discoveries and innovations. The peculiarity is that this structuring of his life is taken by Western man as giving the meaning of his life. It is the first time in known history that both man's personal and societal life are given supreme and sole meaning from a structuring of facts which he receives uniquely by his senses and which he measures and calculates in utter and exclusive dependence on his (aided or unaided) senses, with deliberate exclusion of any *a priori* mind and with no reference to an abstract principle. It is the first time in history that knowing or knowledge has been concentrated exclusively in this area and that the resultant data are taken as the supreme reality.

Knowledge of the meaning of man's personal life consists of a knowledge of the facts which are structured in that life. Knowledge of the meaning of man's societal life and of whatever happens in it consists of a knowledge of the facts which form the structure of that life. Structure is the same as meaning. The meaning modern man seeks is given by the structure only. The method of knowing is statistical and inductive. There has been this change, therefore, in Western society and civilization. The change was not the known objective of any one man or group of men. There is no means of fixing on any particular date or year for the change. This has been a trap-gate of history; man could not avoid it. He has entered it; he must move in this stream. And as far as we can judge, the change is not yet complete. For the preceding essentialist mentality is not yet in complete recession. In the midst of the ever widening and ever more dominant structuralism of modern Western man, we find strains of nostalgia for an unexperienced past and a chaos-bearing yearning for a ground of meaning beyond the hard data of our senses and our microscopes or the interpretations of the polls.

At times, it is as if people heard the faint notes of autumnal music from a distant garden telling them of an unknown gateway to a repose and a unity they will forever seek but never find. We can understand the reason for the raging, the irredentism, the almost freak behavior in young and old, the fringe groups and the subcultures and the street people, the solid but terrifying waves of violence by innovators and diehards. The traditionalist. The utopianist. The visionary. The right-wing law-and-order fanatic. The very aggressive passivist. The pronouncedly Fascist liberal. All hear those notes after their own fashion. At times we find traces of this nostalgia in the factitious behaviorisms of the city dweller and in the pathetic contrivances he adopts in order to feign at being with "nature," at being part of a larger "whole," to escape from the cranking particularism of telephones, traffic, and the treadmill of urban existence. Astroturf on the thirty-second-floor balcony. A barbecue supper in the "open air" of the back-yard patio. An hour or two on the golf course with wind and grass and physical effort.

What is true today of the West, and of the United States in particular, will be true of Europe and the Third World within the foreseeable future. For America is blazing a pathway which all other nations will follow. All who imitate and emulate the values and the success of the United States (and who does not?) will follow the same road. The intensifying structuralism of America prefigures the condition of man everywhere in the world of tomorrow.

12

The Changing Dimension in the United States

Only in America of today, a society of some 203 million human beings, is there concrete and palpable evidence that the human dimension has already changed profoundly and that this change has not yet been completed. The evidence is more than a series of hints or suggestions; it is categoric. We cannot say what form that society will have one hundred years from now. We cannot even say the change will be accomplished by then. The tangible evidence of this change which we can assemble permits us to know only what is being excluded as incompatible with that change. But the change is in no way the revolution envisaged by champions such as Che Guevara, Jean-Paul Sartre, Frantz Fanon, R. D. Laing, Mario Savio, Rudi Dutschke, Jurgen Habermas, Alberto Moravia, Peter Marin, and the other patrons of pessimism and/or violence at home and abroad. It is not a greening of America or anything as irresponsibly naïve and simplistic as Consciousness IV hymned by Charles Reich. If anything, it is a de-greening of America. For historical reasons, it is taking place in an urban or megalopolitan society. But this is not part of its essence. It could, theoretically, take place in a pastoral society.

The change does not imply bloodshed or the Animal Farm of George Orwell, the Eloi and the Morlocks of H. G. Wells, or any science-fiction world of the futurists complete with Green Men, New Babies, perpetuated old age, universal orgasms, and doomsday machines. It does not even require economic prosperity, although this speeds the change. But it has an intimidating aspect.

We have no categories with which to define it. No poet or philosopher has a vision of it and a technique adequate to convey that vision. It is not in the sacred books of Western religious thought. Western religion itself is afflicted with a nescience of the future form. The change has only one enemy: he who resists it either by anachronism of stagnant conservatism or by the insolence of imposed solutions.

The most tangible evidence we can immediately summon in order to acknowledge this change comes from those areas of human identity which hitherto have been basic in defining any particular society of human beings. Up to this point in known human history, any particular human society was and still is given a definite human identity in three accepted ways. The first area includes exterior markings or characteristics: language, skin color, and territory. Individual societies spawned an array of traits from these: their literature, their music, the formulation of their laws, their idea of beauty and happiness, their "national" or "group" pride, their economy, their way of life, their friendships and their enemies.

The second area encompasses the basic unitary form of the society, the family. Not merely father-mother-children, but blood relations and in-laws. From this as a matrix came codes of sexual and marital ethics, family succession, and a gamut of "virtues" and "vices"—obedience, respect, impurity, lawfulness, etc.

The third area concerns the most intimate characteristic of a human society: its national or group ethos. This has always been inner: it resided in blind convictions, emotional ties, and unprovable beliefs; it emanated in a shared and felt commonality; it dictated moral behavior; it commanded the will of individuals as well as of nations; it fixed what was "good" and "bad"; it provided the norms both of personal morality and of societal ethics as well as of the political ideal. Thus has the human identity of any society of men been traditionally recognized and defined.

Today, in all these areas, we see in America as a society not merely disturbances, disputes, doubts, and differences. We see the end of all these recognized categories of the human dimension. Many put the cart before the horse and see these disturbances as revealing the nature of the actual change taking place. They are merely passing reactions, however—symptoms of the deep malaise necessarily resulting from the deep change itself: either resistance to it, or the hubris of certain endeavors to impose personal solutions, or the pathos of efforts to hurry the change or to ride it to political advantage. For all these are sins against history. The intimidating factor, as remarked before, is that we cannot know yet what will replace these categories. It is a field day for the panicky, the insecure, the profiteer, the messianic.

First, as to exterior markings. America is the only country in existence today where officially and popularly the language you speak is not a determinant of your belonging to the society of that country. Americans take this for granted. Foreigners assume that English is the "national" language of the United States. This is simply not true as the term is understood in other countries. Nobody is a foreigner in America today because his everyday language is Ukrainian, Arabic, Polish, Latvian, German, Chinese, Portuguese, Russian, or any other language. In India you are a foreigner unless you speak one of the twenty-four-odd *Indian* languages. There is no *American* language in that age-old sense. But the lingua franca of American society is a brand of English.

There is, then, an almost frightening and certainly unprecedented proposition in America today: to make no judgment regarding a man's rights and duties solely on the basis of his skin pigmentation. I say: proposition. For America has taken almost two hundred years to make this a public undertaking and it will take at least two generations to make that proposition stick and cohere and flow with the viscous cement that binds this society together. There is a time for guilt and for craw-thumping, for bloody riots, for organized effort, and for renewed resolution. This is not such a time. It is the time for seeing the almost outlandish character of this proposition. For the truth is that South African apartheid, with the good and the bad in it, is strictly traditional and in keeping with all past human history.

I say: frightening. For no one knows (1) if it can succeed; or, if it does, (2) what the result will be. It will certainly not be the racial "heterosis" lauded by geneticists in the past, who worked on a veritable cookbook principle: "the epitome of American society will be a John Doe—Polish Irish and Yankee on his mother's side; Italian Jew, American Indian, nisei, and Scandinavian on his father's side; with a German physicist stepfather and married to a black musician from the Urals, now naturalized and living in Muncie, Indiana."

What Americans are attempting today is, historically speaking, anomalous; humanly speaking, unprecedented; and, according to standards entertained in modern France, Italy, Germany, Switzerland, the Soviet Union, and mainland China, repulsive and certainly not to be considered for their own individual societies. None of the major human religions (Christianity, Judaism, Buddhism, Islam) ever proposed this or encouraged it of their own accord. It is unheard of. Yet it is the public proposition of American society. It will certainly be achieved.

There is third the exterior marking: territorial identity. The United States is certainly an identifiable piece of human real estate: about four million square miles of earth, every part of which has been mapped, explored, and examined. It is crisscrossed by highways, roads, trails, rails, and airways. It is surveilled by weather and security satellites every day. In this sense, territorial identity exists. But, in reality, this is territorial integrity, not territorial identity in the traditional sense, such as we find it still dominant in countries of the West and the East. Territorial identity in the traditional sense implies not merely fixed and preserved boundaries of the society's land (territorial integrity). For the identity of the individuals and the groups composing that society, it meant territorial association of a vivid and living kind. The citizen was and is marked by his association with one part of the societal territory; in virtue of this close association, that part stands for the whole. It is a societal meiosis. The whole territory is encompassable in the microcosm of the village, the hamlet, the city.

This territorial identity never flourished in the United States as in traditional countries of Western Europe and Asia. It had a partial existence in frontier days. But today it is excluded by two elements. Such a territorial extent and such a diversity of territory as we find in the United States never belonged before in recorded history to any human group claiming and living within a self-willed socio-political homogeneity. The great empires encompassed greater diversities, but this was imposed. In fact, it is impossible for any territorial identity in the traditional sense to animate the society living in such territorial diversity and extent. No one can identify with a semi-continent such as America in the same way as a Frenchman with France, an Afghan with Afghanistan, or a Peruvian with Peru. It is not "encompassable."

The second element is the mobility, or rather what makes possible the mobility, of the American population. There is very infrequently a sense of deep family roots tied to a particular locality. There are no real linguistic or even dialectal ties. The inhabitants of Ghent, Belgium, refer rudely to the inhabitants of Bruges as Totentrekkers. The latter respond with the Ghentish nickname (equally pejorative) Stropelaars. No such intimate exchange is possible between two big cities of the United States. There are no clan or tribe localities as in the Old World or such as the first Americans found among the North American Red Indians. There is, in addition, the competitive upward-mobile economy which calls for physical mobility. There is, finally, the continual urbanization of the population. The American city effectively wipes out any local ties, obfuscates any primeval attachment to earth and trees and landscapes and waters and particular land configurations.

The total result is that America has territorial integrity but Americans do not have that territorial identity which was as vivid and essential to the mind of Neanderthal Man in his Upper Pleistocene valley as it was to the minds of the Germans in 1939 and is to the British and the Vietnamese of 1971. Territory is not a marking of this human society in the United States of the late twentieth century. For America, in the American mind, was never primarily, if at all, a geographical entity. It was and still is an emotive idea. As an idea, it has a long genealogy going back to Bradford's "beacon on a high hill" and down as late as Lyndon B. Johnson's "Great Society." As an emotive force, it spilled over into feelings, convictions, preferences no different in category from those of a German, a Spaniard, an Irishman, a Pole, or a Chinaman.

Within the society, the change goes further and has lethally affected the traditionally basic unit of human society: the family. Today the "tribal" or "extended" family unity is a dead thing in America: grandparents, blood relatives, and in-laws do not form any dynamic unity with parents and children, according to the ever more prevalent mores. The family was dynamic once upon a time: it ensured the rearing of children, physical security and comfort, economic cooperation, and social living. This is gone, except in some isolated pockets of Orthodox Jews, conservative Christians, American Indians, and in esoteric secretions such as the Amish, the Adamite groups, and in the hinterland of Appalachia.

The change has not stopped there. The "tribal" family reduces itself easily to the "nuclear" family: father-mother-children. But this "nuclear" family is also vitally affected in its traditional *raison d'être*. Furthermore, the roles of father, mother, and children are changing. First of all, the "togetherness," or unity (the old-fashioned expression!), of the nuclear family is on the wane. For a complex of reasons. The emergent motive for any man and woman to get together and stay together is no longer the child or to have children. Nor is their getting together or staying together in function of a societal or a contractual or an ideological reason. The latest reason is "openness of feeling" and human relationship.

The traditional form of the nuclear family itself is obviously being sifted and sieved to see how it can survive on the principle of "togetherness," of "how two people feel about each other," rather than on civil legalities or religious contracts. Even such a staunch and redoubtable proponent of doctrinal grounds for marriage as the Roman Catholic Church is diluting its alleged reasons for the institution and permanency of marriage by placing equal emphasis on mutual love and on child-bearing and child-rearing. It seems, in sum, that the traditional reason for the triad of the nuclear family to stay together is disappearing.

The mutual roles of father and mother are changing. The vitally changing factor here is woman. From being the "vessel of weakness," the "weaker sex," Adam's rib, man's helper, man's playmate, the homebody, the homemaker, the mother of a man's children, she has emerged not as a rival of man but as his equal. Again it would be erroneous to underline either facile contraceptive methods or new job possibilities or the prolongation of life, the increase in single couples and in economically viable single women, greater permissiveness in heterosexual promiscuity, Lesbianism, or male homosexuality, as the causal factors. For these seem to be either symptoms or temporary results of a change, not the change itself. The change lies deeper. It concerns not merely woman and not merely man but the human dimension of the species.

The third area concerns the "national" or "group" ethos. This goes under various names. Sometimes it is called philosophically the consensus, sometimes romantically the "American thing," sometimes bluntly "the reason we stick together," sometimes grandiosely "our American way of life or doing things." Because of its connotation, the term "consensus" is used here.

If some of the changes-in-process which we have discussed can be called frightening, the manifest change in the American consensus is of fatal import. It carries with it an unremitting and ineluctable ultimatum: succeed in this change, and American society will be cohesive and will continue; fail, and it must necessarily fragment, fall apart internally, and dissolve. Again, something hitherto unknown in human history is being attempted.

Expressed simply in terms of what the American consensus

was and what change it is undergoing, the situation is as follows. With the exception of America, any national unit or "country" which we know in history was built on a consensus. This had three elements: an ideology, a national motivation (or moral imperative), and a set of inner convictions stemming from the ideology and concretized in customs, mores, folkways, etc.

Ideology here means an elaborated view of man, his origin, his destiny, his purpose in life, what is "good" and what is "bad" for that life, and his relations to other men. It had a deep foundation in ethico-religious beliefs, and it was usually expressed in theological formulas, credal beliefs, ritual behaviorisms, and, more often than not, philosophically elaborated.

The moral imperative of a nation is understood here as the deepest basis according to which broad judgments and directions are nationally formed and ratified concerning what is morally "good" or morally "bad," as distinct from what is merely physically "good" or physically "bad," economically "good" or "bad," "good" or "bad" for bodily health, etc. Thus a devastating but successful national war can damage a great number of citizens, weaken the economy of the country, can, in other words, be bad populationally (numbers die), economically (drainage of resources to sustain the war effort), and physically (bodily suffering and death), and at the same time be judged morally "good" in the national sense, because its aim is to preserve the national identity.

The inner convictions of a people spring from the mutually shared ideology or outlook which takes in man, man's life, and man's world. The convictions can be conceptualized even minutely. They are embodied in a set of practical principles according to which national life is organized, maintained, and developed. These convictions embrace most activities of the citizens as individuals and as members of the group.

Ideology, moral imperative, and inner convictions—these are the three components of the classical consensus as we find it in all countries of the Old World.

From the beginning, the American consensus had one distinct feature: the deliberate exclusion of any philosophy or ideology as an explicit, implicit, or official basis for the moral imperative or for the practical principles guiding the American union and its characteristic socio-political system. The framers and fashioners of the American Constitution and the later institutions of the Union intended to establish a system where mobility was paramount. They sought mobility. They thus made of de-

mocracy a *process* of socio-political change. They refused to in-
corporate in their system any ideological principles, unchangeable policies, or the tenets of any particularized philosophy.

There was, thus, no explicit or implicit moral motivation, such
as we find in the classical consensus, for this could only have
sprung from an explicit ideology or philosophy. This was excluded. But there was what we can call a *moral presumption.* It
was presumed that religion, Christianity specifically, would
exist and be professed by the vast majority, and that a moral imperative would be derived privately from this religion of the
members and from its intellectual leadership. Americans rested
the justice and rightness of the system ultimately on a moral
presumption. But they did not envisage or countenance it in
any rigid form as a necessary trait of being "American." Within
this union and system, men were enabled to pursue the material rewards of this world—life, wealth, happiness—in freedom.
At the start, for leaders and people, the morally correct pursuit of
these goals was thought to lead to rewards also in the next world.

But within the union there was no official philosophy, no official religion, no official church. There was official freedom for
them to exist and function at the will of private citizens.

Today there is no change in the practical principles of national government and organization. Nor is there any change in
the driving principle that men of this polity should be enabled to
pursue life, wealth, and happiness in freedom. But all the evidence available points to one conclusion: we can no longer take
it that an implicit moral presumption is either operative or even
acceptable to the American people as a whole. In the first place,
the two sources of the moral presumption are inoperative themselves and unacceptable. Second, in the actual working of the
system, any and every moral presumption, explicit or implicit,
is gradually and definitely being excluded as inoperable and
unacceptable.

The two sources. The two sources of the strong moral presumption were religion and intellectual leadership. Originally,
the churches were deemed to and indeed did nourish the moral
presumption. At a certain moment, too, it can be argued, the
synagogues entered the picture. Today, however, neither churches
nor synagogues nourish any moral presumption, and this is due
mainly to Protestant pathology, Catholic chauvinism, and Jewish
neurosis.

Protestant pathology is multifaceted. In essence, American
Protestantism is susceptible to profound guilt feelings, in virtue

of which it is willing to undertake almost suicidal policies. From being radically opposed—on allegedly religious grounds—to all non-Protestants and all non-whites, the Protestant mind has swung over to a guilt-ridden permissiveness that will allow no moral absolutes except two, perhaps: the rights of the individual, and the absolute surety that no moral absolute exists. Thus there has arisen the tradition of thinking that is often labeled "liberal."

Catholic chauvinism started off as the will and intent of the declared underdog to be integrated into the American system in spite of the Protestant Establishment. It has ended up necessarily by becoming merely a social tag rather than the name of a religious affiliation. In itself, there is nothing intrinsically pernicious in this. But because it was paralleled by a Catholic drive to effect political participation and was accompanied by the drying up of Catholic religious inspiration, it has proven a disaster. Roman Catholicism in the United States, while claiming to be different, has become "Protestantized" in thought structure, social cast, sociological outlook, and religious behaviorism. It has partaken, therefore—and with enthusiasm characteristic of all latecomers—of the Protestant "liberal" outlook in all its finer shades.

The Jewish neurosis is particular to Jews. Burdened by memories of dogmatic and authoritarian Christian governments and tyrants in Europe, American Jews developed an almost neurotic fear of anything in public and civil life resembling a moral imperative which had the backing of civil government. Jews have been most prominent in all "liberation" movements of a social nature and in all litigation based on appeals to the Constitution with regard to prayer in schools, abolition of abortion restrictions, liberalization of drug laws, liberalization of pornography laws, as they have been prominent in student revolutionary groups and in opposition to the Vietnam War. It is as if there must be a Jewish reaction—and only in one direction—on these and on related issues.

Protestant pathology, Catholic chauvinism, and Jewish neurosis—these three are only the outward signs of a failure to produce any specifically religious formula suitable for their adherents, which would be reflected in a moral presumption at one and the same time practical and American. This source of the moral presumption, as envisaged by the framers and fashioners of the socio-political system, seems to have dried up.

The second possible source for nourishing the national moral imperative is in the intellectual area, for the chief "ideologues" here are the academic faculties, the professors, the teachers, and the specialists of our universities, colleges, and high schools. They have failed. First of all, they are guilty of a cultural and sterile *parrotism.* They learned the polysyllabic words, acquired the academic trappings, and claimed the privileged dignity of an intellectual culture which they found decaying in Europe between the two world wars and after World War II. But they failed to develop any indigenous American intellectualism, for they merely imitated the pragmatist, who seeks solutions here and now with the materials he can measure. The intellectual seeks solutions in the spirit and the mind of man.

The academicians, professors, and teachers made of this eclecticism a credo and thereby neglected the most significant and strongest distinction between these two complementary personages of the City of Man: the intellectual provides the inner values indigenous and endemic to the material solutions which the pragmatist chooses.

Second, the intellectuals failed to create a humanism genuine for the United States and its specifically different socio-political system and consensus. In philosophy, they adopted German idealism without any of the preceding realism. In social theory, they became pragmatists without any of the rationalism that had made the rise of pragmatism possible. In theology, they became progressives without ever having started at the beginning. In anthropology, they adopted, developed, and perfected the methodology of Europeans, but, like good Americans, eschewed the philosophy that gave substance to that methodology. The result was a science of collections, a taxonomy of ideas, with no cement. Common to all types of the traditional American intellectual was a note of technocracy. The appellation "intellectual" became synonymous with technocrat, and this was really squaring the circle or crossing the Bridge of Asses, in the original connotation of such descriptions of the birth of monsters, the misshapen reproductions of bizarre processes.

Third, they produced no indigenous wisdom for America, their most important social function and their unique professional contribution to the political life of the country. They failed to develop a wisdom concerning human life and human relationships which would match and suit the very new and very different political genre that gave birth to the "American thing" in the eighteenth century. They parroted the apothegms of a parallel European culture wisdom. But there was no native incarnation for America. They never developed an intellectualism to back up the "American thing" in its giant steps from nineteenth-century post-industrialism. Those who should have been the wise men of America adopted without further ado the wisdom and the life view of a culture (European) which arose from a specifically different consensus and was designed to satisfy a hierarchic society sustained by the age-long and aching boundaries of human society as old as Olduvai—color, national language, social classes, ethnic origin, religious beliefs, political "isms," things that are incompatible with the "American thing."

Working exclusion. The moral presumption is obviously being excluded in wide sociological and political areas. What is noticeable is that, by a seemingly general consensus, no argument for any public action or policy can be drawn from what has traditionally been called morality. There is here a subtle transformation or metamorphosis, and it appears in ordinary processes such as the administration of the law, judgment on civic behavior, and gray areas such as drug taking, pornography, marriage, sexual and civic behavior, and in the values of personal life. Judgment and administration of law, for instance, rested in practice on a duo: inner moral (Christian) law, allied to exterior and civil law. More and more, what is good is merely what the law enacts, what is bad is what contravenes the law. Neither the "good" nor the "bad" has any reference to "inner" conditions. Important socio-cultural questions such as pornography, drug taking, male and female homosexuality, sexual freedom, were previously decided on a preponderantly moral basis expressed and upheld by law. It is, for instance, unforgivable and unacceptable to discriminate against or judge anyone because he or she is a homosexual. Such an attitude or judgment will evoke as much protest about violations of the homosexual's rights as today are heard about women's rights in salary parity and equal job opportunity.

What all this amounts to is simple. Theoretically, there is for man no longer a problem of how to relate knowledge to human values. His problem, his occupation, his craze, the big business he is about today, is to know. For knowledge is the only value to be admitted. The values of man lie only in knowledge. For knowledge is what man knows and what man implements in doing. But values, moral and religious, have always been considered as what man ought to be, and what he ought to do by being what he ought to be and in order to be what he ought to be. Within the structuralist mode of society, there is nothing which ought to be, nothing that man ought to do.

No appeal can be made to a revealed ethic (Christian or Jewish, for instance). More starkly still, no appeal can be made to "natural laws," "natural rules of society," "the natural way of arranging things." For hundreds of generations man saw a profound alliance between himself and nature. It was a natural alliance deriving from primeval times, and from it man drew rules of societal grouping. This alliance is scuppered, forever. With it went the rules it implied. For about six generations in America and about fifty generations in the West, man acknowledged an alliance of salvation between himself and God. In virtue of this, he established an entire societal system of moral values and a primary reason for being worthy of the dignity of man. This alliance of salvation has been broken. With it has gone the system of moral values. Between man and nature lies a vast solitude which man overcomes by analysis and labeling of facts. Between man and God there stands nothing. Man's worth and dignity are decided by man on man's fiat. This, as said, is theoretically the situation in the present structuralist change. That is to say, man is acting as if this was the condition. Practically speaking and in the ongoing situation of American society, this is not how things will work out.

The society that is America seems on the evidence to be set on an unalterable course. There were once, as in all human societies certain accepted parameters within which a society or polity was recognized and defined. These are being eschewed. In the national imperative of America, no religious or moral particularism is acceptable. In interpersonal relations, the original units out of which the society grew are losing any justification, explanation, or *raison d'être* which flowed traditionally from particularized and specific moral and religious sources. For national imperative, for interpersonal relationships, as well as for the self-definition of the society, direct appeal is made more and more exclusively to enacted law, and no justification or explanation of that law is sought beyond its character as law.

In sum, the human dimension of American society is increasingly structuralist. It is easy for traditionalists, for "right-wingers," for religionists, to see this development as a degenerative process and to accuse ethnic groups (blacks, for instance), socio-political blocs (Protestant liberals, for instance), or subcultures (Jews, for instance) of having destroyed America. The truth is that elemental forces of American society are at work here, bypassing both the good and the evil intentions of those involved, and engaging this polity on a do-or-die course from which it cannot regress.

13

Prophets, Priests, and Judges

All around modern American man of these decades, there has developed a society based on the structuralist principle. His continual condition in this society is an increasingly painful matter, for he is in transit between one dimension and another. He is involved in a societal attempt by a huge diversified population of vast resources to emerge from a stiff and unchangeable background of ethnic diversity, cultural diversity, hard-core traditions, and ingrained ways of thought. Pulling and tugging at this emergent man are a diversity of doctors and a brood of brainstormers. None of these can succeed in finally immobilizing him; yet they cause immeasurable strain, which only adds to his travail. A suitable image of modern man is suggested by the *Captive,* an unfinished marble sculpture by Michelangelo. It is a study in stone of an unfinished struggle to emerge whole, entire, and viable from a deadening dimension: a bearded figure, an unliberated head twisted in effort, unseeing eyes, one hand still sunk invisibly in the marble, the other half-formed pushing vainly outwards, a torso straining to burst from the stone, the legs contorted and shadowy, the feet still enclosed in the formless, immobile material.

Artists, commentators, poets, and others have showered descriptions and interpretations on the emergent Captive. And so it is with modern American man: as he endeavors to emerge, he is assailed on all sides by interpretations, admonitions, forewarnings, and descriptions of himself by the self-appointed prophets, priests, judges, and prefabricators of his travail.

This travail is taking place invisibly in the American spirit. But we can find one concrete and visible expression of it: viable and newly established institutions, habits, folkways, life-styles, communal norms, commonalities of sympathy and understanding. These are the signs of a change in society. But what changes is something behind these tangible things, something beyond persisting mythologies, practical psychologies, sentimentalities, and the interpretive categories of passing literateurs. The travail has nothing essential to do with the prophets, priests, judges, and prefabricators. These fight against it, or foment it, or comment on it, or block it temporarily, or divagate its energies momentarily, or render difficult the completion of one or other phase. But the process continues inexorably.

For there is something in the people more vital than patterns of thought, something which carries forward cumulatively the traditions we inherit. It is not fastidious nowadays to speak of the American spirit. Nor is it regarded as one-sided—which it is—to confine one's vision to the demonstrable, the palpable, the measurable. Yet no other term but spirit is adequate in this context. Prophets, priests, judges, and prefabricators, however, work in a different sphere. They are concerned with the structure, and they fall into general classes. The pseudo-Romantics and structuralists "intellectualize" the structure. The prefabricators "materialize" or "cosmetize" the structure.

Standing on one side and professedly against structuralism and all its pomps are the pseudo-Romantics, a motley group which includes the Dancers, the Angelists, the Adamites, the Destructors-elect, and an ancillary body of Pathetics. Standing on the other side are those professedly for structuralism: the Intellecters, the Smilers, and the Machine-Men. A fair bid to be the officiating high priest of all growing pseudo-Romantics was made by Charles Reich in his *Greening of America*. But this failed as miserably as Timothy Leary's attempt to be the pseudo-Romantic choreographer of the Joyous New World—but for far different reasons. The fact is that all pseudo-Romantics suffer from a severe case of illegitimacy.

Romanticism from its European beginnings in poetry and politics proposed an escape. It was an escape not merely from the fine wigs, the stiffness of eighteenth-century courtly behavior, and the norms of a class society which held in thralldom the European masses from Galway, Ireland, over to Vladivostok in Tsarist Russia. It went further. It idealized a total escape from all bonds of society. This escapism passed into American art and literature as a quasi-visionary strain.

It ignores society and its bonds, except as contemptible sequels of the individual. He is an empire all alone, a law unto himself, undivided, performing, imperious, all-judging, the last word in all taste and all assessment of what the whole of life is about. Romanticism was born of sixteenth-century Protestantism and formed its basic tenet on the Protestant principle that the individual conscience is the ultimate criterion of behavior. This is the Romantic ego exalted by Emerson as the one "who is able to stand alone," for this is "the end for which a soul exists in the world—to be himself the counterbalance of all falsehood and wrong." The total human scene is, in fact, the domain of the individual man.

One hundred years after Emerson there emerged full-blown the pseudo-Romantics. They are utterly critical of society's corruption and utterly intransigent about its chances of having any value. Society as it is must be dismantled, will be dismantled. People will return to a simple and uncomplicated way of life free from the horrors of bureaucracy and cleansed of the pig-like industrial-complex. Pseudo-Romantics, generally speaking, are as ignorant of history as the Mongols in the thirteenth century, and as full of cant as the sophisticated minds and bored wits of eighteenth-century and nineteenth-century London and Paris, who solemnly asserted from behind their fans, powdered bodies, and pampered minds, that only in Tahiti or Tobago or in the distant "islands of the South" could one find an incorrupt society and unpolluted souls of men and women. As full of cant and, of course, more disastrous. For these fine ladies and scientific-minded gentlemen had no intention of exchanging habitats with the naked, ignorant natives of Tonga. Nor did they wish away the socio-political structures of their society. But the pseudo-Romantics of the twentieth century have gone that distance and even further. There is here a genuine, if bastard, line of descent from the original Romantics to the pseudo-Romantics of today.

The pseudo-Romantics fall into different categories. One group simply proposes to dance while Rome burns. The Dancers of Consciousness IV are as convinced as Marxists and jealous Europeans that the whole rotten thing America has become in their eyes is on the way out of human existence. They outdo the ancient Cynics of Athens in their prophetic stance and their quite unloving fecklessness. They are convinced that they will expand and enlarge their Consciousness IV with their rock music, their bell-bottom–exotic clothing, their psychedelic freedom, their sexual promiscuity, and the freshness of their lives. It is one possible, if rather ineffectual, answer to structuralism. They do not take to nature as such and they are afflicted with alalia or severe inarticulateness. Where Thomas Gray exclaimed in 1739: "Not a precipice, not a torrent, not a cliff, but is pregnant with religion and poetry," the Dancers will mutter breathlessly: "Outasight! A blast, man!"

Another category is formed strictly by Angelists, whose solution is more practical: oppose, subvert, destroy. They have chosen that blend of theology, poetry, blood-thirstiness, and laughter which medievalist myth ascribed to the subtle sadism of Satan and which is best described as Angelism. In a proponent such as Dan Berrigan, the quintessential agent of Angelism, the struggle against structuralism (and the structure) is merely a reenactment of Christ's heroic and bloody struggle against the Powers of Darkness from the Garden of Gethsemane to the hill of Calvary, where, of course, he triumphed. The Angelist is Jesus returned to triumph in blood, or Dietrich Bonhoeffer *redivivus* about to die once more. "In his blood he redeemed us," said the Council of Trent. "God is dead," wrote Bonhoeffer.

Berrigan's exhortation: "Your paint be blood/ your canvas you." His promise: "I touch/ shrapnel and flesh, and risk my reason/ for Truth's sake." His proviso: "Color it not kind/ with skies of love and amber/ make it plain with death/ and bitter as remember." His faith: "Do something responsible and let the chips fall, with a kind of obscure faith that the thing will right itself again." His advice from Danbury Prison to the American populace: "Bring the business of this Administration to a halt . . . Destroy the arsenals with a minimum hazard for human life . . ."

This has as much to do with Christian virtue or the heroic patience ascribed to Jesus undergoing torture and death on Calvary as had Stalin's Order of the Day to Russian armies poised to invade Germany in 1944 to do with the Sermon on the Mount: "For every Russian tree destroyed, uproot three German trees. For every Russian killed, kill three Germans. For every Russian woman raped, rape three German women . . ." The Angelism of Berrigan is merely an echo of what we find elsewhere, in poets like Louis Simpson ("We must/ finally kill them, rid the earth of them/ because they are a diseased species," he said of white men). There used to be in the Roman Catholic Church a tradition of heroic self-sacrifice for the sake of an ideal. The saint was a dreamer touching his absolute dream. But the Angelist is an iconoclast bent on destroying all that is comely, graceful, beautiful, merely because he cannot or chooses not to participate in it.

Pseudo-Romantics further split into the Adamites and the Destructors-elect. The latter category includes mainly young people; the former runs the spectrum of generations all the way from the Nearings who took to the New England hills in the Depression of 1932 (Scott Nearing is nearly ninety years old today) to the numerous "nature" communes on the West Coast. Adamites, in their reaction to structuralism, endeavor to "go back" to nature, to get away from the dog dung, deviates, bums, brownouts, blackouts, pushers, pimps, pollution, dirt, and chaos of "our society." They turn up among the followers of Guru Stephen Gaskin and his family of 270 who forsook West Coast city life for "natural living" at Pegram, Tennessee. They are animated with the hope of "slowing things down, getting back to the land." This is essentially a vegetarian, non-political (but not a-political) grouping. There are fourteen four-person marriages in the group. "We feel all kinds of possible juices here. We feel we've a lot in common with the fundamental, religious people down here. That's why we don't cut our hair," says Gaskin. Adamites such as Gaskin and Alicia Bay Laurel (nee Alicia Kaufman) are not loath to publish books and garner royalties, devoting these monies to their communal life. They are united against the structuralism of American society. We find them very characterizable: socially, they are non-violent and anti-Establishment; religiously, they develop a strong animism infected with a quasi-polytheistic view of plants, animals, trees, flowers, and earth; culturally, they are backward; intellectually, they are starving.

The Destructors-elect are Adamites with a strong messianic urge. Generally under twenty-five years in age and from middle- and upper-income families, their characteristic is an antagonistic disaffection, based on profound ignorance, from the very roots, the flowers, and the values of the culture and the civilization to which we all belong. It would seem that some mysterious hand of human destiny or history has drawn a thin but firm line blocking out anything before 1945 or 1950—or whenever they were born—and decreed effectively: "Of the past you will know nothing, love nothing, esteem nothing. You have no future. Only your present subsists, and that has been fouled up beyond all repair by the structuralism and the formalism of the age." Nescience of the past. Nihilism for the future. Contempt for the present. This is a total disaffection. Destructors-elect do ache with the need to convince themselves that they exist, that their world is a real world of suffering and anguish. This they try to achieve by off-beat lines, by exercising the animal power of rhythmic music, by beating with the hands, by wailing to music, by using obscenities as everyday clichés, by cursing those who refuse to acknowledge them, by violating rules of ordinary conduct.

Some seek utopian visions and self-centered enjoyment and relaxation such as is provided by drugs and certain life-styles. Others become subversives of a major or a minor kind, participating in plots to disrupt the normal life of cities, the operation of government offices, sometimes exiling themselves when their civil offenses and felonies offer no other viable alternative. All Destructors-elect are too mistrustful of the traditions and values of American culture even to bother to learn its by-laws, much less to acquire some self-supportive skill valued in that culture. They find their chief inspiration in a side group, the Pathetics.

The Pathetics do not share either the life-style or the anti-social habits of the Destructors-elect. They inhabit nearby towers of strength, money, and influence, mainly in the world of publishing and of the media. None would be caught dead in a commune, planting a bomb in a federal building, or taking heroin with the hopheads in the Village. For a while, Pathetics tried to make the West Side of Manhattan *their* village. But this effort has petered out since the West Side has become a cross between downtown Thebes of 1802 B.C. and the Parisian flea market and an all-American version of Living Theater. Pathetics do not any longer find dignity there. Dignity is all-important.

Pathetics are mainly editorial commentators, but some are authors in their own right. Sometimes they include a personage from another sphere such as Leonard Bernstein. They included Radical Chic People for a brief period, until Tom Wolfe excoriated the chicanery of all Radical Chic. They have an all-purpose recording in Herbert Marcuse, a martyr figure in Angela Davis, daily messages from God through the *New York Post*, and a phallus-totin' granddaddy and metaphysician of the gut in Norman Mailer. Pathetics, in general, claim no specialized knowledge, are not experts in any particular branch. They do vindicate for themselves the right to pontificate on all subjects. This right, in their case, makes vacuous any knowledge of any particular subject. The strain of comment from Pathetics makes a welcome sound in the ears of the Destructors-elect: America is on the brink of Armageddon and of a dreadful implosion, what with Richard Nixon, Spiro Agnew, Johnny Cash, the King Family, Bob Hope, Roman Catholic bishops, the Wall Street syndics, the Midwest, Eric Hoffer, the Armed Forces, quiet campuses (student apathy), and the U.S. Senate. America is destined to join the dinosaur in deserved extinction.

Many Pathetics are drawing-room socialists and upper-class Marxists. Many of the most influential are Jewish. All claim the name of liberal. Their statements usually take on the garb of universal principles uttered for the betterment and salvation of mankind. It boggles the imagination to find Pathetics making a clear, if implicit, claim to infallibility and the incontrovertible overview we normally ascribe to God. But this they do. "It has become more important to insist once again on the freedom of large areas of human experience from the power of politics," writes Norman Podhoretz. "My bones and the lives of my friends," states Peter Marin, "tell me that we are already two steps into an ice age, a dark age of the soul, what my friends call 'the long march,' a long, bitter struggle for psychic survival," because there is "the immense inner wretchedness and the political fascism already spreading across the land and at work in and against the young." "The East Village, the city and the nation are plagued by gentlemen's agreements aimed to drug and space out the restless natives," Lee Baxandall writes. "The technology-sustained 'villages' of affinity in organization and friendship will be constituted by binding values that carry and leap hither and yon in space and time. In the seventies, we are spreading nationwide."

The opposing groups, the pro-structuralists (Smilers, Machine-Men, Intellecters), are on the whole a jolly lot, but sometimes the laughter is that of amusement at the antics of the guinea pig rather than happiness for the beauty of God or the joy of being human. Being human, in fact, is neither beautiful nor joyous. But, the structuralist insists with steely-toned self-control, it is or can be *interesting*. If ever the structuralists are grim, it is solely because the whole affair is very serious business. For they are, in their own eyes, the architects of change. They water the population at the wells of a new wisdom. They do not do this, again insistingly, with honesty or purity of intention or for the fatal human essence. These are concepts with no appreciable content nowadays. They do it, however, in all objectivity. For, in all the heavens and throughout all of man's earth, nothing but objectivity matters. Now this objectivity is a multiform thing; sometimes it is called "justice," sometimes "science," sometimes "intellectual clarity."

Basically, of course, this new wisdom consists of knowing the facts. It is because of this that one must regard the structuralists as legitimate descendants of the Enlightenment. They do not suffer, as do the pseudo-Romantics, from illegitimacy. Their trouble lies in historical hubris, man's greatest sin. For they are guilty of human impertinence on a cosmic scale, an insolence which can assume a destiny because by chicanery they arbitrarily exclude all other destinies, and a chauvinism that grants them immunity from truth merely because they chose to wipe out truth's distinction from a lie. The pseudo-Romantic will tearfully repeat after the Pathetic, in Auden's words: "The stars are dead. The animals will not look. We are left alone with our day, and the time is short." The structuralist will laugh contentedly and say: "Good old Auden. Brilliant case of a clash between the *Umwelt* and the *Eigenwelt*. The stars, my boy, never shone at *you,* and animals never *looked* at you. We can prolong your life, with any luck. Now, as for time. Well, you know how it is. Time is money."

The Smilers, Machine-Men, and Intellecters all make one common claim: to be intellectuals. But here is where a subtle difference creeps in between them. A Smiler such as John Galbraith, who is first and last a technocrat of both ideas and words as well as of economic analyses, will not claim the dignity of intellectual. He will snipe at those who do, all the while atavistically smiling in memory of his claimed ancestor, Voltaire, and attempting to imitate the latter's caustic wit but generally producing just another "Americanism." One example: "Stettinius was extensively invented by Harry Hopkins to prove a really big businessman could love F.D.R." Voltaire wrote to Rousseau about the latter's *Discourse on the Origin of Inequality*: "No one has ever used so much intelligence to persuade us to be stupid. After reading your book, one feels that one ought to walk on all fours. Unfortunately, during the last sixty years I have lost the habit." But logic is the final answer any Smiler supplies to the human problem. Be logical.

An Intellecter such as John Gardner will deplore with apothegms and neo-Jeffersonian formulations the pragmatic minds and the "New Art" leaders who have allowed power to slip (or be taken) away from the people. He will also speak lugubriously against the theorizers and thinkers of disruption and hate. Against both, he will promote the "common cause" of justice under law. Let us recognize the structure: this is the Intellecter's solution. The Machine-Men like Konrad Lorenz, Warren Weaver, Loren Eisley will speak in the name of intellect and of intellectualism, and of man's "final and only remaining dignity, his mind and his reason." They will speak of the fatal human essence. In the same breath, they will reduce men's problems to the level of molecules, atoms, cell life, and of highly organized and developed biologisms, proposing solutions that emanate from the microscope, the test lab, the statistical index, and the scientific count. The real structure of man and of human psychophysical life—this is the Machine-Man's contribution.

These protagonists, pseudo-Romantics and structuralists, carry on their missions within the little parishes of their localized interests: their university campuses, their limited reading public, the magazine-intellectuals of the Eastern Establishment, and some well-publicized books and a sometime pamphlet. Occasionally, they will make a foray into a really national forum by backing a Presidential candidate, undertaking a public office (a federal commission, for example), or making a loud sound from a national platform. But, by and large, they cannot communicate directly with the signature-caption-TV mentality of Americans at large.

Working away steadily on Americans at large and very concerned with every nut and bolt in the structure of the American way of life is a vast army of hard-laboring, profit-making, honest-to-God-let's-make-a-dollar men. They are not gnomes or gremlins. They are not part of a vast plot. And they have no designs on the life, the liberty, or the happiness of individual Americans. But they are the Prefabricators of the American norm: how an American gets up in the morning, what he eats for lunch, how he smells in a close-up clinch, how he lives after sixty, and what his children do with his body, his estate, and his memory. The Prefabricators make steady proposals about the American type: his blood, his sex organs, his hair, his skin, his flatulence, his spreading middle, his day clothes and night clothes, his choice of girl, his sense of comedy, his jealousy of the neighbors' new car, his marital spats, his drunkenness, what he should be like in bed, in the office, on the beach, entering a 747, in the bath/shower, on the toilet, at dinner, in the street, in his coffin, and in family photographs.

The Prefabricators know a good thing when they see it, and they only want success. They are mainly marketing researchers, purveyors of "convenience" and "necessity" goods, and the hierarchies who own, organize, and operate the paper media (books, magazines, newspapers) and the audio-visual media (TV and radio). The marketing-research companies who "sound" the American market of human foibles for the right-shaped lozenge, the right-smelling deodorant, the right-shaped car, refrigerator, ballpoint pen, the right-tasting peanut butter, soft drink, and the right-looking suntan lotion. But the process is really in reverse. "Right" means "what sells." Across TV screens, on radio commercials, in newspapers and magazines, the "right" product is sold as what you must buy to be "with it," to conform to the American norm. The supermarket owners, advertising firms, publishing houses, food processors, travel agents, furniture-makers, and all makers of "convenience" goods as well as the purveyors of "necessary" goods, all "plug" the "right" product in the "right way": what you must buy to be with the norm. There are, then, the members of the daily, weekly, monthly, and quarterly publishing media and the TV and radio companies who set themselves the task of telling the people "how it is," of giving the people the "facts," and of enlightening public opinion on "what is important to be concerned about" and "how to be concerned."

Again, they are caught in the rat race of survival in a murderously competitive open economy. They are governed by the same fundamental norm: to survive, the people must be given what "sells," what outshines the other competitors in the same field. The nearest approach to indigenous American art on TV is represented by the caustic, ill-phrased, rough-and-ready gabble-and-fight situations of "All in the Family" and Archie Bunker crying: "Stifle yourself, you dingbats!" and a return to Howdy Doody Kinescopes and the Peanut Galleries provokes as much "literary" comment as it does Howdy Doody wristwatches, chewing gum, and hot pants.

There are, also, the pragmatics, men in corporations and institutes who take the discoveries and inventions of scientists and apply them to any and every facet of life. From electronics, from chemistry, from genetics, from medicine and biology, they seek a more efficient machine, a quicker way of doing something, a more labor-saving device. They enter all fields, including the sensitive ones of education, public information, the motivation of personal lives, and the way of judging what is good, what is desired by the great public at large. They thus penetrate the daily lives, the intimate moments and the hours of home privacy, and the personal details of an American's body and an American's mind.

Pseudo-Romantics and structuralists alike join this fray with glee. They are as much victims of the Prefabricators as the latter themselves and the public at large. There results for the body politic a brouhaha of quick change, of keeping up with the Felternbaums, of feeling agonized with the blacks, of feeling outraged with the liberals, of feeling good-smelling with the nice people, of knowing all the American iniquities with the oppressed underground, of eating the right thing, of taking the right trips, of having the latest and most right educational method, of participating in the best knowledge of local government corruption.

In a true sense, the process of change in this body politic is a triple tier. One tier is the area in which the vocal pseudo-Romantics and the structuralists act out their thing. On another tier and nearer to the solid base are the Prefabricators. But in that solid base there is a large body of men, women, and children in a travail of historical change such as the world has never witnessed. Pseudo-Romantics fight against time. Structuralists proudly labor for the future. Prefabricators draw from any quarter, provided that it helps to sell. None of these can undo the trap-gate of history. None can effect historical change.

Many of them fulfill their programs to their own content. Some endeavor to make their prophecies come true. All have momentary triumphs and even disturbing victories. For their effect is never merely physical. They siphon off partial energies into inner explosions. They beget inner hatreds and despair. They emit dreadful uncertainties and doubts within the spirit of individuals and communities. Yet what is changing in America is changing beyond their control and outside their destiny. For at stake is not merely the destiny of a mighty people and of a very young society. The United States in this matter is a trail blazer. It is at the very forefront of men today as they and their society struggle past the inexorable trap-gate of history.

14

The Ordinary and the Touched

"Who are you?" "What are you?" are the questions which man has continually posed for himself and for others. Today we find two types of answers to these questions. One comes from a large body whom we can denominate as the Ordinary (Man-in-the-Street). The other is supplied by and about a smaller but quite vocal body of people who are best described as the Touched (By-the-Sickness, or By-the-Hand-of-God, or By-the-Alienation, or By-the-Anguish-of-the-Ages, or whatever). Among them they compose the entire body politic in the City of Man today.

The Ordinary answers (or is answered for by others) in any of three ways. The answer can be couched mainly in terms of motivations hidden deep in the unconscious, of psychophysical guidelines or fixations laid down in early childhood, and of projections for ego-defense. The emphasis is on infancy and childhood. The dynamics of the present stem from early life. On this basis, the answer will describe a man in terms of his repression of guilt feelings, his sibling rivalries, affection deprivation, of oral and anal types, and of the subtle stratagems adopted by man to bolster his frailties and cover up his weaknesses—repression, rationalization, sublimation, denials, displacement, fantasy.

Refinements of this popular use of "depth psychology," its concepts and terminology, are sometimes added. This is done by use of what Jung called the archetypes of thinking and the time-less symbols of man: mother nature, the sea, fire. Sometimes people refer to the Adlerian novelty of fictional finalism: this is a logical construction they make in order to give meaning to some important episode in their lives.

On this basis, the Ordinary will tell you who you are in terms of what you do and did, do, and will do, and why you do or will do that. In brief form, the answer will be: "You are a dynamic structure who does or will do . . . because of such-and-such fixations and motivations developed because father and/or mother and/or family members and/or friends did such-and-such and you reacted in such-and-such a way . . ." A dynamic structure.

The answer of the Ordinary about the Ordinary can also be expressed more humanistically in terms of human behavior. We are all creatures of habit. "Tell me your habits and I will tell you who you are and what you will do." Habits are grouped into several separate, widely generalized systems. Such habit systems are called traits. Man forms habits by actions repeated from childhood onwards. He repeats changes, and modifies his actions according to rewards and punishments. He thus becomes a dynamic structure of traits.

Refinements are possible. The expert whom the Ordinary apes will apply statistical aids to a content analysis of the Ordinary's traits and actions, producing personal structure analyses, as Baldwin does. Or, aping Paige, the Ordinary will apply the energies of a computer to the statistical data and come forth with an automated content analysis. Thus the traits can be quantified and objectivized.

In answer to the questions "Who are you?" and "What are you?" the Ordinary will tell you what traits you have and what you will do. In brief form, the answer will be: "A dynamic structure who does or will do . . . because of such-and-such traits developed because of such-and-such habits developed because of such-and-such actions stimulated by such-and-such rewards, modified by such-and-such punishments . . ." A dynamic structure. Finally, the answer of the Ordinary may come wrapped in terms of the Ordinary's existence. The Ordinary has a self-view (*Eigenwelt*), social relationship (*Mitwelt*), and an outer environment (*Umwelt*). The Ordinary is here viewed as a being-in-the-world, likely by that fact to be alone, to be alienated, to have anxiety (*Angst, angoisse*). He fashions a view of his assumptive world. He interprets his social relationships and himself according to his own impulses and opinions and thus endeavors to cope with his basic condition of just-being-in-the-world and nothing more.

Success for the Ordinary in this framework consists of forming an integrated meaning in the course of his life. Failure means that he never exits from the aloneness and the alienation of a mere being-in-the-world. In brief form, the answer to the questions "Who are you?" and "What are you?" will be, more or less: "You are a being-in-the-world who has succeeded or failed to integrate your ego (your aloneness) with the society around you, because of existential vacuum or conflicts in outer arrangements or encounters, and thus you can and/or will act in such-and-such a way in such-and-such circumstances . . ." A dynamic structure.

Part or a major portion of these three ways of describing who and what a man is are to be found as everyday currency in the language of and about the Ordinary. The Ordinary, accurately or inaccurately, speaks easily of inferiority complex, autosuggestion, subconscious desires, ego, behavioral aberrations, twisted psychology, dynamic personality, fixation, mother-symbol, frustration . . . He speaks easily of sublimating his feelings (for the secretary), of repressing his unconscious angers (against the boss), of his alienation (failing an exam or being fired), of accepting reality (settling down to married life), integrating his life (getting a divorce and marrying his long-standing mistress), fulfilling his potential (making a million dollars before the age of thirty), or of sibling rivalry (interfamily greed and jealousy over money and estate). We find traces of this in the comico-tragic language of the Ordinary: "My psychology in dealing with that jerk was . . ." "His mammy fed him at the wrong breast." "She's in love with her father." "He goes around looking for a huge orgasm." "You arouse strong emotions in my unconscious." "Life is irrelevant." "My Richter scale registered delicious tremors."

This structuralist view of man and his identity is further ingrained and strengthened by the type of understanding which modern society both suggests and imposes on the Ordinary and which is increasingly essential for him, either for mere survival as an individual or for participation in that society. It is an understanding and a knowledge built on facts and roaming within the confines of facts and of what is deducible from them as factual. The sexual behavior of the Ordinary is a case in point.

Today, by means of reports and studies, encyclopedias of sex and dictionaries of sexual terms, clinics, institutes, and advisory agencies covering everything from orgasm to babies' sex to contraception to fatherhood, motherhood, and vasectomy, to group sex and unmarried sex, to male and female homosexuality, the Ordinary is provided with practically all the relevant psychological, historial, social, and medical dimensions of the basic biological facts which are the setting for his sexual behavior. The Ordinary has at his disposal today photographic material, non-pornographic in any sense, accurately informational, backed up with intelligible writing and presented as not only essential but good and beautiful. The facts of life are given him. Despite all these efforts, sexual behavior thus presented is never more than intimate calisthenics and love is never more than highly organized responses to a biological need. None of the terminology used and none of the emotional armament covered by this information gives any idea that sexual behavior can suffuse the whole of the Ordinary's human experience. Indeed, it could not treat of this for this would imply a meaning beyond the facts, not deducible from the facts but explaining them from another source. It would not be structuralist.

On the wider plane of what makes human knowledge, we find that the knowing of facts both in themselves and for practical use is what is regarded as being educated. In soliciting subscriptions for its publications, the American Museum of Natural History flashes before the would-be buyer an array of facts: that wine breathes; that man speaks about 2,800 languages; that dolphins giggle; that wolves get bored—and what lightning water, Ethiopian supermarkets, microspheres, Mineral King Valley, twisters, Moslem housewives, firefly trees, Tis Abbai Falls, pond ice, aborigine cookouts, prehistoric sculpture, Indian immolations, pipefish, and mammalian retinas look like.

A cover story by *Newsweek* (March 1, 1971) on the American Jew not merely supplied reliable statistics on Jewish beliefs and practices, pollsters' estimates, and substantiated quotes from representative American Jews of different walks of life. It also noted new developments in Jewry such as the marriage of religion and radical politics, and essayed a content analysis and projection on the basis of its statistical analysis. But at heart the total analysis is a description of what major groups of Jews now do and in the future probably will do. The analysis reveals nothing essential about their Judaism and supplies only external traits of their Jewishness. Yet a goodly number of readers would conclude from such a cover story that they *knew* the condition of Judaism and Jewry in the United States.

In other words, in all things human, modern man is inured to the *objective postulate*. Objective: you must deal with objects, not your own subjective feelings and impulses, not other shadowy factors. A postulate: do not question the principle; without it you cannot know; do not examine this condition; take it for granted and act upon it, for otherwise you are going to end up biting your metaphysical tail. You will not know, you will not understand, unless you have facts and the insight which only the facts facilitate. There is nothing else but these two. The sum of your human happiness and of your human knowledge lies in the maximum admixture of both, the one constantly checking the other, in the endless game of leapfrog between rational hypothesis and evidence, according as understanding grows.

Clearly, this principle of structuralism is an irreducible earthbound article of faith. It is beguilingly disguised by its do-it-yourself invitation: you are to think everything through on your own level with no reference to any other plane. Essentially, of course, this article of structuralist faith takes the place of the irreducible faith of our forefathers in Western civilization. The latter related man and all things human to a level which they conceived of and admitted as transcendent.

If man anxiously gets engaged now and again in the puzzlement and the uncertainty as to who he really is, what he knows, and why he desires what he does not seem to understand according to the objective postulate, he is bidden and advised to catalogue and label such subjective elements of his makeup as existential anguish, as unconscious motivations, or as behavioral aberrations. He may occasionally indulge himself with the latest humdinger and whirlpool of oh-my-god horror in films, or attend the season's most original and thoroughly mesmerizing theater chiller, or read with relish a professedly and professionally "lewd and lascivious" book. It quickens his heartbeat. It fascinates for a moment. But it ends up by making any yearning for a transcendent value flit before his eyes in a malevolent form. He returns to the solid world of facts.

With that understanding, man reaches for a world of dead certainties and calculable integrations. He seeks and finds weights, measures, conventions, and transactions. He manages these more and more expertly according as his life becomes more mechanical and more automatic. Truth becomes tautology. Faith is synonymous with knowing. Love is exclusively a group experience. Hope extends as far as the grave, the endless succession of graves or the air-conditioned clusters of dust capsules

preserved in the vaults of scientific crematoria. But death is no
more, for time will not run down or out. Time ceases to have any
stop. Life becomes a monolinear infinite called perpetuity. The
wheel would ever turn. Man's moral being would have no real
choices. His moral behavior and its rules become as common-
place, as known, and as predictable as any other fact of human
biology. Deciding to act honestly or to tell the truth or to have
compassion becomes as functional as urinating or boiling water.
Men need finally undergo no risks, fight no battles, win no victories. Man's world is then no longer credible: it is known, controlled, modified. For man's perception is then coextensive with
his universe.

The structuralist trend in modern man has made a credo out
of a profound alienation. The natural trajectory of man lies in
an alliance with nature and a loyalty to the substance of a wild
hope and the object of irrepressible appetites not fed or satisfied
only with social and moral systems and mental structures which
place that hope in a lethal straitjacket. At times, uneasiness
grows too much, man feels a prickling along his scalp, the passion breaks loose, pouring pain and ache out from deeply buried
regions of our humanity. "Nonsense," chides the structuralist,
"nice nonsense, dangerous nonsense, myth, and primitive superstition. See your analyst. Your fate and your duty are not written
in the stars. (We can listen to them, by the way, with radio
telescopes, will visit them some day.) You have no master. You
have no summit beyond the skies to aim at. Yours, my dear man,
is only the struggle toward a summit. You are Sisyphus pushing
the stone uphill: forget the top; above, there is nothing. Think
only of the pushing: this is your kingdom and your glory. Below
is darkness. This is you. The whole of you. Do it well. It is all
that you can do."

One source of pathos in the changing dimension of modern
man is that religion, specifically Christianity, is not very important either functionally or symbolically. The objective postulate
of creeping structuralism reduces religion and transmutes its
character. Sometimes it becomes a poetic experience as essential
to Christianity as the color of Jesus' eyes was to the Crucifixion.
"At heart," writes Frederick Buechner, "religion is mysticism,
Moses with his flocks at Midian, Buddha under the Bo tree, Jesus
up to his knees in the waters of the Jordan." Sometimes it surfaces as a watered-down existentialism about as specific of
Christianity as anybody is specific of somebody. "The essence of

religion," writes Peter Berger, "has been the confrontation with an *other*, believed to exist as a reality in the universe, external to and vastly different from man. The fundamental religious proposition, therefore, is that man is not alone."

One vision of pathos is provided by a small fraction of human beings who have missed the point of modern man's existence but whose vocation it is to be shrill in dying out. They, the Touched, stand on the fringe of the main body politic, still a part of it, but so much alien to it that they are certainly not going to change its course and will ultimately be absorbed or eliminated. They speak and are spoken of in tragico-romantic terms not new in the history of human experience and expression; but today they have attained a new fury and a special insanity. The Touched appear to be suspended in mid-air between past and future time, culturally, mentally, socially, religiously, humanistically. There is no analogy over against which we can hold their type. Nor is there any ready image to describe their condition. Psychologists, educators, and anthropologists may never be able to tell us who or what has been responsible for the strange strain that has appeared among a small but, for the first time in American history, an identifiably separate minority of America's generation in the sixties.

In any one of them, the memory seems to be a *tabula rasa* as far as the past goes, the cultural and common past out of which they and their society grew. The mind is a closed shell within which no light seems to shine. Darkness seems connatural within it, but it is a darkness echoing with strange parrotings, as if the language of culture and the formularies of civilization as we know it today had been chopped up into inconsequential portions and then jigsawed together higgledy-piggledy end-on-end without the logic of reason and without the clarity of defined emotions. The will seems to have fastened on an unattainable object: "their world." It seems that once it passed them by, smiling and radiant, and then disappeared. Ever since, the will is vapid, flighty, omnidirectional, and hapless.

Our key words of civic culture, personal behavior, and societal norms are meaningless: words like "reverence," "obedience," "piety," "humility," "order," "purity," "kindness," "intelligence," "charm," "endeavor." Their own language is dichotomous, staccato, banal, weak-toned, grammatically incorrect and syntactically ragged, interspersed with exclamations and explanatory nonsense-movements ("wow," "man!"), and clichés such as

"outasight," "a gasser," "tune in." Compared to their linguistic inhibition and poverty, the language of the Ordinary is like the
continuous trilling of cardinal birds.

There is no lodestone for their loyalties, no mental construct
whereby the exterior world can be ingested in an orderly fashion. Each one walks around as closed to the outer world as a
concrete bunker, as if anything impinging on it from that world
is an arrow from chaos, a missile of madness and insanity. They
become, therefore, pathetic pilgrims: in our societal world, but
not of it; alien to what makes that world work, to what holds its
inner tensions apart, to what cements its outer structure together. Separate in psychic bent, physically oppressed by society's configuration, they yearn for their world. That ideal world
bathed in golden sunlight high above the cold, congregated
winds of all the clever games men play at, separated by ethers of
happiness from the steely machines, the chrome rules, and the
windowless habitations, where man eats man. For them, it is a
world swimming rapturously within the very sensoria of God
himself. Sometimes, speaking and singing of it, they attain an
elegiac beauty and dazzling inventiveness.

But the real world commands their attention. Merely to survive, they have to cope. This drags them out of themselves,
pours them out. They are flipped-out. They cannot be "themselves." The temptation for this mind lies in the pseudo-
solution: the psychedelic trip, the numbing noise of music, the
flight to violence, temporary extinction of consciousness, the refuge in weird cults, twisted life-styles, public exhibitionism. For
in the real world they seem to behold some central revelation of
evil which appalls them but appeals to them as the only alternative to dreadful screaming paranoia. Hence the raucous and uninhibited forms in which they find self-expression.

Fundamentally, the revolt of the Touched is a revolt against
the dead boredom as great as God himself which threatens man
in his structuralism. But their solution is a long-drawn-out wail
of rock, pop, and pan-sexuality, an upgrading of fluid identity
and primitivism, a reeking shambles of mixed sartorial styles,
asynchronous assaults on the eardrums, undignity, uncouthness,
fecal language, rhapsodic irrationality, and the degree of grace
and beauty we can afford to an unsightly patch of wild toad-
stools. It is a pursuit of gods without shoes or shirts: Mario Savio
telling six thousand students to throw their bodies on the machines that made them sick; Marcuse promising a "return to an
imaginary *temps perdu* in real life of humanity"; Jimi Hendrix

sculpting lumps of jazz-sick noise; Janis Joplin humming a fearful song of terror, helplessness, and mortality ("We beatniks just know that nothing will get any better"); Lenny Bruce performing as the willing scapegoat of our hidden evil; Mick Jagger as the canonized dybbuk of mob violence ("You are what you are. I want nothing but to turn people on"); and the West Coast rock groups singing the rage and pain of spirits trapped in the malodorous underground of a counter-culture committing suicide.

The character of structuralism, therefore, is clear and its trend unmistakable. Here there can be no confusion of mind, for on this point there is no conflict or antimony in modern man. The course is set. There will be no real effort to regress or change that course. Modern man cannot and will not join in the self-appointed, the thankless, the ingrate task which the Touched set themselves: to mend the rupture with nature, and to forge again the marriage ring of the ancient mystique between man as the child of nature and man as the son of God. Yet it would be an error to conclude that man is ineluctably entering an exclusively structuralist world and that we will all end up in the treadmill of calculated structures, desiccated, dehumanized, bloodless, as it were.

Here is where antinomy and conflict, with the possibility of a huge leap forward in the human dimension, enter the picture because men are unmistakably conscious of another dimension to their humanness. Instinctively, we know that there is no such thing as a moral-free system for human beings and their society: a human society where all is regulated on a quantified and material basis, in which there is no "ought to be," in which no "ought to do" holds paramount, where only "what is," "what is done," and "what can be done" matters. For this would be, indeed, the human anthill. Nobody alive in 1971 can tell us what the society of Homo sapiens will be in A.D. 3000. But the outcome cannot be a totally structuralist society, nor will it be a return to any former state of affairs.

Men are unmistakably conscious of another dimension. Conscious that as in matters of love, so in patriotism, in social relationships, in government, in our play as in our work, the presence of a human being (as distinct from an animal or plant) implies some aspect that transcends material and measurable dimensions. It is some essential connection with a transcendent realm outside society and individual history. Man finds it only in the jigsaw pieces, the bits, and the break joints strewn throughout his real world. He perceives it only in the twistings and the wrenchings of his spirit. For, seemingly, it enters his world only by fragmentation and through breakage. And, no matter how practical the structuralism of his day may be, man cannot shed himself of this consciousness.

This is why organized Christianity as we know it, and specifically Roman Catholicism, does not appeal to modern man. For Christianity by the middle of the twentieth century presented two faces to the world. One was the colorless and ultimately meaningless face described by Buechner in terms of a poetic flourish and a flaccid, nerveless nice feeling. This is fine contemplation for a comfortably installed citizen once a week in his local church or synagogue, but it cannot break the poverty cycle, does not devise a computer, negotiate a nuclear standoff, prevent a massacre, stop rape, murder, or persecution, or tell men how to stop distrusting each other. It does not teach love because at heart it is compassionless. It does not enable man to be noble because it has no moral fiber.

The other is the face of a comprehensive slobberiness described by Berger in terms of a meeting with an existential *other,* a flesh-and-bone "I" facing a disembodied, inhuman, faceless "Thou." Gone is the taut tension of hope in a dying and resurrected man-god. Gone is the compassionate feeling specific to Christianity that all men are brothers because all were saved in the blood of Jesus, not because they all walk, talk, need loving care, defecate, sweat, laugh, enjoy money and pleasure, and die by ceasing to breathe. Catholicism, like the rest of Christianity, has no specifically Christian answer to man's problems. It has taken on the structuralism of the age and drawn from secular studies developed by secular disciplines for solutions of those problems.

This is perfect Pablum for the structuralist mind: the objective postulate will accept and explain all this easily. It will even supply a faceless "Thou" ready-made and overwhelming beyond all man's imaginings. And it leaves men at the mercy of the power within his nature and his world. This is the fatal condition at which Roman Catholicism has arrived.

Part III

---◆◇◆---

THE LAST POPE

15

The Ethics of Power

According to the ethics of power, when the male spermatozoon, with an overall length of 0.06 millimeters and swimming in the upper part of the Fallopian tubes at the rate of about 2.7 millimeters per minute, meets and fertilizes a ripe female egg measuring about 0.2 millimeters in diameter, a human being has been conceived, human life has begun, and God creates a human soul to inhabit this human conception. According to the ethics of power, this soul is immortal—it cannot perish or cease to be ever. It suffers, through no fault of its own but by the very fact of being the soul of a human conception, from a grave lack and deficiency. It cannot ever enjoy God's presence and God's heaven. This lack and deficiency was and is still called original sin. St. Augustine and other early writers had crude ideas about this lack. They thought of it as a horrible spiritual deformity and ugliness which merited only hell-fire for all eternity. Augustine spoke of the *massa damnata*, the mass of such beings (unborn babies or babies born but deceased before their "sin" was cleansed) damned by God to eternal torments in hell.

The ethics of power further stated that, by the simple exterior action of pouring water (immersion and sprinkling were also used), together with special words approved by the Church (this is baptism), a flood of grace was obtained from God, thus filling the grave deficiency and making the child a Christian and holy in God's sight. Original sin was thus wiped out.

But the trouble was not over then. Even though baptism cleaned the essence of this "sin" away, the child as child or as

135

man had deeply sinful tendencies. If these ran riot and were unchecked and he or she committed personal sins (that first one was impersonal), his or her life for eternity could be spent in the same hell-fire and torments, if he or she died without getting forgiveness for those personal sins. The human being, therefore, was seen as someone needing an initial cleansing by baptism and a continual cleansing and guidance during mortal life right up to the very last breath of human existence on this earth. The whole trouble sprang from that primordial deficiency, its crippling exclusion of grace, and, later, the deeply embedded root system of evil tendencies in man which even baptism did not obliterate. Original sin, together with its innate anti-God deficiency and its remaining tendencies, was the foundation of all the ethics of power.

In Pacelli's time, the exact cause of this deficiency in unborn babies had become rather obfuscated. In previous centuries, the whole thing had been traced to the willful behavior of the "first man and woman," Adam and Eve, who disobeyed God in the Garden of Eden. Because of their sin, all their descendants (all human beings came from them) "shared" somehow in their sin. Severe difficulties had been advanced about the Garden of Eden's existence as described in the Jewish Bible. Paleontology had some disturbing evidence which seemed to indicate that human life had begun at several different points and more or less simultaneously all over the globe. Besides, there were strong considerations drawn from the evidence of evolution: it seemed that man and woman had not simply been created by God but that the human form had evolved from lower animal forms.

Nothing was ever quite decided in this matter, except to assert that Adam and Eve were, indeed, the first man and woman, that all men were descended from them, and that original sin and all its nasty later ramifications of evil tendency came from this source. Less stress was placed on the "apple," the talking serpent, the fig leaves, and so on. In other words, the explanation was mitigated, but the main "facts" were reasserted.

To atone for the original sin and to obtain the grace for a good life for all men, God had a plan. The son of God was born of Mary. As Jesus, he grew up, instructed a few "apostles" and "disciples" in first-century Palestine, was crucified, died, was resurrected and after some short days disappeared, leaving those "apostles" and "disciples" as his special presence, with St. Peter their head. They were to tell people that by shedding his blood on the cross he had secured the grace necessary not only to wipe out original sin but to overcome all the subsequent ravages of the evil tendencies. These men formed his Church, which set up its world center under St. Peter in Rome, Italy. In the twentieth century, Pacelli, as Pope Pius XII, was the 260th successor of St. Peter. He was in charge of the Church which had as mission to make sure that as many people were baptized as possible and that the means of forgiving sins and being virtuous were publicly demonstrated and at hand for all and sundry, no matter what their ethnic origin, country, social class, previous beliefs, or present conditions.

It was thus that the Reliquiary came into existence. It was a Reliquiary of power, as we have said, and the ethics of that power consisted of the ways and means by which it, the Reliquiary, made the means of cleansing and virtue available for the mass of men. Now this mass of men was, when all was said and done, a sorry crowd. First of all, they were always referred to as "men," even though the majority consisted usually of women. In the ethics of power, as in the religion of power, the position of woman was very peculiar. She was vital to provide human beings who could be saved by the salvation of Jesus and cleansed by the labors of the Reliquiary. But all else about her was somehow to be included in the term "man" or "men." At one unenlightened time in the Church, she was considered to be a source of badness: she tempted men (males): her menstruations were considered to produce a spiritual pollution in her: even when she bore a child, she had to go through special rites (*churchings*, they were called), because, after all, she had conceived the child in an inherently sinful act. There was no "churching" for males, ever. Even in the Middle Ages, when men were allowed to receive Holy Communion in their own hands, women had to cover their hands with a clean cloth, because, presumably, they had handled the penis of their husbands. Presumably, the husband had handled his wife's genitalia also. But he had not become defiled.

Whether the mass of Christians was considered as men and women or just indiscriminately as "men," they did not amount to much. They were married—mostly. A few, irresponsible or impotent or both, remained single. But they all had a host of sins to be forgiven and a sea of ignorances to be enlightened. Some of them got "vocations" (the work of the Holy Spirit) and they ascended into the Reliquiary. The others had to be shriven of an alphabet of moral filth from anger to whoring all the way through adultery, blasphemy, calumny, drunkenness, envy, falsehood, graft, hate and homosexuality, incest, jealousy, killing, laziness, masturbation, nymphomania, obscenity, pederasty, quackery, rape, sodomy and stealing, thuggery, usury, vanity, and waste. They could produce rainbow variations on the seven deadly sins, violations of the Ten Commandments and of the Six Commandments of the Church, and innumerable errors in belief. There was a mysterious thing called in the old manuals a "sin against the Holy Ghost." This was rather unforgivable, but it was usually said of someone who died unrepentant or unreconciled with the Reliquiary. As for unbaptized babies, Freemasons, suicides, illegitimates, hardened sinners, runaway priests and nuns, they were left to the mercy of God. But for the living and the submissive, the ethics of power provided the means of cleansing and of holiness. The Reliquiary was the source of this.

The Reliquiary relied on a God-given power. Poetically and triumphalistically, it was described as the Keys of the Kingdom. Theologically, it was described as the "power to bind and to loose," based on a saying attributed to Jesus in the First Gospel: "Whatsoever you shall bind on earth, will be bound in Heaven. Whatsoever you shall loose on earth, shall be loosened in Heaven." To bind by rules and laws. To loose from the toils of sin and ignorance. This was the basic idea. But this binding and loosing entailed an entire team of trained experts (priests, confessors, canon lawyers), ecclesiastical judges and courts, forms, dispensations, permissions, grading of sins and offenses, and a vast intricacy of lawmaking. The team included all clerics from assistant priests up to the pope. If, as was claimed, they had acted "as God's representative," or "under the guidance of the Holy Spirit," or "with the charisma of Jesus," or with a rather universal common sense, the ethical system might have worked reasonably well. But this did not really happen. It could not happen, given the dead weight of human aggression and love of dominance, and given the iron laws that govern all bureaucracies. For this is what it was: a Byzantine bureaucracy.

Further, the ethics of power emphasized a negative side of things—man's sinfulness. And it stressed a positive aspect—another man's power to clean him, to give him peace of conscience, to tell him that God was in his heaven and that all was right with the world and with his after-life destiny. The clerical mind made of man's dependency on its ministrations a sharp weapon of attack, a banner of threat and of danger waved at the recalcitrant and the dangerous, and a marvelous source of pecuniary gain, self-achievement, and satisfaction of man's desire to control other men.

It elevated to positions of authority the most extraordinary bevy of ordinary, nondescript, unintelligent, tasteless, lame-souled, ill-educated men. It gave them titles, dignities, robes, ceremonies, canonical protections, and a row of places in the Church to which the eyes of the faithful should always be upwardly directed. It made of the newly ordained priest a veritable caricature of Jesus, to be accepted as the veriest expression of Christian perfection, one who had chosen the noblest vocation and had reached the outside limit of all endeavors. The fresh-faced, narrow-minded, fundamentally fearful, newly ordained priest was an object of wonder and near-worship, clean with a supernatural cleanliness, and a fleshly revelation of God for the faithful, while remaining for himself a mine of indiscriminate desires and carefully covered-over ignorances.

The ethics of power endowed them all, newly ordained, disillusioned pastors, self-satisfied bishops, power-conscious cardinals, divinized popes, with the authority of the voice of Jesus. It dignified their peasant-like presumptions and their parochialisms as the wishes of God's local representative, and put forward their inept, well-padded, and fat-bottomed local administrations as the advance of God's kingdom. It presented their paternalism as God's loving care and their nepotism as God's predilection. It painted their homosexuality as the instinctive shrinking of the pure from the sinfulness of the world, and their suppressed heterosexuality as their greatest pride and joy when in reality it was their bloodiest chore.

It made their lack of education a sign of other-worldliness, their psychic wounds appear as instincts for purity and holiness, their politicking as "zeal for the glory of the Lord's house," their careful apostolate of the genteels as the apostolate of the Gentiles, their cunning and ruthlessness in consolidating real-estate and corporate earnings as devotion to duty, and their well-embedded human greed, jealousy, angers, disputes, and prejudices to be taken as the inspired dictates of men who were more-than-men, whose hands were holy because they had been consecrated with oil, whose bodies were sacral because they said Mass, and whose plans and proposals were wise because they had been force-fed, as chickens are fattened, through a three-year memory course in Church philosophy and a four-year memory course in Church theology.

Once that black cloth and round white collar replaced "lay clothes," all was changed and God walked invisibly beneath them. Once that bishop's ring appeared on the finger, something

more than God himself was present: the authority of God's
Church on earth. Once that cardinalitial purple clad a man's
shoulders, he was now a chamberlain of heaven's portico. Once
the papal tiara sat on his head, however aberrant his spirit, however stupid his mind, however prejudiced his outlook, he now
was more than Jesus was during his lifetime or could ever be
again on this earth. Poor Jesus had to wait, like some Mortician
of Eternity, until someone died, when he could proceed to administer the love and the mercy which he had won by shedding
his blood but which was denied the deceased during life, or, like
a submissive genie in a bottle, he had to function at the beck and
call of the sonorous Latin, the flick of holy water, or the ponder-
ous wave of a bejeweled finger. The great God's grace was bound
to an *Agnus Dei* and the great God's will was bent by repeated
Ave's. It was great while it lasted. But it was no "empire of a
thousand years." It did not last.

On a lower plane of power's activity, the picture was harrow-
ing. The ethics of power was heavy-lidded against all individual
compassion. It made man a victim of supernatural love instead
of love's inheritor. It made of human love a mortgage whose innate dirt and filthiness had to be paid off in the hard-won earnings of human suffering, instead of exalting that love as a gift
whereby man is most like the Trinity. It sanctified the little hell
of marriage incompatibility merely by a written contract, an entry in the parish register, and the blessing of a priest who either
was wrapped in a cocoon of doctrinal phrases and professional
coldness for what happened to married people or was the unwit-
ting minister of a mutual mandate for misery.

The ethics forbade masturbation for all the bad reasons, disallowed contraception for all the wrong reasons, excoriated abortion for all the ignorant reasons, permitted artificial vaginas for
a valid marriage but pontificated on valueless male seed as an
invalidating factor of marriage, made natural illegitimacy a
supernatural stain on the illegitimate, unless it was the bar sin-
ister of people like the Hohenzollern or the zigzag imagery of a
wealthy benefactor. It proclaimed the nobility of a woman who
became a child-factory, looked askance at the childless couple,
snickered ecclesiastically at the two-child family, declared the
unwed mother a blotch on the family name and on civic upright-
ness, provided nuns with a bride-of-Christ psychology but had no
remedies except hard work and self-denial for wombs which fell
from too much kneeling, for frustrations which surfaced at

menopause, and Lesbianism nourished inevitably by close in-living only with other women.

In its finer rarefications, it could close an eye to a man's mistress or boyfriend provided he did not commit a verbal heresy such as saying that Lucifer was, after all, forgiven and in heaven. It forgave homosexuality and sexual perversion with ease but blackballed in public a book whose author praised Voltaire or attacked corruption in high Church places. It laid down conditions for belonging to the Church, by which St. Peter would certainly have been excluded as a heretic and blasphemer or kept on the Chancellery waiting list for five or ten years; but it would have found a suitable place for Judas Iscariot's capacity to make a deal, would certainly not have asked the Rich Young Man to give all his money to the poor, would have devoted St. Matthew's experience as a tax collector to something more tangible than writing a Gospel, and would have disallowed entry to Mary Magdalene as a common whore with gonorrhea and syphilis, which in all probability she had.

The ethics of power were not restricted to the behavior of the individual. It functioned on a wider plane. In fact, the ethics of power, as it flourished by the time of Pius XII, was a carefully studied and minutely applied system of deciding how the Roman Catholic Church as an official body should behave, whether the behavior was that of an apostolic nuncio in Hungary, an apostolic delegate in Malaysia, a bishop in Birmingham, England, or a shopkeeper in Dijon, France. When we talk of how the Catholic Church behaves as an official body, we are referring to its mode of acting in relation to the world of politics and economics in which it lives.

The event which molded the ethics of power was the sixteenth-century Reformation and the Roman reaction to that Reformation. An error of judgment is possible here. The Reformation was not purely and simply a religious revolt or protest. The Protestant leaders, lay and clerical, did not revolt and protest because they had lily-white consciences and angel-pure intentions. The Catholics did not fight back simply for the love of God. If it had been merely good conscience versus the love of God, there would have been no revolt, no persecutions on both sides, no bigotry, no religious wars. The new Christians, the Protestants, looked for concrete results, a piece of the action: booty in the shape of money, lands, buildings, appointments, benefices, trade centers, cities, princedoms, and influence of all kinds. The old

Christians, the Roman Catholics, saw such things disappearing into alien hands. Power, naked, raw, vast, well-desired, long-possessed, was slipping from the hands of the Church. The Roman authorities, besides working on the political and diplomatic plane, set to the task of fortifying the Church.

It is to be noted that the structure which was dictated by the ethics of power was built on fundamentally the same principle that prompted Walter Ulbricht, dictator of East Germany and surrogate for Russian masters, to erect the Berlin Wall in 1949. Primarily to keep the "outside" world at bay, together with its pernicious elements; to keep the freedom-loving citizens inside; not to give them a chance to yield to temptation; and, finally, to make the consequences of yielding to temptation so horrid that they would deter the many by keeping them in the tranquillity of fear of greater ills, and by making a thoroughgoing example of the few hardy rebels so as, again, to deter the many.

The ethics of power exercised itself through an interlocking directorate centered in Roman ministries and tribunals but ramified down through the ranks of the Church to every country and every diocese of every country. Throughout this circulation system there flowed a current of supervision and information. It was think-control, feel-control, talk-control—or, at least, that was the idea. It was a grand merry-go-round of surveillance, reporting, dossiering, card filing, memoranda, reports, recommendations, a Grand Guignol of Italian-speaking churchmen peripatetic everywhere, in the Congo, at Melbourne, in Washington, Hong Kong, Singapore, Beirut, Nairobi, bearers of little purple patches on their chests, purple rings on their fingers, much holy hubris, detailed critiques à la Romaine, frequent references to "the wishes of the Holy Father," and judicious uses of transferable papal blessings.

Rome monitored theology and philosophy professors at universities and seminaries. It screened books, plays, lecture notes, newspapers, and magazines. To Rome a select number of young men were sent every year for special training and indoctrination. They were "Roman trained." Around the Vatican City, a string of regional and specialized colleges stood, housing the nationals of every nation and the avant-garde trainees for new ventures: Europeans of all nations, Americans, Latin Americans, Irish, Australians, British, Russians, Ethiopians, Chinese, Koreans, Sudanese, Siamese, Indians, Afghans, Arabs, black Africans of many tribes.

Professors and lecturers and teachers were made and unmade. Writers were lauded or forbidden. Thinkers were encouraged, rewarded, censured, or condemned. Inspectors fanned out periodically to scrutinize the soundness of theology, of philosophy, of social science, of political thinking in Church-related institutes. Each diocese in the Church submitted periodic reports on all aspects of its life. Each bishop paid an *ad limina* visit to the pope personally and regularly. A wealth of information on social, economic, political, ideological, society, and cultural matters was fed through this marvelous system. For the ethics of power required a tightly knit structure in which all activity and teaching had one sole purpose: toe the doctrinal Roman line and keep free from error.

It was the high period of centralization, not merely in government but in thought processes, in the formation of plans and wishes, and in the formation of aspirations. It was a glorious time for patronage, for influence-peddling, for in-cliques and out-cliques, for nepotism in the cause of God's glory and paternalism in the name of Christ's cross. There were Roman dispensations, Roman licenses, Roman rescripts, Roman permits. There were mass international celebrations called Eucharistic congresses held in different localities each time, to which the pope sent his representative. There were two favorite pilgrimages constantly being made: to Rome and to Lourdes, France. It was the time when Rome-centered and -oriented parish and diocesan organizations pullulated: sodalities, confraternities, institutes, pious reunions, noble knights and loving ladies, collections, funds, contributions.

By the time of Pacelli, the word had gone fast and far: Rome! Rome! Rome! Rome is the Church! Pius XII, our Holy Father, is Pope! Get to Rome! See Rome! Venerate Rome! Have relics from Rome! Be in Rome for Easter! Visit the Seven Churches in Rome! Get your rosary beads blessed in Rome! See Rome before you die!

It is quite true but not sufficiently telling to state that, at heart, an ethics of power is built on a philosophy of fear and a theology of partisanship. The Roman Catholic mind was a marvelously pellucid siege-mentality. Its strength lay in defense and counter-attack. Its glory shone high in gleaming towers of defiance. It assigned its real triumph to an inscrutable aftertime of human existence, and claimed to have the only passport to that triumph, but declared a siege for as long as the Church was not accepted as paramount in this life.

What tells the heart of the whole story is that it was a Christianity built on the concept of power. Over a period of fifteen hundred years, this concept of power had been translated into very concrete historical terms: papal possessions, Church wealth, papal armies and fleets and states and courts, and above all the papal prerogative to make and break rulers, to bind and loose the political allegiance of populations. When this power was threatened and to a large extent abrogated by the Reform and the Protestant ascendancy in Europe, the regaining of that power was a steady aim. The ethics of power was molded along such lines. It dictated papal policy from Paul III (1534–49) until Urban VIII (1623–44), when papal dominion over its former possessions was once again secured. It dictated the creation of the Universal Inquisition in 1542; the approval of the Jesuits in 1540, as well as their suppression in 1773, and their restoration in 1814; the formation of the Index of Forbidden Books in 1559; the assembly of a veritable government administration by Sixtus V (1585–90) and Gregory XV (1621–23). The stress from now on was on universal fidelity to the structure, the commands, the prescriptions, and the ordinances of the Roman system.

The ethics of power on the wider plane of world politics and economics gave birth to the Roman Chancellery and its tradition of diplomacy. One of the most dazzling and heartening aspects of the Pacellist zenith for Roman Catholics was the apparent acceptance throughout the world at large of the Pope's representatives with state governments, as well as the stream of distinguished visitors who came to visit Pacelli in the Vatican. But this also served as a temporary palliative for growing dissatisfaction; the external glory dazzled for a time.

The heart of Pacellist policy, as culmination of papal policy since the late seventeenth century, lay in the idea of papal agreements with the various governments. The policy had been the creation of Cardinal Consalvi (1757–1824), Secretary of State under Pius VII (1740–1823). Consalvi obtained a restoration of the papal states from the Council of Vienna in 1815. Pius and Consalvi then set about throwing a net of concordats, or signed contracts, with European states. The Vatican made demands concerning freedom of worship, schooling, teaching, and the autonomy of local churchmen; the state government in question promised to satisfy the demands on certain conditions, adding its own demands. Once the Concordat was signed, the Pope's permanent representative, an apostolic nuncio or delegate or visitor, was on the spot to monitor its execution. The net was, after all, full of holes. It effected some long-term benefits, many short-term advantages, but in the long run it did not save the Vatican from being stripped of its possessions in 1870 and from continual harassment right up to the end of World War II. Concordats were bits of paper and poor substitutes for the former spiritual power wielded by the popes over governments and the governed.

But in Pacelli's time this expression of the ethics of power had still a glorious aura. The "Roman diplomat" was the archetype of diplomatic perfection backed up by a very big stick—the Pacellist glory and Vatican prestige allied to impressive economic wealth and a network of trained representatives throughout the world. Even for Soviet Russia, its European satellites, and for Communist countries, the Vatican had "its sources" of intelligence and penetration. This arm of the ethics had its efflorescence in a special bureaucracy which served the Vatican Secretariat of State.

All members were clerics. They all got special training in Rome at special centers. The bureaucracy was predominantly Italian, but the lower ranks were somewhat sprinkled with foreigners. A foreigner rarely climbed to a high position. Like other bureaucracies in history, it created its own sacrosanct principle of inertia, and like all clerical caste systems from Pharaonic Thebes to the seventh-century Jerusalem priesthood, the 'Bras Buddhist retinue of the Dalai Lama at Lasa, Tibet, the Greek and Russian Orthodox patriarchates of Moscow and Constantinople, it was a breeding ground for a human rat race uninhibited by cassock, miter, consecration, or the law of love. It also worked according to the same rules: to move down in the system is to be moved out; to stay frozen is to be somebody's lackey; to move upwards is the law of survival; patronage is the ladder, but bite the hand that feeds you only if you have secured another willing to feed you; never climb upward over a dead body unless you are sure it's really dead.

All the infighting, the jockeying for power, position, advancement, and honor, were hidden things for the Roman Catholic public. The pope's representatives bore Italian names, were all schooled in the same dialectic of Church rights and destiny, practiced the same art of diplomacy, did their work, and finished their days, if they had been careful, with comfortable pensions, notable bishoprics, and other rewards. They mixed with high society, figured prominently in the diplomatic corps in each major capital, and moved through the important political and financial circles of each country. The ethics of power taught that this was part of the Church's apostolate. Indeed, it was. For that apostolate (without any discernible mandate from Jesus) was an apostolate of power. Power had to have its ethics. Those ethics seemingly paid off in solid dividends.

It is easy to sneer at the ethics of power and to condemn it outright as a sham and a cover for plain political ambition. Yet the truth is that the claim of Roman Catholicism to have an authoritative voice in all departments of man's moral behavior leads inevitably to situations where the Church authorities must compose their difficulties and differences with the economic and political power structures of each nation. There can be no caviling on this point. Nor can any reproach be urged against the idea of the Church's grappling with such problems. The error lies in the Church's attempt to match worldly power. The day will come, much later in the history of the Church, when men will look back and judge as ludicrous and offensive the Church's past attempts to compete on the plane of worldly power. But today it is still with us. It will continue to produce irreducible irritations in Church life. It will lead to distorted views on the real meaning of the salvation of Jesus.

One incident in Pacelli's power decisions was of this nature. Besides throwing a shadow on his name and discrediting the religious value of Vatican power-politics, it caused the deepest pangs of conscience for Pacelli. There was an occasion in 1942 when he had had an interview with Nazi Germany's ambassador to the Vatican, Ernst von Weizsäcker. A secret report by one Kurt Gerstein had made its way through Pacelli's representative in the Wilhelmstrasse, Monsignor Orsenigo, to the Pope's table. It told of death marches, of mass shootings, of death by gas, of soap made from Jewish bodies, of lampshades made from Jewish skin and inscribed with Gothic characters and the swastika. Pacelli had remonstrated with von Weizsäcker: "We must state that We wish the German people and their Leader all God's blessings, but if such is true and if it continues, We will be forced to speak." And von Weizsäcker: "The German people, led by their Führer, are fighting for their historic destiny and the Christian heritage of Europe against the twin enemies of Bolshevism and international Jewry. Nothing must be done to affect our unity, because nothing can break it. One People. One Leader. One Fatherland. *Ein Volk. Ein Führer. Ein Vaterland.*"

The phrase was repeated as a cant and interspersed his retort to Pius. It spotted Pacelli's sleep and his waking hours for weeks like an ugly snake wriggling in and out of his memory. He had a recurring nightmare that haunted his dreams: he was in bed and the lines of Gothic script writhed around his limbs like vines of evil, around his chest pressuring his lungs of air, constricting his temples and his brain of free thought. He was always struggling to free his brain, but always entwined with the penned script which seemed his own and ran in a nonsensical repetitive way . . . *Führer ein Vaterland ein Volk ein Führer ein Vaterland ein* . . . all over his body. Seeing it moving up his side and disappearing over his shoulder toward his throat, he would wake up murmuring: "It's all over my body, it's at my throat," and then find himself looking at the morning half-dawned.

This was, in cameo, what the ethics of power finally effected in the mass of Roman Catholics. It stifled personality. It throttled initiative. It reduced creativity. It made orthodoxy paramount at the cost of freedom. It vaunted reason as the basis of its themes, but it never enmeshed the will in coils of desire. It defined enthusiasm as calculated quasi-Pavlovian responses to Roman evocations. It placed salvation in an absence of guilt, and holiness in the observance of minutiae, and divine grace in a written form which cost dollars and cents; and joy in the approval of human superiors; and hope in the smile of ecclesiastical favor; and faith in an external panache; and love in an abstract geometric configuration. It all amounted to a nice structuralism of the spirit, supernatural techtonics of belief, and the architecture of passbook religion. It lodged convictions in the mind but they never could catch fire. It was, thus, part and parcel of the structuralism of the age and, of course, was eventually identified as such. It fell in the category of things crushing man's spirit; and when the first dawn of compassion broke for a short twilight, the ethics of power gave way like an ancient fabric torn by a powerful wind.

16

The Religion of Power

The religion of power, as it climaxed in its glory under Pius XII, was a onetime magnificent thing. It took over four hundred years and just forty-one popes to reach its apogee. It was incarnated in Pacelli and it was expressed in the lately deceased Roman Catholic mind. Now that it has, as such, passed from the human scene, it still arouses a nostalgia. For it shed a little glory on all and a cloud of glory on a few. It mirrored glory for those who came in contact with it or who saw it from afar, whether they had an audience with Pacelli as the Great White Father of the Western world—Jews, Moslems, Buddhists, Protestants, Greeks, Russians, or just plain disreputable atheists that they were—or whether they dwelt in Connaught, Ireland, in Pernambuco, Brazil, somewhere in Polynesia, or peered from behind the Iron Curtain. The glory was at least visible.

In religious terms, it concerned three main elements: the salvation of man from his sins, the person of Jesus, and the continued presence of Jesus among men long after his disappearance from human ken. The elements are simple to enumerate. But the religion of power was somewhat more complicated. Intellectually, it was a closed circuit, a self-sustaining metaphysic, a pillar of light. Culturally, it was a Mediterranean product. Professedly, it was an antique Reliquary visible to the tawdry passing show of mortality. It was primarily and self-proclaimedly a Reliquary full of ancient truths, ancient wisdom, ancient instructions, given man by God before man went awry. I say Reliquary deliberately: all in it, from the lingua franca of Latin and the vener-

148

ated basilicas of Rome to the most outlying seminary in Basuto-
land and Upper Egypt, was riven through with the idea of
preserving an ancient truth, of listening to Peter and Paul, of
imitating Roman virgins of the second century, Egyptian monks
of the fifth century, gallant bishops of the fourth century, and
heroic martyrs of the third century. Tradition, the hallmark of
the genuine Reliquiary, was paramount. The main elements of
religion were developed into a full-blown form which can be described as follows.

God was triple: Father, Jesus Son, and the Holy Spirit (prior
to 1960: Holy Ghost for English speakers). The Father was the
Great Silent Strong One (last recorded words at the baptism of
Jesus), but he had spoken extensively to the Jews in the "Old
Testament." Jesus was many things. King. Crucified One.
Leader. Sacred Heart. The Bridegroom of Nuns. Jesus the Monk.
Jesus the Jesuit. Jesus the Dominican. Jesus the Scholastic. Jesus
the Ecclesiastic. Jesus the Missionary. The Black African
Jesus. The Chinese Jesus. The European Jesus (hair-styled).
Saviour. Eucharistic Guest. Baby Jesus. The Boy Jesus. Jesus the
Carpenter. Jesus the Rabbi. Jewish Lamb of God. Two natures.
One person. Bearded. Blond. Brown-haired. Black-haired. Bloodied Glorious. Dying. The Son of Mary. Personally represented by
the pope. Present at every bishop's side. Speaking through the
pastor's appeal for more money. The Holy Spirit was ubiquitous.
Dove. Shafts of Light. He worked. He was always working. Actually, he worked best and only when one of a definite number
spoke or acted: the pope, the cardinals, a Roman bureaucrat
who possessed the seal of a cardinal, a bishop, a priest, a mother
superior, a father superior, and (by indirection) an approved
Catholic layman (rarely a lay woman) or an approved Catholic
organization.

Surrounding these were saints, angels, and the souls of the
saved. Between this motley crowd and the Three Persons stood
Mary, the Blessed Virgin: Madonna of Fatima, of Lourdes, of La
Salette, of Mount Carmel, of a thousand other sites; the Mother
of Jesus. Conceived immaculate. Assumed gloriously into
heaven. Lastly, on earth there was that marvelous Reliquiary:
the Church. It was a very compact affair: headed by the pope,
functioning primarily in the pope's Roman ministries, directed
by the cardinals, bishops, and minor clerics; served by a vast
army of religious orders—monks, priests, nuns and brothers,
and by diocesan priests. A few basic rules were permanently in
honor: talent was the worst of obscenities; success was meas-

ured by officially approved standards of mediocrity; change was
when things became only more so; old age implied more wisdom; there were always enemies outside.

There were then hundreds of millions of "lay people"; these
did not really belong *in* the Reliquary; but they could belong *to*
the Reliquary on one condition: submission. For the many glorious parts of the Reliquary, from the pope on downwards (and
the only direction was *downwards*), were clad in a special privilege of teaching authority and jurisdiction. This was the *oleum
Sancti Spiritus*, the unction and lubricant of the machinery.
Thus the Reliquary, when acting as a whole, was infallibly correct. It could not err.

The Reliquary moved forward by means of an intricate and
delicate series of mechanisms under the direct control of God
the Father, Jesus Son, and the Holy Spirit. But actually the functioning parts of the Reliquary knew what *they* wanted and man-
aged it all for them. There was, first, the mechanism of Christian
perfection. This was fully implemented only by those (1) who
took vows of poverty, celibacy, and obedience, and (2) who occupied high positions. In that order. Lay people did not get perfect; they saved their souls or at least aimed at that. The mechanism was a perfect hierarchy of little cogs, bigger cogs, large
flywheels, all grouped around the central dynamo expressed as
the "Vatican," the "papacy," the "Church." These transmitted
grace from God to the faithful. Seven sacraments acted as immediate discharge outlets for that grace. Only consecrated hands
turned the faucets.

There was then the mechanism of truth. This was primarily a
pronunciamento in exterior form. Of course, invisibly, the Holy
Spirit accompanied it, authenticating it. The pronunciamento
appeared primarily in a papal letter, bull, encyclical, brief, *motu
proprio*, or any document that could be described as "papal."
This actually was anything which emanated from a Vatican
office. Next best in this order was the pronunciamento of a cardinal, an archbishop, or a bishop. Of course, a pastor or a priest
was normally deemed to be merely reflecting one of the really
authoritative pronunciamentos.

Normally subservient to the pronunciamento-makers in the
mechanism of truth, but sometimes engaged in quasi-"dangerous" and -"venturesome" doctrines, were theologians and philosophers. These polished and refined and honed a series of Latin
terms and philosophic concepts which were translated into the
vernacular in all lands by popular writings and by sermons.

They were, by and large, completely unintelligible to the lay folk. But it was submission that was required, not understanding. At Pacelli's height, lay people were told that they should be monogenists (not polygenists), that the mystical body of Christ was not an organism but an organization, that actual grace did this but sanctifying grace did that. There were further subtleties about baptism by desire, virtual contrition, the relations of the Trinity, limbo, purgatory, hell, predestination, mediation of all graces by Mary, parthenogenesis, literary forms in the Bible, meritorious acts, sacrifice and oblation, in-dwelling of the Holy Spirit, and a host of words and phrases which were bandied around over the heads of the people by pastors, priests, and writers. They meant nothing for the people's problems; they were rarely understood by the ordinary priest; they answered doubts by stifling protests at ignorance, solved mysteries by substituting further mysteries, and contributed to the dead weight of Catholic luggage.

There was finally the mechanism of triumph or the organized triumphalism of the Reliquiary. This aspect of the religion of power characterized Pacelli as the most successful of the forty-one popes since 1534. Leo XIII (1878–1903) had yearned for mass popularity; only Pacelli achieved the marvel of the repeated mass audience on a sustained and astounding level. Pius VII (1800–23) and Pius IX (1846–78) had both dreamed of political influence and territorial sovereignty for the papacy; Pacelli enjoyed it within the tiny Vatican City and his irresistible access to all world leaders. Pius V anathematized and excommunicated Elizabeth I of England; Pacelli received the future Elizabeth II and Prince Philip at the Vatican. Pius XI (1922–39) had planned a broad sweep of missionary work in Africa and Asia; Pacelli lived to see it in action: colleges flooded in Rome with neophytes from all over Africa and Asia, and a steadily growing infrastructure of schools, convents, orphanages, clinics, and centers throughout these areas. Whereas Benedict XV (1914–22) died brokenhearted because he did not witness the peace he struggled for, Pacelli lived through a more horrible war and was surnamed the Pope of Peace, mainly because he had survived in spite of his error of political judgment in sanctioning Mussolini, not taking a stand against Hitler, and tempering Roman Catholic reaction against Joseph Stalin's brutal materialism as long as the last was the needed ally of the West against Nazi Germany. Pius VI (1775–99) was taken prisoner in Rome by the French; he was deported and died in captivity at Valence, France; Pacelli was named Liberator of the City by a grateful populace after World War II. Pius X (1903–14) had desired to communicate with all men. Pacelli's addresses to the world by radio and his continual stream of allocutions reached a variegated array: gynecologists, Vespa-riders, atomic scientists, biologists, midwives, Ethiopian Boy Scouts, Irish pipers, the Harlem Globetrotters, Chinese schoolchildren, Tibetan lamas, and lawyers, architects, farmers, bankers, brokers, rowers, cooks, Olympic champions, husbands, wives, children, from all over the world. The message throughout was triumphalistic and centered on the Roman Pontiff, on Pacelli.

This Pacellist triumphalism had a negative side: those who did not submit. These were: Jews, Russian Bolsheviks, Chinese Communists, Soviet satellite governments, Protestants and Eastern Orthodox Christians of all and every description, Christian ecumenists, anti-clerical Irish Republicans, Freemasons of any degree, and "dangerous" thinkers (interim "dangerous" thinkers and permanently "dangerous" thinkers). The last were silenced and/or excommunicated temporarily, until they submitted; all the others were permanently excluded.

Pacelli's attitude and the triumphalistic reaction is very well summed up in how a gentle, peace-loving, and fraternal initiative of His Holiness Patriarch Athenagoras of Constantinople was received. The latter sent a letter to Pius, proposing that the two men meet and discuss mutual problems. There was no official, public papal response. It was made known to the Patriarch and to all interested that His Holiness of Rome first of all required submission. Then the talking would begin.

Triumphalism was a heady wine. It intoxicated the Catholic mind. It gave the impression of victory already won. It stifled half-objections. It obfuscated real difficulties. Above all, it cast an opaque cloud of seeming success over what was happening in the mass of the people of the Roman Catholic Church; and it blinded Roman Catholics both to the nature of world problems and to the deeply felt changes taking place among Christians elsewhere. It made the value of religion reside in a dictated orthodoxy. It minimized the value of other Christians by labeling them, hatefully and discriminatingly, heretics, atheists, rebels, cut off from Peter's bark, out of communion with the pope, and so on.

This religion of power could have developed logically and by natural extension, if it had been something more substantial than a structure. Triumphalism would have died a natural death, if it had been merely the overflow of a felt commonality, the bubbling cream on the milk of human kindness and human sympathy which is man's first and fundamental reaction once he reaches truth and lives it in his life. But Pacellist triumphalism was as contrived as an intricate Madison Avenue public-relations campaign. Unfortunately, it was dealing not with anything as banal as soap, perfume, or automobiles, but with the potentially explosive things of the human spirit and of human aspirations. This spirit and those aspirations could not be caged long in the structure.

The religion of power was, after all, nothing more than a gigantic processing system perfectly molded for the purposes of a clerical caste but inevitably bound to pall the spirit. The Catholic was structured: Catholic parents; First Communion; Confirmation; Catholic schooling with the nuns or brothers; Catholic junior high, senior high, college, and university; Catholic professional organizations; Catholic marriage; Catholic newspapers, books, radio stations, and political parties; Catholic-approved films; Catholic holidays; Catholic neighborhoods; Catholic political officials; Catholic hospitals; Catholic chaplains, doctors, lawyers, architects.

All this would still have been viable, if it were structured on the reality of intense socio-cultural and political evolution which was silently brewing not only in the United States but in Europe, Asia, and Africa throughout the fifties and sixties. It was not, unfortunately, so structured. It was the Reliquiary. Its religion was sprung from a Mediterranean culture that had been plowed and fertilized by Greco-Roman religions and cults for a thousand years before it. Its concept of religion, of religious authority, of individual freedom, of individual rights, of the character of the "people" vis-à-vis the "authority," even an impressive amount of its liturgical paraphernalia and its theological conceptions, sprang uniquely from that culture.

This could and did hold together rather admirably as long as the dead center of Western civilization and the technological fulcrum of its urban culture remained in the European delta. In the first thirty years of the twentieth century, the Roman Church may not have had Roman roads fanning out through Europe to carry its missionaries or Roman aqueducts to bring the baptism of Rome to the nations. But it was at the center of Western civilization. The biggest change, effected by two world wars and the decease of all European colonial empires, was the shifting of that dead center and that fulcrum to the North American continent. Christianity here was not founded on any ancient peasant culture of the gods of nature. It was professedly and from the beginning a supposedly Christian and urban culture. Pacelli did not realize it, but the silent beauty of the Catacombs meant nothing really to blacks in Mississippi or, for that matter, to the very Catholic ladies of Boston, Philadelphia, or Brooklyn. The canonization of Maria Goretti as the exemplar of chastity did not affect the heterosexuality of the American man or, for that matter, the mores or the desires of the Dutch clergy. And the discussion of Christ's Mystical Body was of no use to the assistant in a slum parish of Detroit or the pastor of an Indian village in Guatemala.

The deepest deficiency, however, was in the thinking and outlook of more sophisticated members of the Church, the educated Catholic layman in New York, San Francisco, and St. Paul, Minnesota, in The Hague, in Milan, in Beirut, in Dublin, in Rio de Janeiro, in Paris, and in Düsseldorf. All felt increasingly the pressure of structuralism throughout their lives as citizens and as individuals. All experienced more and more the need, not for opposition, not for siege conditions, not for triumphalistic dwelling on the glories of Saints Peter and Paul and the resounding meaninglessness of Church ceremonies, but for compassion, for relief from the fear of being submerged as individuals, for a reassurance that, under further dissection at the hands of structuralist society and the impersonal reach of government, they would not cease to be the men they were or lose the hope of being the men they planned to be. In the triumphalistic religion of the princedom of power, there was by definition no compassion. There was a power structure. There was boredom. There was standstill contemplation of abstract truths. There was oppression of the spirit and impoverishment of the mind as condi tions of the all-important submission to revealed truth.

This religion of power was overpoweringly boring for the layman and the cleric. Not just the boredom of a rainy Monday morning, of stale beer in darkened bars, or the boredom of sameness in food or repetitious work. It was the boredom of lives emptied of meaning, the solipsism of being alone with dead rules and deadening strictures, the final iconoclasm in which every fair image of beauty, of hope, of aesthetic urge, of enthusiasm for life, and of first fervor is shattered so as to leave the open spaces of the spirit empty and free for the ultimate mechanization. This religion of power lay on the spirit like a divine incubus. It oppressed by the very weight of its prescriptions. It numbed the mind by the opaqueness of its explanations. It explained nothing, but facilely explained all away. It did not appeal to authority; it cited authority with a take-it-or-leave-us gleam in the eye. It endowed religion with a minatory value which cowed the spirit. It demanded everything. It tolerated no initiative, but commandeered total loyalty.

Of Church punishments in this life and God's anger in the next, it spoke ominously. Of God's love for his Church, it spoke authoritatively. Of the beauty of Christ's Church, it spoke rapturously. But it meant the beauty of liturgical pageants, the grace of virgins, the clarity of scholastic theologians, the faithful obedience of the masses. And the Church in this case was the entire bench of Roman Catholic bishops, topped by the Roman ministries and the cardinals and the pope, the whole flanked by hundreds of thousands of submissive monks, nuns, priests, and religious. This was the Church, the beautiful Church, the Bride of Christ, the Church which God loved, which Stalin offended brutishly, which Pacelli defended, from which the heretic and the schismatic departed, which the Jews hated and the Moslems despised, against which the sinner sinned. In essential Christian teaching, however, this "Church" had as much to do with Christ's salvation as Pacelli's slippers had to do with the circulation of his blood. Now, Pacelli was one thing. The Pacellist concept of the Church Catholic mind was another thing. But the religion of power relied on both.

Pacelli, first of all, was the most delicately contrived façade in recent European history. In the divinizing terms of the princedom, he was noble, persevering, misunderstood, of lofty and elevated view, and the Vicar of Christ. In human terms, he was a cold appraiser of opportunity, a supreme egotist, and he had a genius for the PR gesture. For years, permanently, as everyday conduct, and seemingly without extra effort or ever tiring, he nourished the image: a gentle exemplar of dignified horror, of ethereal communication and conversation in heaven, of aristocratic revulsion from evil, of priestly condescension, of godlike statecraft. But he was a consummate practitioner of what his contemporary and not too friendly fellow leader, Charles de Gaulle, called the mystique of the leader: the maintenance of a deep and definite gap between himself and all mortals, the inaccessibility of a mystic basking in the Cloud of Unknowing, the untouchability of an unscalable peak, and the studied and permanently conveyed impression that he was the bearer of a wisdom nobody shared with him and the Holy Spirit, and the seer of a vision common only to himself and God.

He thus could not afford the common touch. He could not
laugh heartily, publicly or privately. He could not permit himself
a ludicrous remark about his person. His preoccupations gave
him no time to think about the reality of the common man or the
pressures wielded on the masses. He was engaged in the Great
Enterprise of the Ship of State, the governance of the Kingdom,
the wielding of the Power, the increase of the Glory. By exclusion, therefore, he was wholly indifferent to the actual pains of
the common man, cared little for the bread and butter of the
peons, the pain of the excommunicated, the yearnings for unity
among other Christians. He was wholly dominated by the dignity
of his office and the supreme privilege of his destiny for himself
and all others. Only Charles de Gaulle in this century equaled
him in this achievement: the identification of his own egotism
with a supreme cause, thereby claiming an inviolability and personal precinct only violated by the sacrilegious and the profane
and only terminated by the omnipotent hand of the Great
Witherer.

The lately deceased Roman Catholic mind was a suitable tail-
piece for this magnificent concept of Leader. A word about its
genesis will illustrate its nature. When the Roman Catholic
Church closed its ranks and built its fortifications against the
sixteenth-century Reform at the termination of the Council of
Trent (1563), there was a lull of about one hundred and fifty
years. Trent gave Rome a centralized government, and the popes
a program of action. The Counter-Reformation and the political
upheavals of Europe occupied all attention. At the opening of
the nineteenth century, it was manifestly clear that the new in-
dustrialism of the West and the birth of scientific inquiry presented categoric challenges to Roman Catholicism.

There arose a need for answers: answers to the rationalists
and, particularly, the encyclopedists, to the physicists, to the
archaeologists, and to scientists of all kinds. The ideal of "muscular" Catholicism now began to appear. In essence, this included two elements. First of all, a perfect submission to the
decrees, commands, decisions, and wishes of the pope and his
representatives. A submission characterized by a childlike acceptance of what they offered in worship, in credal statements,
and in political partisanship. Second, a mental agility and expert
capacity to answer objections, to reconcile the "truths" of faith
with the data of science as well as with the objections of the
objectors (the scientists, the philosophers, etc.). It produced
noble minds and it created ludicrous situations. It had intellec-

tually capable men submitting, for fear of offending, to interminable Church pronouncements mouthed by Roman bureaucrats who acted out of fear of losing something and not out of genuine desire to reach greater clarity.

It produced, for instance, the amazing measurements of Mediterranean whales' mouths (to show that Jonas *could* have stood at the back of a whale's throat and thus survived for three days); the almost insane efforts to find and identify the "tomb" of St. Peter; freewheeling suppositions about Moses' handwriting and his flock of busy secretaries in defiance of all paleographical evidence from the Canaanite period of Palestinian history; astounding theories about female ovulation (to counter attacks on the conception of Jesus by the Holy Spirit); geographical surveys of the Red Sea and the Sinai Peninsula to find where exactly the waters stood up to allow the Israelites to pass; firm assertions about Noah's ark and Mount Ararat in Armenia; and volumes of arguments destined to provide the Catholic mind with an arsenal of telling replies to the scholarly prejudices, religious bigotry, as well as the strictly scientific findings of non-Catholics.

The resultant Roman Catholic mind was set on two springs. One was coiled and ready to unleash a series of counterarguments to "defend the faith." It was important to have the answer. They already had the truth. Only the answer was important. Another was wound up gently and easily triggered by a series of prearranged signals, resulting in reverence for the pastor, respect and reverence for the bishops, and veneration for the pope. It was ideal for that period of Roman Catholic history. It satisfied the Reformation mentality of British Catholics long used to live cowed beneath the hatches of learned and polite Protestant Establishment society, while allowing them to perfect themselves in secular pursuits. The sign said: I am an ordinary citizen like the rest of you, but I have popish answers if you get controversial. Let's have a beer and discuss the cricket at Lord's. It provided a new field of endeavor for French, German, Spanish, and Italian Catholics still reeling beneath the combined effect of the Enlightenment, the Kulturkampf, and nineteenth-century rationalism. The sign said: France is the eldest daughter of the Church; we can prove it. Or: The Faith satisfies German demands for logic. Or: Faith and reason are mutually related. It provided the nascent Irish-American Catholic Church with the clubs it needed to beat down the heads of its enemies. The sign said: The day is coming when we will be just as educated as the WASPs. In the meantime, take this.

But this Catholic mind was never more than a suppositious intellectual stance based on the power to argue your opponent blue in the face and come out of the fray uncowed, not having left the last word to the adversary. It provided no mental furniture. It created no new philosophic trend. It nourished parochialism and smug satisfaction. It depended on the power of the princedom: its panache, its glory, and, finally, its threat to be bigger, to be more numerous, to be more vociferous, to wield more political clout, to be more profuse in books and papers and lectures. When Pacellism died, when power went with it, the Catholic mind was a vast and indeterminate wind blowing through the desolate spaces of man's questionings. Its handy verbal solutions were assaulted by waves of concrete problems. Its creations were liquidated overnight by the aching to have done with the contention, to find a brother and not an enemy.

17

The Humanism of Power

The cookbook formula for the humanism of power was extremely well defined. Take a grown man. Strip him of his clothes. Lacerate the fleshy parts of his body (back, buttocks, thighs, calves, arms, hands), until he is caked with blood. Having driven sharp points into his scalp and forehead, hammer a sharp nail through both hands and one large nail through the insteps of both feet, thus pinning him to two planks of wood placed in a T-shape. Stand the planks up in a socket cut in the ground. When he gets thirsty, soak his lips with vinegar. He will try to "stand" on the big nail driven through his insteps so as to relieve the strain on his arms and ease his breathing. Break his legs so that he cannot "stand." Result: within a short time his chest cage collapses; no oxygen reaches his brain. He dies. Just to make sure, stab him through the heart. It is essential, by the way, that this man be the son of God and, furthermore, that God accept this horrible death of his son as atonement for the sins of all men.

According to the humanism of power, because of this mode of death, it follows that: a rose is a thing of beauty and a joy forever, a man can legitimately make love with his wife, the child can be educated, and man can find throughout his world that beauty and aesthetic rapture over beauty's image which are expressed in man's humanism and given form in the recognized works of art—poetry, sculpture, painting, dance, theater, writing. Without that particular mode of death on the part of this individual who was the son of God, no humanism is possible.

159

Now, humanism in this context is not science, or technical
prowess, or technology. Properly speaking, it concerns the aesthetic life of man. In the textbook of the Prince of Power, this
was the meaning of Jesus' crucifixion for man's humanism.

The reasoning behind this humanism is simple. This death, in
terms of basic value, bought power. Power for Jesus: he became
the sole and unique Saviour of all men for all time. Power for
man: he could escape the consequences of his sins. Power for
the Church of Jesus: it, alone and uniquely, could enable true
humanism to flourish. Toward the end of the first half of the
twentieth century, whatever energy the humanism of power had
displayed was spent. Its artificial nature was about to yield to
more vibrant pressures. But a humanism was an essential part
of the Princedom of Power, and as such it would deserve more
than a passing note in the latter-day history of the Roman Catholic Church. A more compelling reason for commemorating it
here is that this helps in understanding the nature of that power.
Of itself, neither beautiful nor unbeautiful, power must align
itself with beauty, if it is to be reckoned truly human. The power
we discuss is the power claimed by the Prince, God's Vicar on
earth, and by all those associated with him in the exercise of
power. Its claims embrace all things that interest and move men.
As such, it had to develop a humanism characteristic of it and of
it alone.

For the humanism of power, the essential note of man's lean-
ing toward aesthetic beauty and his spontaneous enthusiasm for
dance, for theater, for poetry, for writing, was one of danger.
Aesthetic beauty and aesthetic activity moved primarily in the
world of forms and especially of the physical form of man,
woman, and child. It was axiomatic for the humanism of power
that any real interest in the body was just plain lust and lechery
under a handy disguise. Jesus had suffered untold pains in his
body merely to atone for that lust and its vagaries. Adam and
Eve's original trouble was, undoubtedly, lust. St. Paul himself
had complained of trouble in this direction. And St. Augustine's
whole triumph seemed to have been in dominating his lust. A
long tradition in the Church looked on man's sexual and genital
powers with as much loathing and suspicion as it did his elimination system. Aesthetes, therefore, were toying with danger.

But the artist, the poet, the playwright, the sculptor, the
writer, presented another and more serious danger: freewheeling diffusion of ideas, of impulses, and of passions. Their medium was dynamite: it had immediate access to the mind; it

emphasized the value of the senses while titillating them. It was thus that intellectual error was sown; and it was thus that libertine instincts were aroused. It might be a *pas de deux* in ballet, an arabesque or a camel spin in ice skating, a nude female statue, a lover greeting his beloved. Sensuousness was sister of sensuality. Sensuality was sin. The exposure of legs and bellies and breasts and buttocks and thighs and panties and the "private parts," the expression of human love—all were dangerous. In theater, there could be subtle blasphemies against God and his Church, criticism of the pope, the bishops, the priests; or overt approval of "illicit love," of "successful crimes," and the godlessness of people who were happy without the blessing of Mother Church. There could even be religious heresy or political sedition of the wrong kind in a play.

In the humanism of power, therefore, the approval of the Church was required for any worthwhile aesthetic or humanistic activity. Unless there entered into the picture that power of cleansing, of purification, and of discernment, conferred uniquely on the Church by the power of Jesus, man was bound to go off the rails and be enmeshed in the lust of the flesh, the lust of the eyes, and the pride of life. On the other hand, holiness and retirement from the temptations of this world had best be embraced. There was sufficient grace and beauty and visual representation in the liturgy of the Church.

The humanism of power thus made beauty the hostage of a ritual purity instead of recognizing beauty and purity as twins. It made purity a filter of the suffering which power demanded as its meed. It made suffering a necessary concomitant of godliness. It made aesthetic perception a hair shirt and an occasion for renouncement, made joy an artificial mumbling of formularies, and channeled man's dramatic talent into a performance of liturgical gestures that were, in the final analysis, bad theater, dead mime, meaningless celebration, ridiculous symbolism, childish recall, and tasteless choreography.

This humanism was propagated primarily in the educational systems, which the Church controlled in various countries. There arose in these centers the concepts of a Catholic art, a Catholic aesthetic, a Catholic poetry, a Catholic view of history-writing, a Catholic view of theater, of ballet, of dance, and of the Catholic aesthete. It reached its most prominent English expression in the writings of a man like G. K. Chesterton, who endeavored, idiotically enough, to revive the idea of "merrie England," joined to a vibrant persuasion that in all things the Church had the answer. Chesterton's "godliness," and his superior use of paradox and antinomy to destroy his opponents, was marred by his convert's excessive zeal for Rome. He was "a pope's man" and proud of it. Chesterton and Belloc, the famous Chesterbelloc combination, proposed nothing less than a complete human manifesto coming from the Church and solving all man's ills, if only man would listen. It was a paroxysm of the humanism of power.

But that humanism entailed a dreadful price. Artistic faculties were stunted. Powers of sympathy, of understanding, and of perception were curtailed. Capacities for dramatic and poetic achievement were asphyxiated in the young. It was a high price for the ordinary man and woman to pay: to renounce thought and to limit their perception. It was the pain of aesthetically impoverished people and intellectually contained minds. But it was an old story in the history of the Church. The lesson had never been learned. For even before the humanism of power took on its definitive form, power had always been to the fore in the Church at the cost of all else, including love. Eight hundred years before, it had been acted out. It was the brilliant Breton, Peter Abelard, castrated and impotent, condemned as heretical by the Council of Sens and retired in a Cluniac monastery, still gnashing his teeth in passion for the powers of the mind. It was Héloïse growing old and gray and wise in her nunnery, and it was Peter the Venerable writing consolingly to her: "Soon you will be reunited with him, there where beyond these voices [their detractors] peace subsists"; and to St. Bernard of Clairvaux, their untiring enemy, caustically: "You perform all the difficult religious duties: you fast, you watch, you suffer, but you will not endure the easy ones—you do not love."

The humanism of power received its big impetus in the first half of the nineteenth century. It had political patronage, was based on a socio-cultural fear, and was centered on the authority of the pope and the glory of the Roman Catholic Church. It had no direct lineal connection with the Hellenism of ancient Rome. It was not even a waxen reproduction or a robot version of the Neo-Hellenism created by the European Renaissance. It had nothing directly to do with the carriers of Italian humanism in the eighteenth and nineteenth centuries: with Pergolesi, Cimarosa, and Paisiello in opera, with Canova in architecture, with Goldoni or Alfieri in theater. It was a new effort. But it drew on decadent currents and the remainders of past European humanism.

The political atmosphere immediately following the Council of Vienna (1815) was favorable. A century of revolutionary chaos and of wars, and the appearance of "anti-throne" as well as "anti-Church" political views led to a new popularity for the pope and the papacy among European rulers. Protestant monarchies came to see that the papacy and the pope's authority provided one of the best bulwarks against the rising tide of socialist and Communist doctrines and movements, as well as against nascent nationalisms. The old governing classes of Europe felt the foundations of their society being shaken. The pope was again installed in his possessions in the former papal states. There arose in Europe a first current of literature and aesthetic writing which expressed in essence the humanism of the Roman Catholic Church.

The humanism of power was primarily an intellectual thesis proposed with passion and propagating power as the guarantee of all humanism and of all else on the human scene. It was the theme of Joseph de Maistre (1753–1821) in his *Du pape*, where he asserted that all things in man's world derived their beauty and value from the spiritual absolutism of the pope. It was Chateaubriand (1768–1848) romanticizing pope, papacy, and their Christianity in his *Génie du Christianisme*, an amazing concoction of classical idyl, romantic pains smoldering at hidden beauties, and lavish praise of Rome. It was Lamennais, Lacordaire, Montalembert, Gerbet, de Salinis, Guérin, maintaining that society could only be regenerated within a revival of Catholicism. Roman Catholicism meant the pope and the papacy as the central pieces in a reconstructed Europe. The tragedy of this group was that early on they realized the formula would not work. But their attempt to separate Church and state ran counter to the power claimed by Rome. Lamennais died excommunicated from the Church. His humanism was of no use, if it did not serve the power. It would happen again to Charles Maurras in 1926. There were desultory attempts at Roman Catholic humanistic writing, such as Cardinal Wiseman's *Fabiola*, and J-K Huysmans (1848–1907) satirizing escapism and lauding the semi-monastic life led in expiation for one's own sins and the sins of other men, and Léon Bloy (1846–1917) writing as "the artless clamorer" and "for God only."

The humanism of power went on to receive its most forthright expression from the redoubtable Pius IX. By 1864 the papal states had been taken away from the Church; the end of Rome as the pope's city was in sight. Everywhere the humanism of power and the papal claims to universal sovereignty were being challenged by nationalism, by socialism and Communism. In his encyclical letter *Quanta cura*, together with the list of condemned errors (the Syllabus), Pius IX declared again loudly and intransigently that all culture, all humanism, all science, and all educational systems should be under the control of the Church. It was of no avail. On October 2, 1870, Rome was annexed by Italian troops and declared the capital of Italy. Pius IX went into the Great Sulk of Christ, refusing like all his successors to leave the Vatican. It lasted nearly fifty years, until 1929, when the City of the Vatican was created by a Concordat between Mussolini and Pope Pius XI.

From 1930 onward until the mid-1950's, the humanism of power had a little heyday. The Church-controlled educational system of the United States reached its apogee, promising to turn out a new generation of Rome-oriented Ph.D.'s, doctors, lawyers, architects, politicians, writers, philosophers, artists, publicists. The humanism to nourish them appeared all over the Catholic world in a cluster of local magazines, newspapers, and periodicals, such as *The Catholic Herald, The Downside Review* (England), *The Irish Monthly* (Ireland), *Études* (France), *The Messenger of the Sacred Heart, Commonweal, America Magazine* (U.S.A.), *L'Osservatore Romano* in Rome. The humanism was extended by writers to cover all social and political ills and problems afflicting Europe and the world. The watchword was: if the Church is allowed to implement her principles, the world will be saved. A journalist such as the British Arnold Lunn reached the peak of his career within this movement.

This humanism received a "spiritual" expression in devotional writings of people like Dom Marmion and Father de Grandmaison. It attempted "higher flights" in a literature of "mysticism" and an apocalyptic vogue of thought. Raïssa Oumanoff, wife of Jacques Maritain, celebrated this mysticism in her *Adventures in Grace,* while her husband analyzed man's metaphysical intuition of God in philosophic terms. Raoul Plus told the mystical story of a young girl in his *Consummata.* Thomas Merton popularized the mysticism of John of the Cross and Teresa of Avila in a suitable form for businessmen, housewives, and seminary students. The correspondence of Jacques Rivière and Paul Claudel talked back and forth about immediate perception of God. There was a revival of interest in the Victorian Gerard Manley Hopkins because of the Christocentric mysticism of his later poems. Simone Weil and Henri Bergson were claimed as at least crypto-members of the strain. The movement embraced the apocalyptic threats of the Fatima revelations and of visionaries such as Père Labry, making its own the onetime phrase of Léon Bloy: "I am waiting for the advent of the Cossacks and the Holy Ghost."

It was all very insular, because it radiated only within Catholicism and then only to the elite. It was illegitimate because the "mysticism" was cut off from the main stream of the Spanish tradition. It was ineffectual because no real creativity was born; it was imitative, reproductionist, repetitive, and barren of new forms. It was self-defeating because it did not spring out of cultural diversity or even reflect socio-cultural problems such as the inequality of blacks, the poverty cycle of city ghettos. It had nothing integral to do with the literary tradition of the West, which had already reached its uttermost limit in the enchanting cacophonies, the unpronounceable word-forms, and mutate epithets of James Joyce, and the existential silences of Samuel Beckett. The frightening meaning to life which these latter perceived and endeavored to convey was ungovernable by the power of the Church. By midcentury and more than halfway through Pacelli's reign, all efforts at a Roman Catholic humanism were in vain and practically spent.

Those efforts had depended on the brilliance of the glory shed by power and derived awe from the fear and the respect which power inspired. Something more moving than the glory of power took over in men's minds. And something more fearful than the threat of religious power began to cast long shadows over man's existence. From 1945 onwards, the life of Western man was spent in the penumbra of fear that a nuclear war would end him completely; and his daily life was increasingly invaded by a structuralism which effectively blotted out any brilliance of the glory because of the intricate network of complex living systems to be coped with, if life was to continue. Reminders that he should fear the power or admire the glory seemed, more and more, to be willful distractions from the job of survival, mere palliatives for his problem of remaining at least human.

There was no point in maintaining a Catholic view of art, if art was increasingly despairing and a glorification of the ugly. To place a Christ Crucified atop a city dump or dispense holy water from a discarded Campbell's Soup tin seemed inane. The dump should be cleared from the ghetto. The hungry needed soup and bread and vitamins. It was a graceless pirouette to reflect on the beauty of Gregorian chant in the Vatican choir singing of the Church's glory and man's new dignity in Jesus. In

Latin America, in the Southern United States, and in the large cities of the world, it was not a question of dignity. Men lived like animals, were treated worse than domestic pets, and were liquidated like dangerous animals. The power of the Church could not effectively claim to author the beauty of love between man and woman and their grace of mutual devotion which poets expressed, or trumpet its wardship of the child and the child's marvelous symbolism for innocence and fresh humanity. Sexual psychology as evinced on the analyst's couch and in the five-dollar manual was more essential for a greater orgasm, breaking frigidity, or correcting incipient homosexuality. The double helix of the chromosome was more vital so that the child should be born without genetic defects.

A seeping disillusionment crept through Catholicism. The essence of Catholicism had been presented in terms of power, and its religion, its ethics, and its humanism had been stated categorically as syndynamic with that power. Now, however, that power had nothing really effective to say or do concerning man's constricting dilemmas. It could not even compete with the detail of research or the skill of technology. The power had itself structured its adherents and organized their minds, their lives, their pocketbooks, their politics, and their allegiances, without warming their hearts, foreseeing their dreadful wants, or elevating their vision.

It is not remarkable, therefore, but altogether logical that what crippled and killed the humanism of power was what still cripples and kills any true poetry or aesthetics today: the narrowing of all human vision and reflection to a question of coping with what man has wreaked on man. This, in sum, is a power system of facts and a pattern of activities that fragment the unity of individual consciousness. The effects are felt all over, limiting modern drama and theater to so-called "realistic" stagings that either leave audiences cold or plunge them deeper in their pessimism and their fears; presenting as art the offal, the waste, and the incidentals of human life, plastic bags, glass tubes, garbage cans, wrecked automobiles; and degrading poetry to blank prose statements about hubcaps, the writer's hemorrhoids, one man's reactions to the draft, the contrast of hamburgers and human flesh, and how painful it is for the human spirit to have a Congress and a White House. No great theater was ever built around the "realism" of the pustules on a leper's face. No great poetry sprang from injunctions on how to negotiate the billy club of an enraged policeman. No aesthetic literature or plastic art consisted in mere accumulated details about childbirth, exhaust fumes, the eruption of a volcano, the disemboweling of a pregnant woman, the color of human excrement, or the length of the penis in a state of erection. True, in such examples, there is either power or the effect of power or submission to power.

Humanistic values arise when the human mind seizes on these as occasions to treat of the things that move man's spirit: compassion, hope, trust, humility, love, repentance, joy, expectation, gentleness. It is the motive power of these great human themes which light up the dormant mind, engage man's will, and stir him to those endeavors that have always characterized man as man. The humanism of power treated of such things as consequences, as of secondary importance. Stress was laid on the power of Jesus' salvation and the power it put in the hands of the Church.

The cookbook formula for the humanism of power suffered from a fatal defect: it was not human, and therefore it was not authentically Christian. If it was not human, it could not be divine. For according to Christian doctrine, the divine was built on the human. The formula was composed by the power mentality in order to convey one persuasion: power in the temporal order. A sacrificial death, even of a God-man, which evinced only power as its dominant note was a miscarriage of communication between God and man.

The formula had erred in its summation of the Man's death on the cross some nineteen hundred years before. He had not been the pawn of power. His pains and death did not win power, consolidate power, justify power, or make power the backbone of man's salvation. He was put to death because he loved, because his Father loved. And what he won was love: love of man for man, love of man for God. God already loved man, so much so that he had sent his son to die for man. He had transformed all human things, it is true. But this did not place all human things beneath the power of any man or group of men. In the Christian paradigm, he was the willing prisoner of pure pain and the gentle God of grace. The pain was proof of love. The grace was guarantee of love. Because of him, all man's world is proposed as a theater of love. No extra blessing of a cleric is needed for this. What he won was grace. What he left to man was a promise of compassion for man's problems as well as man's weaknesses, and a vehicle to carry the message of that grace and that compassion for all generations of man's dwelling on this earth.

18

The Death of Pacelli

When Pacelli died, he was eighty-two years of age and staying at Castel Gandolfo, summer residence of the popes. There, the last layman he received in private audience was British actor Alec Guinness, recently converted to Catholicism. On October 6, a stroke hit him, leaving him totally blind and not lucid. By the seventh, he had recovered sufficiently; shaken by unceasing hiccups, he prayed and listened to Beethoven's First Symphony. He made his confession to Father Robert Leiber and received Holy Communion. His everyday Jesuit confessor, Father Augustin Bea, lay seriously ill of intestinal poisoning in Rome. By evening, the Pope's sight had returned. With a temperature of 99° he was allowed a glass of red wine. At 7:30 A.M. on October 8, a second and final stroke paralyzed him. The word went out: the Pope is dying.

He lay alternately on his brass fourposter bed or on a couch placed at its foot, trying to die while gasping oxygen through a tube held by Suora Pasqualina. A priest stationed at his bedroom door issued frequent bulletins. Italian radio broadcast organ music, Frescobaldi and Bach, interspersed with the Catholic hymn of triumph, *Christus Vinxit*. Listeners in Europe, the United States, South America, and Africa could from time to time hear Pacelli's labored breathing on their radios.

For the world outside, the figure of Pacelli was a key and a symbol: no one thought of Europe without him; no one could imagine world events in any realistic way without the element of

168

his person and his intervention. Pacelli was Rome and Rome was Pacelli. Pacelli was Vatican power. Vatican power was Pacelli. Vatican prestige was Pacelli's prestige. The men of that October 1958 were acutely aware that a figure of power was slipping from the human scene with that inevitability only exercised by death. His life and achievements, his face, his voice, even his personal characteristics such as the shape of his nose, his bespectacled eyes, his delicate hands, his weakling voice—these had been linked with lists of exclusive names which had become household words for over a billion and a half men and women in a matter of five short war years: the most hated—Stalin, Hitler, Mussolini; the most loved—Churchill, Eisenhower, De Gasperi; the most respected—de Gaulle, Roosevelt, Chiang Kai-shek. He had shared, consequently, in the regnancy conferred on them.

The regnancy transformed the most unnoteworthy facts of his personal existence. Elements and facts quite insignificant in the lives of ordinary mortals acquired a mystique, became somehow luminous parts of revelation when found in Pacelli. His daily dinner at 8:35 P.M. (eggs, bacon, milk products), his favorite composers (Bach, Wagner, Verdi), the name of his favorite canary (Gretel; she used to perch on his hand while he shaved every morning), were known to the faithful. In 1954, after his first stroke, when his doctors allowed him an egg whipped in Marsala wine, the story was recounted with relish and significance. His white portable typewriter and his white telephone became symbols of his marvelous modernity. His use of the telephone was regarded as a phenomenal papal breakthrough. So it has always been with the regnant: Louis XIV's fistula, Washington's wooden teeth, Stalin's gusto for a whole roast pig, Churchill's cigars. Their regnancy confers significance on all details. I say this of Pacelli, as of any veritable Prince of Power: regnancy was his first characteristic.

Death, when it finally came, took him fast, so fast that only five people were present. There was aging Suora Pasqualina, his housekeeper for forty-one years. Two Vatican monsignori, Nazali Rocha and Quirino Paganuzzi, were there. Both had feared him in his lifetime. Both had frustrated Pacelli's wishes. And both stood to gain in advancement after his death. Bartolomeo Migone, the gentle, sad, realistic ambassador of Italy to the Vatican, was there on behalf of the state to certify officially the Pope's death. Lastly, there was Dr. Galeazzo-Lisi, the Pope's physician, an oculist by profession. Once the death agony set in,

Galeazzo-Lisi busied himself taking photographs of the dying man from different angles. He also kept a minute-by-minute diary of the agony. He would try to sell both after Pacelli's death, thus provoking legal action and professional repudiation by his colleagues.

Shortly after 3:50 A.M., on October 9, Pacelli's breathing quickened for some brief seconds. Laboriously, he drew in one last deep breath and exhaled it lengthily. But he never drew another. It was exactly 3:52 and three seconds in the morning. Pacelli was gone.

Galeazzo-Lisi certified the death medically. Eugène Cardinal Tisserant, roused out of bed, arrived shortly after with tousled hair to certify it ecclesiastically. He tapped Pacelli's forehead three times, asking ritually: "Eugenio, are you dead?" There was no answer. Ritually intoning "Pope Pius XII is truly dead," he removed the Fisherman's ring from the third finger of Pacelli's right hand. Ritually it would be broken and buried with Pacelli's body. At 5:00 A.M., the gates of Castel Gandolfo were barred with a heavy chain. At 5:03 A.M., the papal flag was lowered to half mast. A light morning wind flapped it idly against the plaque bearing the papal arms and the crossed Keys of Peter. It was a misty morning with a reddish sunrise.

The removal and breakage of the ring was by now a symbolic rite. Originally, it was mandatory: no one must be able to usurp the legitimacy of the pope's power by using a dead pope's seal to legitimize documents, decrees, decisions. But, by the force of his personality, legitimacy in the person of Pacelli had been transmuted for the adherents of his Church beyond mere formal protocol and the stuff and matter of a decreeing, deciding, and governing authority. It had been transmuted to the point of human divinization, much as god-heroes were in ancient Greece and Rome or the Dalai Lama in modern Tibet. But it was not crass with the former's follies or ridiculous as the latter's mock-court of heaven. That legitimacy was paramount for all true believers, friends as well as enemies. Among those kneeling around his plastic-covered body was Monsignor Tardini. He had been part of the bitter and very subterranean opposition to Pacelli. Now he knelt and kept repeating in a whisper: "Pacelli, forgive me. Forgive me, Pacelli." Participation in Pacelli's legitimacy had become a mark of Pacelli's triumphant Catholicity, no matter what sacrifice it entailed, no matter what suppression of opinion or inclination it necessitated, no matter what it cost in terms of personal suffering, omission of compassion for the sake of truth, or obfuscation of lesser claims for the sake of major statal politics. I say that this paramount legitimacy was the second characteristic of Pacelli as the Prince of Power.

Suora Pasqualina and the attendants stripped off the sickbed clothes, washed the body, dressed it in a white vestment and red velvet cape and cap, laid it on a bier, and covered it with a sheet of transparent plastic. Suora Pasqualina then packed two suitcases and placed Pacelli's half-dozen pet birds in one cage. She had stood between Pacelli and many would-be sources of botheration, had obtained the cardinalate for two clerics and blocked at least three from getting the cardinalate. (The Italians had maliciously nicknamed her *Virgo potens*, the Powerful Virgin, a title taken from a litany in praise of the Virgin Mary.) But once Pacelli died, she was refused car transport by all. Cardinal Tisserant finally secured it for her. Two days later she departed, never to return. Three days later Pacelli's body was buried beneath the Bernini altar in St. Peter's Basilica, Rome, near the spot which Pacelli himself had designated in 1950 as the grave of the first Bishop of Rome, Peter the Fisherman.

There was this touch of rightness about Pacelli throughout his Vatican career, even down to the location of his tomb. It clothed him, his adherents, those who obeyed his dictates, accepted his decisions, worked in his employ, and acclaimed his greatness. All seemed to be so right about him; about his person, about his reign, and about his final resting place.

Even though he died, the condition in which he left his Church seemed to be spiritually so right, as a direct result of Pacelli's rightness. Roman Catholics had grown in number from 388,402,610 in 1939 to 496,512,000 in 1958. He canonized thirty-three saints. He proclaimed a new dogma to be held unshakenly by all the faithful: that Mary the Virgin had been taken body and soul into heaven. He had one private vision of Jesus in 1954 and another vision in public but reserved for him alone in the Vatican gardens: the sun danced around the sky as a sign of God's power. In a record-breaking number of speeches and letters, he outlined Catholic principles on everything from automobiles to mercy killing to rocketry to silence and to yoga. His fluency in six languages seemed right. His friendship for Gary Cooper was right. His attempted cure of Red Skelton's son was right. Even his very appearance was right: "He is straight, strong, taut as a watch spring, thin as a young tree, but tranquil and tranquilizing, a Gothic figure whose vestments fall about him in Gothic folds, whose long hands are raised in Gothic gestures both still and graceful," wrote Anne O'Hare McCormick.

When violent controversy with ugly implications arose about his role in the Jewish Holocaust of World War II, the smell of any wrongdoing or even bad judgment could not really touch Pacelli. Whatever happened, whatever he did, whatever he did not do, he must have been right—this was the core argument of his defenders and admirers in their steadfast rebuttal. So it was throughout his Church, its bishops, and its people: the Pope was right. I say this rightness was the third characteristic of Pacelli as the Prince of Power.

There died, then, with Pacelli in Rome, the charisma of power. With the burial of its last bearer, there was buried forever any substantive hope that such regnancy, legitimacy, and rightness would ever again characterize a pope as pope. Jesus on his second coming would achieve all three, but on a supernal plane and as a matter of course.

At the height of Pacelli's prestige from 1945 to 1958, the malaise of Catholicism ran deep and yet was near the surface. But it was a time when stereotypes would do, when the easy answer was accepted, when offered images were swallowed whole. The mass movements of men, of nations, of global fortunes, facilitated this acceptance, anyway. Never again, however, would there be a Prince of Power as pope. For, despite appearances, power no longer enjoyed an effective ascendancy throughout Roman Catholicism. And the world at large needed only death to unshield its eyes once blinded by the brilliance of any great man.

Pacelli had chosen only a little love with his tragedy and had spiced his history with only a little wit. Catholicism at his apogee was spent in its humanism. Its people were weary of formulary holiness and stamped passports to a Roman heaven for Romans. Since the Protestant Reformation in the sixteenth century, three hundred years of happiness on command, of morality by ukase, of holiness by licensed rubber stamp, and of salvation by tight-fisted bureaucrats had left a huge debt to be paid off in human understanding and an almost impossible void to be filled with warmth, welcome, and willingness. This debt and that void—Pacelli's failure—are only ancillary themes of this study. At the moment of his death, compassion was needed. In October 1958 the hour of its need was later, much later, than anyone guessed.

Part IV

———⟨∞⟩———

THE GREAT GAMBLE

19

The Ice Age

Unmistakably, the election of Angelo Roncalli as pope in 1958 fell flat. Mind you, there was the usual fanfare and the traditional Roman circus: the white smoke, TV cameras, traffic jams, delirious nuns and seminarians and cheering crowds in St. Peter's Square, the radio broadcast of the new Pope's blessing ("Sounds just like any one of five thousand other guineas I used to know in Rome," grunted one young American bishop), ecstatic trumpetings from *L'Osservatore Romano* (after all, it *is* the pope's paper), a spate of congratulatory telegrams from foreign governments, sudden pullulation of the new Pope's picture and biographical notice in newspapers and magazines, reminiscences by cardinals returning to their home towns, assessments by pundits. But when all was said and done as it had to be said and done, as it had always been said and done about a new pope, the election of Roncalli was a classic example of the letdown. In more ways than one, and for different people.

For the veterans of the Vatican ministries aching all over their political bodies from nineteen years of Pacelli's authoritarian and disdainful treatment: a promise of relief, a breathing space, no worry. Good old Johnny. One of "us." Even the name sounded inoffensive. For the Reformation-minded Catholics of England, for the blindly faithful Catholics of Ireland and Spain and Portugal, for the ebullient trust and uninformed good will of American Catholics: a glorious thing, a new "Holy Father." For the ramshackle and disheveled Catholic intellectuals of France, Germany, Belgium, and Holland: another fat Italian cardinal had

175

made it; more Italianate ruling, more centralization, more Romanism. For those living in the long unrelenting winter of condemnations, expulsions, censures, silencing, muzzling, for "errant" philosophers, writers, artists, and for divorced Catholics, homosexuals, defrocked priests, runaway nuns, and "lapsed" Catholics: more of the same, more of the ostracism, more of the condemnation. For the confirmed progressives who had squared their beliefs and their opinions with their consciences, it was all over: a bloody bore. The election provoked yawns. So what?

For the Protestant churches and sects: another Roman affair, a non-event for them. For the Eastern Orthodox Churches: another round in the rampant imperialism characteristic of Rome, naughty children trying to spell God's name with the wrong alphabet blocks. For the Jews (those who cared about it): the replacement of one who had refused to help six million of their number. But no great change. All popes turned out to be the same. For the Moslems (those who heard about it): an infidel process with an interesting bearing on Middle East oil. For the Soviets: a negative benefit. At least, their ardent enemy, Pacelli, was gone off to inspect his divisions in eternity. He and Stalin. "We sent our cosmonauts up into outer space. They searched. They didn't find God. Hee! Hee!" laughed Khrushchev. For the Chinese Communists: of no significance. For the diplomatic corps and their reports to the home governments: nothing new. Certainly a kind reign, probably an uneventful reign, possibly a weak reign, all in all, a stabilizing factor for the rickety Italian government.

For nobody did it bode anything extraordinary. Give or take a pound or two of papal flesh, give or take a Vatican document or two, an appointment or two, a new face or two at diplomatic-corps gatherings, the status would remain precisely quo. Above all, it heralded no change, no new era. Now, all this was logical in 1958. It was a world of congealed attitudes. Particularly the immediate world from which Pacelli exited. It was a known thing. An architecture in rigid, cold sureties and of accepted incalculabilities. An assemblage of power centers frozen into counterbalancing stances, little mortals and big mortals either sunk in their subordination or drawn up taut and watchful in their dignity. Controlled channels. Determined distances. Predominant policies. Regulated rationales of back-scratching, backings and forthings, what-have-you-been-doing-for-me-lately exchanges, diplomatic tightrope walking, and cud-chewing bull sessions on "safe ground," in "neutral territory." The arrangement was not made in the image of man's compassion. It was an ice age. For the greater glory of God. And in the name of Jesus. Whatever you made *him* out to be. Why expect Angelo Roncalli to melt and liquefy all that?

As in any ice age: nothing could really move, but great continents were surging beneath, and new regions as yet invisible and untrod were forming. On the surface, no warmth of hope. No springtime burst of life. No new birth. No maturing. No golden days. Darkness alternating with light in unjust sequences and unbearable lengths. This is the beginning of the Book of Roncalli's Analysis. In the beginning was the Word. But it became very ecclesiastical. In the beginning, God created the heavens and the earth. But man split their atoms and strung his own chromosomes in a necklace. And this was Roncalli's analysis.

For traditional Roman Catholicism at the time of his election, there were Four Worlds. The Old World. The New World. The Alienated World. The Other World. They were defined, of course, in terms of power. The Old World had the power of divinely authorized salvation. It included any country or nation where Roman Catholicism was either officially or as a matter of fact the recognized religion of the majority or of a significant mass of the people: Austria, Belgium, Canada, England, France, Germany, Holland, Ireland, Italy, the Philippines, Portugal, Spain, and all countries in South America.

The New World was, exclusively, the United States and it had the power of newly born Roman Catholicism. New: because its Roman Catholic Church had only lately flourished in numbers, in wealth, in fidelity to Rome. Australia might some day become part of this New World. But there was too much independence down there, and not too much wealth.

The Alienated World fermented with the power all error generates. It included all other masses of Christian churches, sects, communities, and persuasions. A gaggle of heterodoxies, esotericisms, wild aberrations: Armenians, Copts, Ethiopians, Greeks, Mormons, Protestants, Quakers, Rollers, Russians, Syrians, Unitarians, *et al.* One and all, either heretics, schismatics, or erring sheep. Alienated: because, for the nonce, they were not in their rightful home; prodigal sons, runaway daughters, historical dropouts from God's house that they were.

The Other World was firmly locked into the power of sin and hatred. It was an unholy grab bag: Jews, Moslems, Buddhists, Shintoists, Confucianists, Hindus, Communists, socialists, athe-

ists, agnostics, and "pagans" of every kind—well-heeled ones in
suburbia, academia, business, and government, as well as splay-
footed aborigines in Australia, cannibals in the Amazon basin,
as well as delightful gourmets and the "beautiful people" in
every Western capital.

The Church had definite attitudes to all Four Worlds. It supplied a life of supernatural grace to the Old World and preserved
its Catholicity in its purity. This was the Church's official stamp-
ing ground, otherwise known as the "family of Christ's house."
The Church drank from the New World, under God's marvelous
providence, enormous draughts of money, financial advice and
facilitation, manpower, material supplies (medical, dental, food,
cigarettes, clothing, equipment), and plain old-fashioned "pull."
American Catholics were, indeed, children. The Church kept the
Alienated World at a safe, aseptic distance, then prayed ardently
for its conversion and set about converting it piecemeal, man by
man, woman by woman, child by child. Some day. Somehow. In
God's hidden plans.

The Other World was precisely that: an other matter. God
only knew how *that* would end. The Jews had to wait anyway
until the end of time. Serve them right for having killed Jesus.
The Muslims were the carpetbaggers of the Truth, plagiarists of
the Gospel, but not unlikely to be saved withal. For all others,
save Communists and socialists, there was a vast missionizing
effort. Communists and socialists were mortal enemies. The former, sometimes indubitably linked with a Jewish-Masonic plot
against Christ's Church, were the last word in satanic hatred and
the first word of Antichrist's arrival.

Obviously, this Four World conception left no room for an ice
age. Rather, four very active spheres. The Old World active in its
life of supernatural grace. The New World bursting with the
ebullience of supernatural youth. The Alienated World laboring
in exile from home, kneading and eating the bread of its bitterness. The Other World as busy and as lively as a vegetable garden overrun with weeds, virulent with poisonous and unseemly
growths, choking in a magnificence of ugliness. But Roncalli disagreed with the Four Worlds outlook. Rather, he no longer held,
as once he did, with the Four Worlds topped by a white-maned
Father, a radiant half-naked Son bearing a shiny Cross, and a
Picasso dove Holy Spirit enclosed in a milk-white isosceles tri-
angle and shedding supernal rays. Besides, all this was rank
ignorance, culpable ignorance, of stark facts. He saw an ice age
with all its implications. His starting point was different. It was

reality. He was the first pope to think as man. The problem for
him was neither natural nor supernatural, a question neither of
converting pagans nor of reconciling dissident Christians, neither
of opposing nor of appeasing Communists nor of forming working alliances with socialists. The problem was man, the human
species as a whole at this juncture of human history.

The most important and inescapable fact about men does not
stem from the color of their skins, their religions, their racial
origins, their political opinions, or their economic conditions. It
is that all men, wherever and whenever they existed, exist, and
will exist, belong to a "human family." Not a father-mother-children family. Not a vast lineal family descended physically from
an Adam and an Eve. Not a supernaturally elevated "human
family." Not even the "human family" outlined by the anthropologists, the Homo sapiens. But it is the family men constitute
because each man shares with every other man the equality of
being human and the dignity of equal human rights.

The "human family" character of man is, however, an abstract. It does not imply any unity, or equal dignity, or equal
rights, in the concrete. A medieval philosopher would crush the
mind with equally abstract arguments to establish the unity ab-
stractedly. At the same time, outside his door, outside his house,
outside his city or state or country, men could be setting about
proving the opposite in the concrete order of human life, by hate,
by opposition, by inequality, by all man's inhumanity to man.
Roncalli was not concerned with any abstract unity. He was
dealing with concrete history: living men in definite locations on
the planet earth, working, begetting, and dying, around the
middle of the twentieth century. Their concrete conditions defied
and rejected the abstraction of the philosopher.

In this concrete order of history, there is manifest, only in our
modern day, the beginning of a unity among men which was
never achieved before in human history. This unity has yet to be
achieved. No abstract principles of belief or philosophy can
forge it. At midcentury, and at its most base level, it is merely and
poignantly a community of increasingly pressing needs. Men today are truly interdependent as never before. "There has been an
increase in the circulation of goods, ideas, and of persons from
one country to another." Thereby, relations between individuals
and communities have been created now which did not exist before. Second, "the interdependence of national economies has
grown deeper . . . so that they become, as it were, integral
parts of the one world economy." Third, "the social progress,

order, security, and peace of each country are necessarily connected with the social progress, order, security, and peace in all other countries."

These needs, however, could conceivably be satisfied—and peacefully, if it were not for the awesome fact that some radical change has been effected within the lifetime of twentieth-century man. Roncalli only specified this to a degree. "This," he asserted, "is an era in which the human family has already entered, has already commenced, its new advance toward limitless horizons." He is speaking of human horizons. Horizons on this planet. It is evident "in the present course of human events . . . human society has entered a new order." As a further specification, he spoke of the present "dynamic course of events," declaring that present human relations must be "adjusted to the era of the atom and of the conquest of space." There lies at the back of these assertions some intuitive grasp upon which Roncalli did not expatiate very much further.

But he did explain the ice age, the deathly freezing and immobility which afflict the present institutions of human society. He is talking about the relations between governments of different nations: their disputes, jealousies, suspicions, fears, and clashing interests. In brief, human beings have world-wide problems today which will not go away. But, as things now stand, they have no means of solving them. The profound changes wrought in our time give rise to these grave, complex, and extremely urgent problems. The changes are permanent. There is no going back. These problems must be solved. On the other hand, men today do not have the means of solving the problems, because there is no public authority in existence with world-wide powers corresponding to the world-wide dimensions of the problems. Roncalli listed the incapacities of modern man: "No matter how much they multiply their meetings or sharpen their wits in efforts to draw up new juridical instruments, they are no longer capable of facing the task of finding an adequate solution to the problems." He included in this negative assessment the United Nations Organization.

Thus there arises in our world the tension of world powers, the reliance on nuclear deterrents, the sustained efforts to attain first-strike capacity, the dividing of loyalties, and the reign of fear. None will establish a world-wide public authority. None will submit to such an authority freely for fear of losing their juridical equality and their moral dignity. International relations are thus frozen into set motions, mutually maintained opposition, and the chilly silence of equally destructive opponents.

The social structuralism of the twentieth century is, on another and more personal level, part of the ice age. The individual is being hemmed in by a complex web of duties and involvements necessary for survival in our modern countries. Individual governments are being hemmed in by an ever increasing complex web of juridical and bureaucratic machineries necessary for running the country.

> Rules and laws controlling and determining relationships of citizens are multiplied. Opportunity for free action by individuals is restricted within narrower limits. Methods are often used, procedures are adopted, such an atmosphere develops wherein it becomes difficult for one to make decisions independently of outside influences, to do anything on one's own initiative, to carry out in a fitting way his rights and duties, to fully develop and perfect his personality.*

If these social relationships multiply more and more, they can produce men who become "automatons and cease to be personally responsible." Man's society will cease to be genuinely human. It will be Orwell's Animal Farm, and the iron reign of Big Brother. For, as things now stand, it would have only the excellence and achievement of the age to help it. These promise only "scientific competence, technical capacity, and professional experience." Every modern government depends on these, as does every modern army, every modern city, every diplomatic move. "To regulate the price of butter, to control drug addiction, to exit from environmental pollution, to cope with overpopulation, to defeat disease and starvation, these are necessary. Yet none of these is sufficient to elevate the relationships of society to an order that is genuinely human." For the genuinely human order is of a very particular kind. Its foundation? Truth. Its measure and objective? Justice. Its method of attainment? Freedom. Its driving force? Love. But love, freedom, justice, and truth are not generated by scientific competence, technical capacity, and professional experience.

Within this framework of human need and human helplessness, the most discouraging note for Roncalli was provided by Christianity and particularly by the Roman Catholic Church.

* Quotations throughout this chapter are from the speeches and writings of John XXIII.

Not only did it not provide a solution; as it stood and as it acted, it only served to perpetuate the ice age. Precisely in those places where the Roman Catholic Church claimed at least nominal paramountcy in its Old World, the human problem seemed insoluble on the basis of Roman Catholic principles.

This was the curse of the Princedom of Power: it froze mortals within a framework, destroying initiative, decrying change, exalting the status quo. As the only means of salvation, it proposed Jesus Crucified, God Almighty, Holy Spirit Wise, Mary the Virgin, hell, purgatory, heaven, and the Seven Sacraments as administered by the Church. And it held them up for man's view like so many mummified forms poised against the grill gates and the bars of the ecclesiastical Church, warning each man and every woman, him that he was an animal, her that she was man's perennial source of sin, both that their salvation depended on a blind and passive submission to an "authority" which, come what may, always "knew better." Now, in Roncalli's mind, the reckoning time had come for the Princedom of Power. Nowhere in its "good" and "reliably Catholic" Old World could it do anything. In the other Three Worlds of its fantasy, of course, it could do nothing.

The position in Latin America was very clear. Latin America supplied Vatican statisticians with a 1963 cliché number of Roman Catholics somewhere in the region of 235 million. This was over one-third of the total estimated number of Roman Catholics in the world of Roncalli. These were the faithful. At that time, there was not one nation in Latin America which the Roman Catholic Church did not claim as a Roman Catholic nation. Everywhere, the Roman Catholic hierarchy was well organized and well entrenched: archbishops, bishops, monasteries, convents, schools, lands, and possessions. Everywhere an apparently obedient and submissive faithful. Yet, despite this apparently roseate picture, Latin America had been recognized for almost a decade as an international disaster area in the Roman Catholic world. The reason was simple: nothing, apart from a miracle, could save the vast bulk of its population from Communism or Sovietization (in practice, the same thing). Latin America was coming apart at the seams.

All its trouble and each of its woes were reducible to a simple formula: overriding and profound poverty of the millions held within an outworn social system, an economy dominated by national and foreign monopolies, and a political condition that rarely, if ever, permitted even the initial maturation of true democracy. Government by the people, for the people, through the people, was a myth.

The Roman Catholic Church—i.e., the hierarchy and its organized power—stood solidly with the Establishment. Coming in the main from the powerful families, they stood with the landowners, the big companies, the military juntas, the reigning families, the financial power centers. A few churchmen made heroic but futile gestures. Chilean Crescente Errázuriz y Valdivieso, Bishop of Talca, surrendered 366 episcopal acres of land to some eighteen destitute families. Colombian Botero Salazar of Medellín handed over his episcopal palace to workers and went to live in a shed in a town slum. These and a few others were exceptions to a centuries-old rule.

There was, even according to Vatican traditionalists, very little to do for Latin America, except to pray and rely on the North Americans. The Latin American masses were ignorant, superstitious, utterly impoverished, a prey waiting for the political demagogue and the skillful indoctrination and utopian promises of Marxist and Communist. What anguished Roncalli was the inability of the Roman Catholic Church to provide even the beginning of a solution. Latin America within one generation would be lost. This inability arose from the static immobility which the Church maintained as a condition for its existence. Nothing could save Latin America for the Roman Catholic Church. The continent was going by default. The four-hundred-year-old jig was up. The ice age.

In North America, in Europe, and in Australia, the picture was no less desperate, although few would have agreed with Roncalli in 1960 that a crisis was impending. The Church seemed so solid. Compared with Latin America, here the causes of crisis were different. The results promised to be as drastically the same, however. According as these countries advanced in social sciences, technology, and the good life, the structuralism inherent to these developments was taking over. There was no "Christian," much less "Roman Catholic," solution or answer. "In traditionally Christian nations, secular institutions, although demonstrating a high degree of scientific and technical perfection and efficiency in achieving their respective ends, not infrequently are but slightly affected by Christian motivation and inspiration." The reason was clear: "an inconsistency in their minds between religious belief and their actions in the temporal sphere." Roncalli was charitable and mild; he spared the evildoers, the neglectful, the morally responsible. In the centralized system of the Roman Catholic Church and according to the ethics of power, those morally responsible were, primarily, the Vatican administration; secondarily, the hierarchies and the priests throughout the world.

These men were responsible for the reign of intellectual terror rife in seminaries, university faculties, institutes, among writers and thinkers; for the ghetto mentality of the Spanish, the Portuguese, the Irish, the British Catholics; for the dead-weight conservatism of Roman Catholics all over the world. They were many and they were diverse in character, but all churchmen. They were heads of operations. And they were, chiefly and principally, the heads of the powerful Vatican ministries in Rome. By the end of the fifties these Roman bureaucrats had practically completed a stranglehold on all intellectual and scientific development in the Roman Catholic Church and its institutions.

The non-Catholic and very often the Catholic himself is not aware of the general structure of studies, of research, and of intellectual activity within the modern Roman Catholic Church. Study, research, and intellectual activity depend vitally on a supply of teachers, books, and learning centers. A distinction must be made between ecclesiastical studies (theology and philosophy) and secular studies (science, humanistic subjects, etc.). The stranglehold mentioned above was intended to include both ecclesiastical and secular studies, research, and activity. The path to such a stranglehold was clear: control of teachers, books, and learning centers.

By the time Pacelli died in 1958 and Roncalli was elected pope, the stranglehold was practically accomplished. A few last stages were necessary. But it was a grandiose plan. It was proposed that all ecclesiastical learning centers in Rome be brought under the direct control of a new creation in Rome: the Lateran University. The university would be under direct control of the Vatican ministries. This meant that approval of all future teachers in Rome and of all books used in Rome would be subject to the Roman bureaucratic and conservative mentality. It also meant, in the long run, that approval of Catholic centers, teachers, and books throughout the world would be subject to the same source.

In the meantime, throughout the Catholic academic centers of France, Germany, Belgium, and Holland, the principal and really professional intellectuals, researchers, and students had been silenced, removed from their posts, sent into exile, restrained, or censured. It was a rather frightening atmosphere of suspicion and inhibition. Scholars disappeared on an indefinite "sabbatical" to Jerusalem, to a monastery in northern Italy, or to some quiet mission field in darkest Africa. Rectors of institutes and provincials of religious orders resigned without rhyme or reason, suddenly, quietly. Some of the finest minds were cloaked off: Lubac, Congar, Chenu, Teilhard de Chardin, Lyonnet. All feared being secretly reported to Rome. Professors never knew if their class notes might not find their way to a Roman censor. There was no defense, no explanation, no trial.

A similar watch was kept over publications by Catholics in subjects other than ecclesiastical ones. Studies in books and magazines were forbidden or put on the Index of Forbidden Books, expunged from ecclesiastical libraries and Catholic book-shops. The imprimatur (ecclesiastical approval) was sought after by any serious nonfiction writer and intellectual. Local bishops and the censorious authorities in Rome were immediately suspicious of anything new in the fields of Bible study, of anything at all to do with psychology and psychiatry. The net in which this vast catch of intellectuals and churchmen were held fast was simple: Roman ministries could make it impossible for a bishop to run his diocese from day to day. Only Rome could grant special dispensations for marriages in certain cases, and ordinary permissions for the ordination of priests, the organization of financial drives, the building of churches and convents. Rome held the power. Without it, no bishop or churchman could hope to govern happily, or even unhappily, his diocese.

Thus the ice-age conditions were reproduced faithfully within the structure of the Roman Catholic Church. The immobility of development. The strangling of initiative. The steady pumping of stay-as-you-are principles into the body politic. The swift and ruthless elimination of any contrary element. Finally, the dominating presence of irredentist, intransigent, and backward conservatism at the keystone of this structure. It was, as said before, a power structure. The Princedom of Power.

It would be invidious and unfair, however, to lay the responsibility for this at the door of any one man or any small group of men. Pacelli was at fault because he lived out the role as Prince of Power. Cardinal Ottaviani and Archbishop Parente, both the most powerful members of the Vatican bureaucracy, were responsible because they aped Pacelli's power stance and they capitalized on the docility of all believers. But in their own way, and either because they actively collaborated or because they sinned by default, so also were responsible, for instance: Cardinals Pizzardo, Cicognani, Siri and Ruffini (Italy), Heenan (Great Britain), D'Alton (Ireland), Tappouni (Beirut), van Roey (Belgium), Gilroy (Australia), Pla y Deniel (Spain), Caggiano (Buenos Aires), McIntyre (United States), to mention only a few. All over the world, archbishops, bishops, monsignors, university rectors, and diocesan officials were at fault. It was nobody's fault in particular. It was everybody's responsibility.

In the final analysis, however, as in every human bureaucracy, as in every known caste system, and as in every corporate lunacy, the cheapest and readiest commodity is the scapegoat, scapegoats aplenty. It was really the system which had taken over, though. In the long view of human development, blame in itself and excoriation after the event do nothing useful or beneficial. This is so for several reasons. First, because responsibility in the system is always delegated and hierarchized; there is always someone to whom plaints, complaints, or attacks can be diverted. Second, because by and large it is impossible to accuse anyone of blatant insincerity or deliberate ungodliness. At most, one can tag them as ignorant, timorous, stubborn. And, finally, because, as someone once said, in world history both are right—the hammer and the anvil. Only the iron is wrong, is heated, is molded by strong blows. It is this molding which occupies us.

20

The Great Un-need

No matter how we turn it, the last thing needed by either the Roman Catholic Church or the world at large in the middle of the twentieth century was an ecumenical council held in the Vatican, Rome. An ecumenical council of the traditional type (what other kind can there be?) is just what is not needed. The great un-need. There had been (before Roncalli's Second Vatican Council of 1962) twenty previous ecumenical councils. They were councils: the participants discussed problems and took decisions. They were ecumenical: bishops from all over the world were active participants in the discussions. The subject matter was religious, ecclesiastical, theological, and philosophical. What could all such discussions do to affect the concrete problems of human society?

A council can talk itself to death, produce resounding declarations, high-sounding condemnations and recommendations. When all is said and done, the Roman Catholic Church and, for that matter, any of the Christian churches, lacks the power to do anything in the concrete order. It can nudge no military arm, has no bombs or divisions, does not control even economic power of a world-wide potency. Whatever power had been sought by the Church, it had ended up as a sclerosis and not as a kingdom assaulted. There was no handwriting on the wall. No Mene, tekel, u-pharsim. The Princedom of Power had not been weighed in the balance and found wanting. Not even divided and given over to others, to aliens, into the hands of strangers. Nobody lusted after its power. God had not abdicated from its throne. He had never sat on it.

Another facet of un-need: the Church itself did not need a council. All twenty previous councils were needed (more or less) either to define a belief so that the faithful would have some clear ideas, or to condemn and lambast heresies, schisms, and errors of an extraordinarily virulent and dangerous kind. No such thing existed in the Roman Catholic Church at midcentury. A few aberrant German, Dutch, French, and Belgian theologians needed a wrist-slapping (which they got promptly). An occasional book needed expunging or total excision from existence. It was expunged. But erroneous books were not what they used to be, and heretics and schismatics had died out of fashion. Anyway, the Vatican already had in operation quite an efficient machinery of elimination for all undesirable elements. Error, heresy, schism—these things really had no chance. If the pope really wanted to find out what his bishops all over the world thought of a doctrine or belief, he had only to write them a letter. He could even call them on the telephone and have their answers recorded, sifted by computers, and so produce a statistical rundown. Pacelli had conducted a world-wide consultation by letter in 1954 and thus arrived at a justification for decreeing that Mary the Virgin had been taken body and soul into heaven after her death. He did not have to call an ecumenical council.

Roncalli himself underlined the great un-need more sharply than any one of his predecessors. "Our work here," he said at the inauguration of his Council, on October 11, 1962, "is not to discuss some particular headings of doctrine or to repeat only more profusely what former and recent theologians and Church Fathers have handed on to us." If that were so (Roncalli termed such procedures "discussions of this kind," with a wry dismissal), then we need not have summoned an ecumenical council. Of course, he remarked, whatever we teach must be in keeping with our faith, but "our job is not merely to preserve this precious treasure and to dwell on its antiquity."

In a letter of January 6, 1963, he thrust the knife deeper into any illusions on this point. "If we get held up exclusively in our Catholic affairs or if we stay inside the limits of the Catholic Church, would this way of acting really be an adequate response to the command of our Saviour?" Then he spelled out what churchmen could do with a tranquil conscience, persuaded that they were doing all they had to do: preserve the integrity of Catholic teaching, as found in the Bible, in the Fathers of the

Church, and in statements of previous popes. When all that has been done, he went on, we still have not fulfilled God's commands.

These commands are chiefly two: "Go forth and teach all nations," and "God entrusted each man with his fellow man." Roncalli quoted a statement of St. John Chrysostom as a final exclusion of all partisan mentality: "You have to give an account [to God] not only of yourselves but of the entire world."

There was another and more hair-raising aspect of this great un-need. An ecumenical council, as a collection of men, could quite well turn out to be less than the sum of its parts. There were approximately 2,500 bishops in the Roman Church. All had a right to participate. Among them, by and large, there reigned a sincere desire for the good of religion and the safety of mankind. Among them, also, there were intelligent, well-educated, hard-nosed, frank men, who would not quickly blanch before a difficulty or easily misunderstand a concept or a situation.

But all were part of a juridical order. All were governed by a mentality to a large extent determined by Rome. Very few of them exercised power in Rome. And that bureaucratic power was all-pervasive. It could defeat Roncalli in the everyday administration of the Vatican and the Church. It could hamper his decisions, refuse him the aid he needed, prevent his receiving letters, documents, or news magazines. It could make appointments, remove officials, create posts. Could an ecumenical council possibly achieve anything relevant to the world outside the bureaucrats? Rather, it might serve to ensconce more deeply the already deeply entrenched bureaucracy; it could spread *Romanità* further among the bishops from the universal Church. It could defeat its own purpose: it could turn into a very undecorous in-Church squabble camouflaged in clouds of meaningless hot air; it could devolve either into a reproduction of itself in terms of the world around it or into a narcissistic parade; it could, finally, lose itself in a new assertion of its ancient dominance.

An in-Church squabble. This was more than a possibility. The exercise of juridical power untempered with love over the Catholics of Europe had succeeded in holding them down as a mass. But since World War II a certain irrepressible ferment had been noted by Rome, noted and pursued and castigated whenever the opportunity arose, and in its more extreme forms. Two currents of theological thinking and one current of social action in particular had come to Rome's notice.

Young and recently graduated theologians in Germany,

France, and Austria started speaking of a "return to the sources of Catholic belief." They meant, of course, to take a new look at the early Church Fathers, theologians, and Church practices. But to Rome this sounded like a reproach: Rome's present-day teaching mirrored faithfully all facets of the early sources. Rome was the early source perennially living right up to this moment. It was as if Herbert Marcuse and Norman Thomas told Mao Tsetung or Joseph Stalin in the privacy of that leader's drawing room that one had to reread Marx, Engels, and Lenin to find out what was correct party belief. A second theology current concerned the Bible. Catholic scholars had absorbed the recent findings of archaeologists, linguists, and historians concerning the ancient Near East. They realized that the official Roman interpretation of the Bible lacked veracity and factual foundation and that sometimes it included sheer nonsense.

Over the postwar years up to and including Roncalli's brief reign, there were many hurt feelings, many bitter words, much human suffering, and an ocean of suppressed convictions on these two theological points. In the social order and especially in the ambient of big cities, industrial centers, and urban agglomerates, a certain experimentation was taking place. In a desperate effort to retain the ordinary layman's interest, priests were talking, thinking, and doing something about Masses in the vernacular languages (instead of Latin), greater participation by the laity in Church ceremonies and Church matters, and closer contact with the life of lay people. The worker-priest movement in France was one result of this. That and similar movements were received inimically in Rome. Again, many were hurt in the process, and they still hurt at the time of the Council. To cap it all, discontent was noticeably building up among foreign bishops. They resented the growing imperialism and highhanded manners of Roman churchmen. They felt neglected in many of Rome's periodic prescriptions, ordinances, admonitions, provisos, and commands. They paid a large total of Vatican bills, yet they had a disproportionately small say in matters of internal Vatican government. Many bishops lived in new countries of Africa and Asia; they were close to severe difficulties arising from local conditions. What could a Roman official in the Vatican whose peregrinations took him as far as the Campagna to see his family, or up to the Alps in a communal outing, know of polygamy in the Congo, Chinese rites for ancestors, poverty in Brazil, work hours in Detroit and Essen, and the agonies of contraception versus anti-contraception laws for struggling New York executives?

Given a suitable opening and a sufficient number with burnt memories, sore hearts, and humiliated hours to their credit, an in-Church squabble could easily ensue. These clerics could invade the sacrosanct Roman landscape, writhing through it like cautionary wraiths. The Vatican could become the fire hydrant for every outraged underdog of ten years and up who felt the moment had come to show his contempt. French wounded in their unseasoned pride, Americans struck in their pockets but maintained in an ecclesiastical kindergarten, Germans stifling with new concepts, Dutch boiling with stiff and throaty rage, and Irish together with the Spaniards outraged by such disrespect to the Holy Father and his high office, could turn up at the Council with about as much good effect as a group of masochists arriving at a white-tie dinner complete with boots, whips, and leather underwear to prove their point. A debacle of that kind and magnitude could reduce the Vatican in the eyes of the world to the status of a hoary banyan tree presided over by a definitely impotent hoot owl. Needless to say, the Church needed such a disgraceful exhibition as much as it needed the persecutions of Diocletian complete with man-eating lions all over again.

A more likely possibility was that the whole affair would turn out to be a cross between an exercise in narcissism and a wordy description of God's Church with new concepts and freshly baptized terminology drawn from the religious ambient of the century.

The temptation to narcissism was very near the heart of many, at about the time of Roncalli's Council. For so long the Roman Catholic Church had been a parochial affair: overshadowed by the Protestant ascendancy with its derived glory from Protestant powers and empires, in Northern Europe and the United States; relegated to ghettos in Ireland, London, Glasgow, Brittany by the intelligentsia of the late nineteenth century: looked on and described by Protestants as the religion of mere Celts, Dagos, Levantines, Mediterraneans, and other greasy, superstition-ridden human beings; bludgeoned by scientists and researchers in all fields; out of touch with the ancient churches of Constantinople, Damascus, Cairo, Moscow, Beirut, Armenia. Now could be the heaven-sent opportunity: observers coming from all major Protestant and Eastern Orthodox Churches and sects; government watchers and observers from all major gov-

ernments. Let them see the beauty and strength of Christ's
Church. The panoply of magenta and white, the strength in
numbers of 2,500 bishops with their theologians and experts.
And at Rome. The whole affair could be a vast one-act drama set
over against the deathless immortality of Rome which had seen
Caesar rise and fall and had outlived every other living capital in
the world.

"Come and see how good it is for brethren to live in harmony."
By the sheer force of their presence, the unity of doctrine, the
calm patience with error, the treasures of their teaching, the
modernity of their awareness, the bishops of the Council could
effect an éclat which might even elicit a new desire for the old
unity among the guardians of Christianity, all in a new movement of rebirth. But such narcissism would be a terrible intro-
version. It would only paper over the cracks in the wall, not
repair them. It would be a reckless exercise in triumphalism,
clericalism, and juridicism.

It was also possible that some small dosage of such narcissism
be mixed with a goodly flood of new concepts and refurbished
terms. The purpose of the new admixture would be to "modern-
ize" the Church, to make it more "intelligible" to other Christians
still separated from Rome, to High Church Protestants, Greek
and Russian Orthodox, even to Lutherans and Methodists and
Calvinists. In fact, a lot of Martin Luther's original concepts and
words and even hymns could now be safely adopted. Lutheran-
ism was a spent force. No threat really. And Martin Luther was
with God. He now had the light.

This modernization of Roman Catholicism could take a few
more steps. It could, for instance, tackle the Mass, clean out
some of those long, obscure, and now meaningless prayers, the
litany of unknown martyrs; it could simplify the ceremony by
omitting gestures intelligible to a Roman of A.D. 200 but without
any significance for twentieth-century man; it could render the
Mass in English, give the laity more words to say, a few of Luther's finer hymns to sing, include some new "group" gestures
(standing together more often, shaking hands in the middle of
the Mass). There could be simpler forms for the other sacraments (baptism and marriage, for instance).

In theology, a lot of new things could be said with complete
impunity. The Roman Church could emphasize things which ap-
pealed to other Christians, could even use words that the latter
used. After all, it was not words which mattered but the power to
permit this word or that. There were other theological points to

be stressed: the primacy of Scripture; the dignity and relative independence of the bishops; the role of the laity; the value of the simple priest. A move could be made toward the hitherto banned ecumenical movement once the exclusive province of non-Roman Christians. A little footwork would be necessary here so as not to fall between two or three stools at the same time: to be so nice to the Constantinopolitan Greeks that the Muscovite Russians sulked and stayed away—or vice versa; or to be so nice to both of them that the World Council of Churches became afraid the Vatican was trying to wean them away from the WCC.

The Church could also declare itself on important new factors in the world of man: the news media which infiltrated minds so subtly; the plentiful crop of agnostics and atheists who believed that existence had no meaning and loved every minute of it; even on Jews, Buddhists, Moslems, who were in an impossible position today, anyway.

The whole Council would then be an exercise in deliberate translation. Translation of the age-old doctrine received from Peter and Paul into terms understandable by non-Romans, even by non-Christians. With a series of carefully honed declarations in hand, with enlarged permissions actually to pray together with non-Romans as well as to pray incessantly for them, with new juridical bodies of bishops and theologians and laymen to meet in Rome periodically and aid the Holy Father in solving problems—by advice and consent, the Church would be modernized, opened up, ready to mix with the world outside, would learn a few practical lessons, act out the sessions with impressed outsiders, and no longer just sit out a long isolated wait for the returning errant and sorry sheep. The Church would be right in the middle of things.

It is obvious that such a development was not needed by the Roman Church or by the other Christian churches or by the world at large. Granting that all this were achieved, it would not bring Christianity any nearer a solution of its modern dilemma. Nor would it enliven the aging bones of the Roman structure. At most, it would usher a surcease of life, induce a dangerous proximity to those in error, and a fake principle of identity between Romans and other Christians, and stave off any serious consideration of Christianity's role in the history of human society, if indeed modern Christians were capable of recognizing that role and then fulfilling it.

The truth was that, along with Roman Catholicism, all other forms of Christianity were likewise affected by rigid senescence.

Protestantism in all its forms had taken refuge either in philosophical theology or in activist sociology. All Eastern Orthodoxies were mummified with dynastic clichés and by canonized nationalisms: "Holy Mother Russia," the "Ancient Armenian Faith," and the "Greek Witness to Orthodoxy." And no one ever thought that Jews, Moslems, Hindus, and Buddhists could teach the Church anything. In fact, Roman Catholicism would, by this needless occupation of a council, merely approximate more nearly to the dry-boned fossilization of other Christian churches and sects. They would all go down together to the compost heap of effete human structures. But the death cry would not be only in Church Latin.

In terms of the great un-need, none of the above would vitally affect the Roman Catholic Church for its own betterment. It would mean more disassembly and a further aggregation of rigid, isolated structures in an ice age of man's religion. The tall icebergs of official beauty, the swirling floes of catchy words, phrases, and ideas, the flat and monotonous surfaces of created unities, all this would be whipped by the cold winds of human calculation and drenched in the numbing of foamy declarations, the sting of spindrift ideas, and the eternal inhumanity of an all-embracing sea of history.

21

The Time

In 1959, America is still young, the Roman Catholic Church is still calm, the world is still open to all possible solutions. No irrevocable Rubicon has been crossed in the Middle East between Arab and Israeli, or in space, in Vietnam, in pollution, in drug addiction, in campus revolt, in black resentment, in Catholic frustration, in South American Big Brotherism, or in Czechoslovakian rescues. It is late, but not too late. For everyone.

There is, in addition, what is notoriously and promiscuously called a vacuum. Sometimes it appears as the fresh vacuum any opening springtime promises to fill. The youthful towers of Camelot appear in Washington with President Kennedy, as of 1961. Sometimes it is felt as the peculiar vacuum of unknowing, as when a hard, impermeable, and obtrusive sight melts into indistinguishable mist. The hard, hypnotic glare of Stalinism is broken, and a jug-eared peasant from the Ukraine of indescribable *chutzpa* and unpredictable goodness and badness replaces a whole tradition. Sometimes, indeed, it strikes the men of 1959 as the vacuum of weariness at the end of a long waking night in which too many terrors were lived and too much pain inhabited the darkness. The Cold War should now be ended. The economic struggle should now be pacified. The Third World of Asia and Africa should now be free of colonialism. And, finally, it was a general vacuum of solutions, like a sole survivor treading water in the middle of an ocean with no land in sight, or a bell swinging to and fro in a high belfry but emitting no sound when its hammer strikes its insides.

However we describe it, it is a simple situation compared to that of ten years later. There is no trace of the multiple cancers which will gnaw and tear at the vitals of world society in 1971: the governed still want to be governed; the unfree do not throw bombs but still ask to be free; the unequal do not panic but aim at equality; the public morale is not sapped by official lies; the young still have their elders. Man's situation on the planet reduces itself to four definable components related to each other in a tension of mutual dependence and the agony of mutual distrust. Uncomplicatedly, it is merely the mutual international relationships of the United States and the U.S.S.R. as the only superpowers, of the United Nations Organization as the overfull spittoon of international differences, and of Communist China as the ostracized son of the international human family, aloof, xenophobic, torn internally, raw. The lopsided tetrahedron of man's 1959 world.

There is, in effect, a visible and appreciable human problem: the good universal to all nations and common to each one is at stake, but no one can agree on how to secure it. This is a hard, undigestible fact. But all the problems can be reduced to that lump sum of mutual distrust, mutual fear, and mutual need between the international Greats. None of the protagonists can accept the other in trust. None can obey the other with love. None can submit in freedom. None can promise justice. It is too dangerous. The analysis of this is simple. Roncalli writes: "At this historical moment, the present system of organization [between nations], and the way its principle of authority operates on a world basis, no longer corresponds to the objective requirements of the universal common good."

Patently, there is no inkling in Roncalli's mind and no echo in his language of the oft-repeated reproach made to the world by popes, Roman Catholic writers, and Christians in general: "If you people would only accept Christianity and let us organize this family according to our Christian principles, the whole mess would be cleaned up in a short time." Pacelli, speaking over the radio on June 1, 1941, when the world was divided into warring and hating camps, claimed demurely and somewhat superciliously that the "Church has indisputable competence to decide whether the bases of a given social system are in accord with the unchangeable order which God our Creator and Redeemer has fixed both in the natural law and in revelation." Such language was unacceptable. Worse, it was unintelligible, as much to Hitler's Nazi Germany, Mussolini's Fascist Italy, and Tojo's militaristic Japan, as it was to Stalin's Bolshevist Russia, Churchill's imperial England, and Roosevelt's American democracy. It was a cold, unthinking, unapt, infertile breath of air blown over a desert of stalking prejudices and clawing fears.

Roncalli is held by another vision and preoccupied with a different problem. Neither is dictated by the blind exigencies of the Princedom of Power. He draws simply the conclusion which any man can accept: "Today, the universal common good poses problems of world-wide dimensions which cannot be adequately tackled or solved except by the efforts of public authorities endowed with a wideness of powers, structure, and means of the same proportions; that is, of public authorities which are in a position to operate in an effective manner on a world-wide basis. The moral order itself, therefore, demands that such a form of public authority be established."

He is speaking of a supranational and world-wide public authority. Its structure is obvious. It cannot be imposed by force or fear. It must be freely created by all, superpower and tiny nation. It must be freely but faithfully obeyed by all, tiny nation and superpower. It must be impartial, sincere, and objective. It must solve problems of an economic, social, political, and cultural character which affect the universal common good, but only those. It must "create on a world scale an environment in which the public authorities of the individual political communities can more easily carry out their specific functions." As a coda to this he adds: the United Nations Organization is all right but inadequate.

At first sight, this seems to be a rehash of a very old dream, a papal version of previous proposals. Indeed, Roncalli was not the first world leader to think of a supranational authority. In his own lifetime, two such proposals took concrete form: the League of Nations and the United Nations Organization. But such proposals were bitten off and chewed unmercifully by the mordant facts of man's suspicion, distrust, and vulnerability. The League became a laughingstock for some nations, an imperial forum for others, a huddling-house for still others. The U.N. had fared a little better. But it had merely achieved a world forum for all important opinions (except Communist Chinese) and a source of economic help for poor nations. Neither of these organizations ever enjoyed even a shadow of the genuinely supranational authority which Roncalli vindicated as essential. Neither got off the ground. For into neither was put a common supranational will, a willingness on the part of all member nations to obey a supranational authority in supranational affairs, and to provide that authority with the moral and physical means of discharging its functions, of coercing the recalcitrant, and of championing common causes.

"There is not an earthly hope of such a common will," says Roncalli in the spring of 1959, "as far as the individual governments and peoples of the earth are concerned." He adds: "Such a common will to trust, to submit, to cooperate is greater than the sum of all peoples and governments together." For the men of this time, it is a somber moment: an international impasse clouded over with the threat of terror, in which all conversation of human society is reduced to the stark unpleasantries of daily clashes and the chilly encounters at the occasional summit meeting.

Throughout this, Roncalli discourses unshakenly and from the beginning of his reign as pope. His real enemy: pessimism. "We have known some spirits to be so struck by the sight of these difficulties as to see only darkness about to engulf the world." His advice: "Have nothing to do with such prophets of doom who are always promising worse things." His message: "We must seek a suitable means of binding the souls of men more closely together in preparation of the great event."

It would be unjust and a gross misreading of Roncalli's human sense to think, as is commonly done, that the great Event was merely or chiefly an ecumenical council. If it were, Roncalli would have indulged in the great un-need—the very thing he rather caustically decried.

But the great Event was something else. For his Roman Catholic enemies: the outermost tip of his imagination and a monster of his fantasy. For many of his friends: merely opening windows for clean air in his Church. For himself it was the child of many interlocking intuitions: man at play; man at work; the failure of his own organized Church; men's manifest and growing desire to be at peace; the nature of human reality. All these intuitions coalesced.

Roncalli reads lessons in the banal: man at work. He intuits reality in the contrived: man at play. He acknowledges failure: Catholicism never succeeded. He feels men's needs: they act as they act because of such needs. But he is not attracted first and foremost by the hard glitter of action. Some more evasive illumination shines out in the mundane and the everyday. The Winter Games of 1956, for instance, or the 1960 Olympic Games in Rome. Here, all participating put forth their best efforts, measured up to the same ideals, submitted to the same rulings, cheered the victors whoever they were, and, withal, remained individual nationalists. It was an event. Not precisely the actual Olympic Games themselves but this communal act of participation. It was exterior and superior to all participants, yet it included all participants. Man at play.

Or man at work. Especially at work to help man. Roncalli was struck by the behavior of Americans, Russians, French, Germans, British, and others at particular crises of human misery and human compassion. Two of many: the Quetta (West Pakistan) earthquake of 1935, and the Congo famine of 1960–61. International rescue teams hurried to help; all participants contributed of themselves and their goods, put forth their best efforts, measured up to the same ideals, did not hinder the overall effort, and, withal, remained individual nationalists. It was an event. Not precisely the actual earthquake or the actual famine, but this communal participation in relieving human misery. It was exterior and superior to all participants, yet it included all of them.

He had no illusions about ideological motivations and political ambitions. Of course, the U.S.S.R. made the status of athlete a privileged one, and at home mouthed shibboleth phrases about the "peace-loving principles of the Marx-Engels teaching," in the same breath with exhortations to do a better high jump or throw the javelin further than any white dog of a capitalist. Of course, it sought political mileage. Of course, the United States also sought political mileage, as did the French, the Japanese, the British, and all the others. Nor did he simplistically believe that anyone who aided the stricken ones in an international disaster did so from sheer goodness of heart and for a purely altruistic end.

But he refused to confuse collaborative competition or multination teamwork with the ideologies or political motivations of the masters in the home countries. He would not, could not, identify a good act with the explicit or implicit motivation of that good act. In that act: generosity had been exercised, compassion had been given; obedience was rendered to an ideal, submission was given to local rulings and to alien needs. What mattered was the act. The sum total of these acts, the thing generated by all such acts, was superior to all, enveloped all, outshone partisan motives, created a human beauty. It was an event.

An event in the Roncalli sense had very definite outlines and components: men of differing motivations; a desirable ideal; no manifest danger for individual nationalisms or ideologies; undoubted impartiality in the results; effort-demanding conditions; some self-renunciation; implicit benefits for all participating. Above all: it needed a physical meeting and getting together in one place. It could not be done by letter writing, by a thousand sermons preached in thousands of churches, by hundreds of parliaments voting in hundreds of different countries. It needed the physical union of the participating men, at least of their leaders and representatives. In its very nature, also, the event had one negative ingredient: no matrix of suspicion or distrust. The event needed something as impartial as a pelvis shattered by an earthquake, something as above distrust and suspicion as a competitor who swims one and a half times faster than anyone else, something as innocuous for partisan ideologies as starving children in Quetta, Ethiopia's Abebe Bikila running the marathon barefoot and faster than any modern athlete, populations in shock, a decathlon and pentathlon winner like American Indian Jim Thorpe, or homeless victims in Skopje.

The time for such an event on a grand human scale was now, concluded Roncalli. "Men are beginning to recognize that their own capacities are limited, and they seek spiritual things more intensively than before." He had spent the best part of forty years watching, waiting, asking, listening, noting. No matter whom he was with, Gaullists, Turks, Russians, Americans, Italian Communists, Arabs, Jews, he noticed the same desire: to have done with contention, the same dissatisfaction with purely technical and juridical means of regulating the human situation. "All of which," he concluded, "seems to give some promise that not only individuals but even peoples may come to an understanding for extensive and extremely useful collaboration." But in January 1959, except for some professional French and Belgian anti-clerical dog-watchers, people did not even laugh when he decided to call an ecumenical council.

Roman Catholics thought of all those bishops sitting together with the Holy Father—God bless them all, or bad luck to them all (depending on your status). Protestants and other non-Catholics hearkened back somberly to the first Vatican Council, when the pope was declared to be infallible. Secular governments (the first to understand, somewhat later, what Roncalli was about) told their protocol officers to look after this ceremonial affair. They all saw the Council as the "great event." But the intended Council was not Roncalli's great Event.

There was at the heart of Roncalli's proposal a bias and an

intuition which sprang from his faith as a Christian. It requires understanding and discernment. It had nothing of the Princedom of Power. This is hard to grasp. Surely Roncalli envisioned a major and predominating role for the Church, One, Holy, Roman, Catholic, and Apostolic—is what believer and unbeliever would automatically say. The answer is that he did not envisage any such role: Protestants "returning," Greeks and Russian Orthodox "submitting," Jews and Moslems and Buddhists "converting," Russians saying that little-caressed word "yes" to a pope, and everybody scurrying in a holy haste to be baptized with the baptism of Peter in Rome.

His bias was twofold. Most people would concede it as justified. The Roman Catholic Church alone of all major religions and of all the Christian churches was sufficiently universal to call together a truly international gathering of representatives standing for a truly international membership. Second, it alone had sufficient economic power, historical panoply, and personal prestige in the diplomatic and financial and political world to attract universal attention.

The intuition was also twofold. First, the pure and undiluted content of Catholic faith held the key to man's dilemmas and problems. But never yet in its centuries of history had that pure and undiluted content been exposed to man.

In the Council, wrote Roncalli, we must strive "to expose the truth in its own light." What about the teachings of previous popes, previous councils, previous theologians? Have they not done that? This was the question of conservative opponents. By this Council, "we will have much more plentiful hope and force, if we exercise ourselves in stating the whole truth," Roncalli wrote imperturbably. "We must," he stressed, "know our teaching more fully and more deeply and imbue and mold our spirits more fully with it." Roncalli is speaking, not to ignorant and unformed laymen, but to Church officials, to everything from a cardinal downwards to a seminary student. Many a Catholic was condemned in the past for suggesting that the leaders of the Church did not possess full and deep knowledge of the faith. Most Roman Catholics would not dare state this. Many might not dare think it. Some have been suppressed in various ways for mentioning it. Most non-Catholics would at least ask pertinently: What do you mean by "pure, undiluted content"? Roncalli would answer: We do not yet know. We have never yet known.

Roncalli's reasoning was clear on this point. But his statements were discreet and restrained. In a certain definite sense, he was feeling his own way from intuition to concrete realization on the human scene. He could not dislocate all by jettisoning some fifteen centuries of Church organization all of a sudden. He could not disillusion weaker spirits or scandalize the small-minded. He had himself jumped over mighty and ancient thought-barriers. He was ahead, but the organized Church he led, its leaders and its people, was behind him.

The nature of human reality was something which had preoccupied Roncalli ever since his years in the Near East. Before that, he never entertained a disturbing thought. What does man, the life of man, and human society signify—this was the question which had been forced on his mind in spite of his religious upbringing, clerical training, and professional calling. He never underwent "reverse indoctrination," never doubted his faith. But his reason clamored for answers to a concrete enigma.

This could be expressed as follows. If Christianity had the answer to man's problems, that answer must be satisfactory. To be satisfactory, it must answer problems concerning not only the good of individuals but the good of man's society, and in the twentieth century the universal common good. But that universal common good demanded a solution to the central problem of international relations. Concretely: what can Christianity and the Roman Catholic Church do to effect the creation of a truly international public authority acceptable to all nations?

In Roncalli's time, the answer was: nothing. Nothing, but a reiteration of abstract principles, a spelling out of laws, and a sustained assertion of Christianity's divine mission in general and the special mission of the Roman Catholic Church in particular. Quite a while before he became pope, Roncalli had admitted to himself: (1) that the Roman Catholic Church once upon a time had a splendid opportunity to establish a society completely based on Christian principles, and (2) that it failed to do this.

By the time he became pope, Roncalli knew the truth. In the human reality of his century, the laws, practices, and doctrines of Catholicism did not belong. Explicitly: in her prayers she mirrored the sentiments of men who lived five hundred, ten hundred, fifteen hundred years ago; there was very little specific to modern man's anguish. In her stated doctrines, modern man was served the mere verbiage of juridical minds and today it lay as a large dry wad of cotton wool stuck in his throat. In her so-called social doctrine, modern man unearthed merely the incorporeal beasts of the philosopher's memory and the unsubstantial gremlins of the theologian's speculation. In her central beliefs— salvation by Jesus' cross, resurrection, the Real Presence, heaven, hell—modern man stubbed into rock piles of theorizing which might titillate his mind, if he could just for a moment get that mind away from the problem of survival. Early Christian and Catholic teachers had dared intellectualize all. This was unforgivable hubris. They had tried to stare down the sun. All were blinded. Teachers and Taught.

Human reality lay primarily in human experience. The expression of that reality as experienced was the truth. "And the Word was made Flesh and dwelt among us. And we saw his Glory." The divine had entered the human reality. The Church's expression of that divine presence should spring from the perennial experience of it. But it did not. Whatever experience the Church had of the divine, it had taken and locked away in a book like a rose petal stiff between the pages, in the mind like a bee preserved in amber, in a Latin formula like an alchemist's secret known only to the initiate, in the blessing of a cleric's hand like the mystically fertile gesture of a creator. Roncalli's realism was never careful. His thoughts were never ironic. He spoke with a healing grace of humor and a smiling understanding for the weakness of man and the darkness of his soul. But it was clear what had to be achieved.

An event, a great event had to be achieved. An event on the scale of human society in the twentieth century. Whatever vitality, drawing power, and self-renovative ability still subsisted in the drying bones of organized Catholicism had to be marshaled. Not for a clerical éclat on an international scale. Not for a Roman Catholic junket on a high-theology diet. Not for a pleasant (or unpleasant, as the case might be) in-conversation with each other, a thunderingly great bonking of mammoth clerical heads with much trumpeting in high places. He had to gamble on the Spirit and on Chaos; so that what lacked to man could shine out from among men, shine and catch fire, melt and warm over the iced face of human society, liquefy its members, and let all men of good will live just one shattering moment and experience their unity as men. Just one such moment would suffice. This was Roncalli's planned Event.

22

The Event

In January 1959, the Event was what everyone secretly desired but nobody believed could happen. Nikita Khrushchev in Moscow, Eisenhower in Washington, Mao Tse-tung in Peking, Charles de Gaulle in Paris, Gamal Abdel Nasser in Cairo, Ho Chi Minh in Hanoi, Francisco Franco in Madrid, any national leader, and any and every John Doe engaged in the somber struggle. Even today, ten years after Roncalli spoke of it, it is the latent wish of all; but it is regarded now as idle dreaming. No one, no practical man of politics and no highly placed cleric, conceives the idea of it, much less speaks in favor of it or acts on its behalf. In the long attic of could-have-beens, the Event is already gathering dust.

At a much later date in human history, when the men of this century have been long in their graves, it will be remembered. The barbarism and the foolishness of our political leaders, "West" and "East," will be noted. Or, at the very least, they will be dismissed as pygmies on stilts who wandered into high places. The self-serving cowardice of our religious leaders will be underlined. Except for Roncalli as John XXIII, no pope (there have been 262 to date) will escape the calm censure of future men that they refused to jump old encrusted thought-barriers, and the rueful reproach of future Christians that they sacrificed the truth to parochial fear, and that, in order to preserve their own privilege, they denied love a chance to be born among men.

But, at that later date, the word "men" will have been changed to "brothers," and the word "Christian" will be purged of its parti-

san sting. Not on paper merely. Not in utopian statements by a
rump Council of God. Not on the lips of a perfervid few halluci-
nators waiting for Godot. But in accomplished fact, in the streets
and houses and factories of man's city as well as in the rooms of
his governance at home and abroad. Even though the Event is
now laid away quietly in the temporary never-never land of
man's vital needs and his summary desires, we should consider
today that what is said of it here and what is recorded in writing
concerning Roncalli's breakthrough in spirit and in human time
is still valid. With one proviso: we cannot at will recall, re-
create, or revive the magic moment Roncalli lived, so that we as
a community of men be finally at peace. Truth, justice, peace,
love—these will have to come to man in another way and in
bitter travail.

The Event was not the Ecumenical Council which Roncalli, as
pope, summoned to open in Rome on October 11, 1962. But that
Council was his calculated occasion for the Event. Nor was the
Event any one statement or body of statements to be issued by
his Council or by himself. He did envisage statements, but not
concerning doctrine as such, or of the morally good or bad, or of
the morally advisable or feasible, in men's actions. Nor, finally,
was the Event the creation of an international public authority
such as Roncalli concluded was essential for the preservation of
human society. That authority was perhaps the foreseen and
prime result of the Event.

There is only one central experience in their 1,940-year-old
history which has never been repeated for Christians. It took
place in Jerusalem. Its year and month and day and hour and
the exact location—these we will never know. It happened to at
least twelve Jews, the twelve chosen by Jesus before he died, to
be his messengers and to tell his story to the world. Possibly,
more people were there. Possibly, Mary, the mother of Jesus,
shared the experience. We do not know. And it does not matter.
History does repeat itself. But this event never has. So far, in
Christian time, it took place only once. According to the oldest
account, the twelve were in an upper-story room praying together, when it happened.

Jews rarely pray silently or individually, when they are together. The prayer is communal. There is always some noise of
mumbling and muttering, some swaying of the body, some gestures of the hand, some raising and lowering of the eyes and
head. It is an irregular orchestration of voice and movement, a
swaying and liquid motion with a common rhythm and individ-

ual colorings, a viscous pool of rising and falling supplication, atonal beat, breathing syllables, and uncoordinated beginnings coalescing periodically and irregularly either in a quick silence with trailing murmurs or on a word said unexpectedly with one voice, or against an agreed-upon gesture. Suddenly a silence. As if some wordless command has been issued, or a hidden clock has struck, telling a sudden end of all talking. All are aware of the others in hush.

At first, some think that only they hear it. Each one looks around at the other faces and along the narrow walls and ceiling, in surprise and questioningly, seeking and straining to know if others hear the remote and strange sound coming from no definable direction but apparently with gathering speed filling their ears increasingly. The busy multiplex movements of praying have stopped in their tracks. By the time each one knows that all are aware of the same thing, it is too late to ask: what? That something is happening. The sound has become the rushing as of a strong wind issuing from immeasurable distances. It is caressing their faces, their clothes, their hair, their hands. Without ruffling. Without chilling. Without speed, until its full, volatile body envelops them invisibly with air beyond breathing, announcing itself with sound beyond human music and further than any human melody.

The feeling is awe and recognition. The totally Alien is among them, taking them. They have never known It. They have always known It. It is the Impossible become the real. It is the Unhoped become realized. Remaining as they are, they are filled with senses of inner proportion and outer form. It is not in their brain or their skull or their heart. It is in the whole of them and around them. It is them. But it is distinct from them. It is not a sight. It is a seeing. For that moment, it is the living of a mind-known and heart-loved landscape they have never named out loud. It is not an experience. It is an experiencing. It is an overhanging vision of themselves in contours of being where the sun shines but does not burn; where the light is bright but not blinding; where the air is crystal clear but not dazzling, where warmth pervades but haze does not make drowsy, where peaceful silence reigns as a vocal welcome cloaking all the unearthliness in a harmony of earth colors, green, brown, dark gold, purple, red, black; and where all the puzzling and the painfully loose ends of their lives lie shimmering and clear and understood in a seamless pattern. Life. Death. Pain. God. Jerusalem. Moses. Abraham. Prophets. Priests. Jesus. Crucifixion. Resurrection. Romans. Gentiles. All is understood in the all of knowing all, living all.

Each fact is the same as it was. And each fact is now different. All is different. The experience is without end but only seemingly so, merely because they did not count out the seconds. They have lost count of time. They have no sense of the room space which holds them. They do not feel their feet on the floor, the hair on their foreheads, the touch of their hands. Then they are aware of each other again, suddenly. And as they look, one at the other, each finds himself straining unsuccessfully to know the Visitor, the subtle Spirit which effaced itself while possessing them and departed leaving no perfume of a memory and no echo of a voice. Unique Pentecost. Solitary visit of the Holy Spirit.

Today we must read the account in the Acts of the Apostles, remembering the fluid mind of the Semite. He lacks any static concepts. He takes ready refuge in physical metaphors to express the unimageable and in visual images to describe the unimaginable. In this light, we must read of the "sound from heaven," the "rushing mighty wind," the "cloven tongues of fire sitting on each one of them," the "speaking in many different languages." What happened and was important was the group-experience of the Spirit. As a group, they emerged changed, made one, welded together in a shared moment and mutually held knowledge. They communicated to others, not what they thought or felt, but primarily what they had become.

Such an experience has never again been undergone by any official Christians. Individuals have claimed it. Private groups strive to attain it. Psychologists try to reproduce in created circumstances the glossolalia, the speaking in different and unknown languages. All this is factitious. And the officials, the clerical caste, of Christianity as a body have evolved in quite a different direction.

It was inevitable. The content of the Spirit was translated into a human word. Its authority was vested in a person, a dress, a ring, a sentence, a book, a building, a gathering of men, a body of laws, a set of customs. It was hierarchized with dignity. It was mechanized with processes. It was doled out in certain quantities. It was colored with certain qualities. We cannot say when the point came, but one human day it was practically indistinguishable from the other quite human and non-religious hierarchies, mechanisms, processes, quantifications, and qualifications. It took on their structural rigidities and their frozen composition. It froze into the human landscape and contended with nature and reason for supremacy. The struggle was unequal from the start. For both nature and reason move with power and dominance. But the Spirit, if it moves, moves with love only, with truth only, and with compassion only.

The Princedom of Power marked the end of this struggle. The conquering invitations of nature and reason threatened to seize the whole of man. Roncalli, as the Prince of Compassion, understood that reason leads men to hold, as he wrote, "that the sense of religion is to be regarded as something adventitious or imaginary, and hence is to be rooted completely from the mind as altogether inconsistent with the spirit of our age and the progress of civilization." And he knew that knowledge of nature was of itself useless for the human quality, that "scientific competence, technical capacity and professional experience, although necessary, are not of themselves sufficient to elevate the relationships of society to an order that is genuinely human: that is, to an order whose foundation is truth, whose measure and objective is justice, whose driving force is love, and whose method of attainment is freedom." But this was the unmistakably true and the deepest compassion. For it aimed at saving man from the tyrannies of reason and from the dead weight of nature.

First, from the tyrannies of reason. It is a question of keeping man intact and fully human despite the cold, metallic victory of brain over heart, of thought over feeling, of rational plan over intuitive sense, of reflex over instinct, of dictates over wishes. For man's reason, as it goes today, will tell man more eloquently than ever before in his history that up to this he has been awry and quite amiss. Man's reason has a speech.

You are no more, really, than a very intelligent insect, a highly developed biologism. Your forebears lived, you could say, but half a month in last midsummer. They knew nothing of your full summer, autumn, winter, and spring. So much for you, the dupe of myth, locating all your origins in a fool's paradise figmented by an ancient Semite somewhere in the Fertile Crescent, who lacked grass and trees and water for his camels and his donkeys and his nomad followers. Your ancient dream of heaven is but his desire for pasturage. As for you in this spaceship of your earth: now you are adrift and spinning regularly upon an ocean, bound for nowhere. But cheer up! At last you know the truth indubitably. You are moving fast nowhere. So cease to have this trusting look for a hoary helmsman to guide you safely over waters of the passing centuries and human time to some eternal permanency of being on an unknown shore. There is no such thing.

With reason as your guide, you will construct all that must convey your knowledge, your good things and your bad things, to your children's children. But even as you live, do not align the horizons of your world of wishing with the stars. Gaze steadily, directly at that which lies in front of your nose. You will at times feel the tug of something, as it were, more than human. Fear not. This is still you, man, caught in the eternal spiral of life into death back into life, and of order into chaos back into life, of the past into the present back into the past within the future on another level. Open up a porthole and passage in your reason and your conscious mind. For as your body is at one with all material things, so your mind and reason are enveloped in a field of interpersonal but quite impersonal communication. Let the logical projections and productions of that field flow through and pour around your conscious thought, your poetry, your painting, your loving, and your hope. For thus you truly are a human. If your world goes amok, you can drink yourself to stupor and mutter with Captain Boyle: "The whole world is in a state of chassis and confusion." If you ever fantasize a vision of eternal beauty, be sure and repeat with James Joyce: "Gauze off heaven! Vision. Then. O, pluxty suddly, the sight entrancing! Hummels! That crag! Those hullocks! O Sire! So be accident occur is not going to commence! Can you read the verst legend hereon? I am hather of the missed. Areed!" The vision will disappear in a cackle of laughter. Human laughter of amused reason. Call it, if you will, the "last bleat of the good pagan." But it is human and reasonable.

Second, to save man from nature, man's first temptation and his last recourse before calling on God. Nature has a very simple direct and telling speech to make to modern man. For man was nature's first of all, before man thought of spirit and of books, of empire, of genetics, of conquering the stars, of altar, priesthood, and of God. Nature bids him have the confidence of all doomed and dying things, but asks him to be quite content as complementary part of all, promising with utter surety and faithfulness that he will live forever in the cloverleaf, swirling with the molecules of nettles and of lilies, of rocks and stone and stars beyond the Milky Way, be immortalized with atoms in a dandelion. Nature has a speech.

You can emerge from the last dreary thickets of your preoccupation with the spirit and the spirit's convolutions. You can stop all further efforts to take off and soar above the human and be more than human. Just feel a moment how my good brown earth receives your feet! It soaks their energy and drowses them with natural sloth of soft and yielding natural things. For this is me: I am the womb, the tomb, and the silence of contentment. And if you should today get frozen in the rigid canyons of the City, trust me, for I rule there too. When you are barbarian, I am barbarian. When you are kind and gentle, I have gentleness and kindness to match. All you now fabricate within the walls and all you learn to do and make by cunning symbols and the harnessing of energy, all that too I can do, but infinitely, with endless patience. For I know no night as you, no need for rest, no sundown, no grave, as you will surely know.

The only thing I cannot give you is the meaning. I have none to give. But meaning only tortures. So desist. And be content with knowing how the world works, but do not seek to know what works within the world. For this again is weariness on top of weariness and pain piled up on pain in mountains. Men once fashioned such a mountain and set a cross on top of it. They hung a man upon it and he died for love of you. And all the world is weary from the climbing of that mountain. So be content on my broad plain. But do not think to harness chrome and steel and quick computers to raise your spirit. Turn alchemist, technologist, and technocrat, if you must. But do not look for goodness from the wheel beyond the sound and steam and speed, or purity from the fire beyond the purity of carbonized material. Fear no defeat; I will lay your victor dead as you, beside your grave. Tremble at no pain; on pain I thrive.

When your knowledge goes beyond the limit, it must decay. When your will contracts, it must self-destruct. In either case, I will possess you for the aeons of your disappearance. You are a stone in my long wall. You are a sod in my limitless earth. You are one tiny strand in the enormous intricacies of my webbing. For a while you may walk upright like a prince, think proudly like a god, and sing sweetly like a nightingale. When you first love. When you kill your enemy. When you outlive a mortal danger. When you beget a child. But, in the end, I will ground you to the earth like a onetime flashing meteor, and pin you tenderly like a butterfly to be preserved in camphor. I will provide all for all: hardness for your hardness, softness for your softness, beauty for your beauty, hate for all your hating, love for all your loving, death for all your dying, and dust for every speck of dust you will become.

Somewhere between the hours of 5 A.M. and 7 A.M. on January 6, 1959, Roncalli was at prayer. He is due to preside at ceremonies at the Church of St. Paul Outside the Walls later on in the day. He also plans to address his cardinals, who will be present. For two months he has been wrestling with a problem of mounting proportions: painful news of an ever more desperate situation. In sum: decadent and inept Roman Catholicism, grave social problems, threatening world crises. Nothing he had been able to think of seemed adequate as a solution. All plans proposed were dry and fireless. All advisers were a hundred times more learned than he ("I will never understand the international monetary situation," he told one definitively), but their ideas were just that, ideas.

"Pope Pius XII did consider an ecumenical council, Holy Father, but to what purpose," said Bea. "Christians are torn and disunited. How could we unite the world? What forum can we provide that will attract them all?" "If we could step outside ourselves," he remarked one day to his collaborator, Tardini, "outside our Latin, our rings, our rules, our protocol, our dignities and grades, and love and feel love and act out that love, we would see our truth in fullness. All men would listen." "Holy Father," said the ever ready-tongued Tardini, "at present this would mean chaos from pole to pole. God would have to show his face in order to save us all."

John's prayer this January morning is simple. It is a prayer for light, the request of a man facing two courses of action, each one clad in its own special attraction, both fraught with the same danger. John's decision not only will affect the daily life of millions; it will set the course of his Church for unborn generations. No matter how many counselors surround a pope, in the end the decision is his. His is the responsibility. The world will never know—perhaps it would never understand—the subtle alchemy that took place within this old man as he knelt struggling with his fears, his loneliness, his daring, and his hopes.

Men today easily decry or explain away in the facile terms of an overpopularized psychological theory the genuine "face-to-face" communications between the spirit of man and the God who fashions that spirit. Angelo Roncalli's experience in this matter was his privilege. It is sufficient for this narrative to state that when he rose from prayer it was not merely his will which had been strengthened. His mind was clear.

The Event now took shape in his mind. For the next three years he would unceasingly express its contours. Time and time again, it will be pulled out of shape and distorted by ignorance, by prejudice, and by blind zeal. The conservative traditionalists will endeavor to reduce it to a close-in discussion of pre-approved thoughts. The "rubber-stamp" Council so many feared. Progressives of narrow vision will try to convert it to an arena of new ideas, some to a dictionary of new terms. Still others will try to make it a parliament of proposals, a weapon against the Roman bureaucracy, a Roman Catholic version of the World Council of Churches, a celebration of bishops' rights over against the pope's prerogatives, papal and Vatican power for purely political ends. All, unfortunately, will succeed to one degree or another. But the real debacle was spared Roncalli during his lifetime. As far as one can judge, Roncalli died without ever knowing how far he had failed.

There were to be initial preparatory stages before the Council. But Roncalli's Event, as he planned it, would take place as the last of a three-stage development at the actual Council. A short initial stage for the elucidation of the "integral truth" of the Christian faith within a new unity. A second stage, when this integral truth took hold of all those attending the Council, Roman and non-Roman Christians together with non-Christians, and spilled out through them to the peoples they represented on their individual home grounds, thus forging a greater unity. The Event itself; when the spirit of the Council thus enlarged spread to governments, thus forging the greatest unity. As one of its prime effects: a rapid coming together of the relevant leaders and people bent on the creation of an international public authority on the basis of the achieved unity. This, simply and briefly expressed, was the Event, and this was what Roncalli's Council was all about.

The main and only purpose, the *multiplex graveque opus*, as he termed it, of the Council was not to explain ancient doctrine, not to affirm traditional teaching, not to reassert episcopal rights over against the privilege of the pope, not even to elucidate the ancient message in a modern dress. *Aggiornamento*, dating, in this sense, was a secondary consideration. The main and only result of the Council was to be a *human* one: "Council discussions must enter the very marrow and essence of human affairs," he wrote. He continued: "Today it is required of the Church that she inject the perennial and vital divine power of her good news into the veins of today's human community." No objective could be more clearly stated: "The near-future Ecumenical Council will give all men of good will an opportunity of undertaking and promoting counsels and plans for peace." The three stages he foresaw should end with such concrete and human results.

It would be easy to lampoon Roncalli's Event as merely a Pentecostalist's dream: babbling participants, wild emotions, unknown languages, emotionalism run rife in the aisles, venerable cardinals screaming, eyes shut, at swooning patriarchs, careening bishops and jigging monsignores, an orgy of the "spirit" clad in the hubbub, the brouhaha, and tohuwabohu of clerics caught in a Midsummer's Night frenzy. Roncalli was not thinking or talking of this.

His belief was in two things: the Spirit as a really existent force, personal, all-powerful, divine; and the truth of men's brotherhood in Jesus who had saved all men. Somehow, that brotherhood had been obscured—in the Roman Church and in Christianity. Among men, its place was being taken by man's reason and by nature. It no longer stood at the forefront of minds, Roman Catholic or Christian. It had to be regrasped, relived. And somehow the Spirit had been silenced, been dampened, been caged. It could no longer fill men's minds. Now, Roncalli believed in both with more certitude than men have in knowing that two and two make four.

He intended to create a newly apt forum for this Spirit, so that within that forum his Roman Catholics, then all Christians, then other men of good will, could be filled with the Spirit and discover their brotherhood in the salvation of Jesus. The forum of the Spirit which he desired to create was a specific thing. It was neither a mere physical getting-together and an airing of views in a public reunion nor a religious banquet of wild abandonment where caution was flung to the four winds of heaven and all gorged themselves on undiluted irrationalism and the wild highland fling of minds jerked and dislocated out of proportion by mob feeling. It was rather a mental disposition, backed by inflamed wills, a combination of hope, expectation, and an openness to ask so that they could receive, to seek so that they could find, to knock so that a door be opened giving full view and knowledge of that unity of which men already were members and of that unity in action which only the human community could achieve. To create that forum, Roncalli depended on the Spirit, and on "the love of God which kindles and consumes all things," as he noted in December 1959.

The emergence of this forum lay in Roncalli's concept of the "full truth," the "full and perfect unity in truth." Along the cen-

turies-old way of Christianity since Jesus died, it had been only
partially made visible. It had been obscured. The Roman Catholic Church was at fault as much as any other church. All were to
blame. All had stood to lose. All had lost. Nobody in particular
but all in general were astray. No body of Christians could find
their way to that "full truth" unless the Spirit illumined once
again their minds, communally, as a group. Roncalli was gam-
bling on the Spirit. We have no words to describe that "full
truth" or the effect of its acquisition, as he envisioned it. But it
had to begin there. Gently. Lovingly. With all the comforting
assurance that only full acknowledgment of truth can bring.

To begin with, Roman Catholics. A profound change was required. No abandonment of precious teachings was necessary.
Rather was there required an exclusion of any dwelling on that
preciousness or even on any one teaching or group of teachings.
Such dwelling would merely entail a biting of doctrinal nails, an
ecclesiastical hurdy-gurdy. Rather a birth, in the hearts of 2,500
bishops, of a fresh light. Light to avoid the hypnotic particularisms of exact wording, just phraseology, and "safe" treatment of
beliefs. Light to understand as men of their time the mystic rationale of all Christian beliefs, so that all in general and each
belief in particular would fall into a new synthesis of love,
understanding, and compassion.

Roncalli expected a happening within these 2,500 bishops. A
coalescence of what they all were singly and collectively into one
homogeneity, like a fresh coal ready to be plunged into the
flames of the Spirit. A happening in the silent recesses of each
heart. A quick illumination in which all would be accomplished,
all loose ends tied together, all particularities sunk. An utterly
simple process, a-logical, non-reasoning, a-conceptual, in which
all customary mental processes of the ecclesiastical mind and
method would be performed and completed in an instant, as it
were. To reconsider, relive, and thus illustrate anew in their
bodies, in their eyes, their language, and their minds the height
and depth of Christian riches for the human spirit of today
which is unwilling stranger to the substance of Christian godliness: the tenderness of Jesus of which the saints have spoken;
every look of maternal care and love the master artists have read
and painted into the Virgin's eyes; each subtle silent inspiration
which all the mystics from Epiphanius in the fourth century to
Jean Vianney in the nineteenth century have said the Spirit does
let fall into man's soul as quietly as snowflakes.

To do all this and much more by an instant sifting of the

essential from the unnecessary, of the substance from the accidents. All this was to shine with a glory that immediately communicated itself. It would make one thing evident and clear to all those nearby and watching. Roncalli was thinking of the observers from other Christian churches, of the journalists who covered the Council, of the representatives from non-Christian religions and from foreign governments. That one thing: "the key to human happiness, the solution to our human problem, the truth about man, is here possessed by these men." Gone is the stridency of Romanism and the overshadowing threat of Roman Catholic primacy which brooded over men's pain in these latter days with the air of a dying lioness watching her recalcitrant and starving cubs. There would not necessarily be any statements from the Council as such, in this first stage. There would only be a vital communication, an understanding passed from man to man, men to men, group to group, among all.

It was to be a dawning, a mystical light breaking in all hearts and giving a new understanding, an understanding which neither Christians nor Catholics nor non-Christians ever before possessed. It was to be a new mode of speaking about Jesus and luminously, harmonizing all the old irregularities, healing all wounded pride, hurt hearts, crushed minds, and telling of a veritable wonder in human feeling. It was to be light so illuminating and speech so convincingly human and so accurately modern that all those near in space would stand up and say: "Surely this is the truth and this is the sum of all our searchings." Light and speech would well up and spill over, drenching all those near with its wisdom and its enthusiasm. Thus would begin the second stage in a movement outwards, an embrace of those nearest in space. The overflow envisaged by Roncalli was to overcome all obstacles of pride, the barriers of fear, the resistant growths of sectarian belief, and the hard knobs of prejudice, pouring out like a rich sunlight over a once-darkened city where men had lived a long night with lamps of their own making and huddled in defensive dwellings of their own choosing. It was to be an emotional enrichment because everything would be felt more intensely by the proximity of the Council. All these would be affected, each one throwing in his lot with the others as with his brothers, sharing a great climactic moment of understanding of what was wrong with them all and of what was right about man, speaking and acknowledging and communicating.

"Wrong were we Roman Catholic churchmen who stopped living the truth and insisted on intellectualizing it, forging a religion of words and concepts and neglecting the spirit and the heart, developing theories and formulas which shut out Jesus but imposed a Christ of no humanity incarnated in officials, administrators, inquisitors, judges, rulers, suiting one culture and one frame of mind in all our doing. Deceived were we Roman Catholics who became sleepers in the great caravan of Jesus provided by an imperialism as human as Caesar's.

"Mistaken were Luther and Calvin and Zwingli and Melanchthon and all the Reformers who arrogated to themselves the right to decide what God alone could decide. Maliciously ignorant have been all those clever teachers who laid unbearable burdens on man, repelled him with their cruelty and then condemned his rejection of their unthinking cruelty.

"Stupidly proud were we Greek and Russian Orthodox Christians, who nationalized the Gospel and conferred Greek and Russian citizens' papers on Jesus, making Tsarist Russia, Communist Russia, Byzance and Greece the tabernacles of Jesus' dwelling—on our own whim, and persisting in a regular mumbo-jumbo of ancient Slavonic and Classical Greek, with incense and robes and bearded magnificence to cloak our pathetic impotencies.

"Naïve were we multiple sects of Protestantism, with our theologies, philosophies, compromises, slobbery comprehensiveness, spineless beliefs, social fatuities, our following of imperial flags, our Mary Baker Eddys, John Smiths, Friends, Pentecostalists, Spiritualists, Baptists, all of us taking the trees to be the wood and fashioning fads and isms to suit diminishing congregations.

"Pathetically wronged but unjustifiably bigoted did we Jews become, because we could not bear the success of early Christianity, even before it left our shores in Palestine, and because we closed our minds to the truth, partially changing our own beliefs and practices in a chauvinism God can forgive only in Jews because his son was one of us.

"Unrealistic were we Moslems, who, not understanding either the Jewish or the Christian Bible, decided that we alone had the final say, affixing the label of infidel to all others, pursuing a course of bloodshed, cruelty, and imperial design, assigning pleasures and profits to ourselves, and resisting the clamoring voice of modern need and modern conditions.

"Punished were we all, all of us. Christians and non-Christians, because we never lived the full truth of our faith and we consoled our weakness saying that our Leader was God, and re-

fused to succor man, saying that our Leader's kingdom was not
in this world and anyway that it was reserved for us alone."

At such a climactic moment, by an inner instinct and a common illumination, all would come together, united, as men in a
now lightsome city pour out of their once dark houses in a strong
current, flowing through the streets, ever augmenting until they
merge into a great central conclave of commingling emotions,
dignity, brotherhood, feeling, compassion, sympathy, shared by
all and transfused by the unrivaled experience of unity, with a
force and a sweep that promised to wash over all men alive, and
to transform all human institutions.

It was Roncalli's expectation that the Spirit would create such
a common experience. It would let Council participants and observers and guests share in such a living moment with such impact for the common mind that it could not be held or restrained
to the Council in Rome or merely to Christians in Rome and
elsewhere. It would spread by word of mouth, by television, by
press and radio, by person to person, to the home peoples of the
bishops, of non-Catholics and of non-Christian observers, carrying a sense of renewal and of hope.

The sense of renewal was again a thing of the Spirit, bearing
all the fruits of the Spirit: gentleness, cleanliness of the mind,
clarity of thought, deep taste, openness. It had really nothing to
do with the hooting bad taste of the divinely disobedient and the
tasteless newness of invented underground liturgies which lack
the smell even of body deodorant. And it is alien to the false
mysticism and impudent appropriation of the Dark Night of the
Soul (hymned by John of the Cross and Teresa of Avila as man's
ascent to God in holiness and poverty of the spirit) in order to
beautify some ragged and harum-scarum efforts at dislocating a
legitimate government. There is as much significance for life in
a corbie perched on a gallows cawing over the swinging corpse
as there is hope of renewal in society through self-styled Dietrich
Bonhoeffers, as it were, returned to life, setting bomb timers to
the lyrics of Jesus Christ Superstar, dodging F.B.I. agents with a
prayer to the Guardian Angel, and thirsting for neo-Nazi concentration camps in Amerika the Ugly, and fresh Roman crosses in
Amerika the Krass, in order to shed all that lovely, lovely, red, red
blood. Rabbit blood. Christ's blood. A fuzz's blood. Hell! What's
the difference. It's all just blood.

Out of this would emerge the Event. Once an experience of
this kind has been undergone, it communicates itself. It speaks
to the ordinary man in the street, to the afflicted John Doe of

every modern nation, of its cities and its isolated countryside. Always with the burning substance of that experience. It is, in fact, that experience relived in its substance by all, but now concretized and expressed in terms of the lives of ordinary men and women. The chimera of life ceases to oppress with its apparent ineluctability. The reality takes over from the viewpoint of man. It becomes his own, earned by his mind, warmed by his heart, churned through his blood to his heart and his mind.

The truth of the Gospel, the Jesus of the Gospel, now cleared away of all the initial myopias that afflicted the Gospels' first writers and commentators, that Jesus is now telling them: let the dead bury the dead. The experience is thus a sword to free the living from the bounden deadwood of tidy ritual. It is an evolution of the one to the many. It is an individual as a free man. It is the poor who were always there as driftwood cast up, poor because bereft of hope, poor because lost to the center of themselves. It is not merely those who lacked clothes or shelter or food. It is all of them now surging to a warm Niagara of humanness. Not to a judgment or a hearing, but to a living God, an immanence among men. All feel the need now to live in the actions of their inner gift, to move toward other men and against the waste, the brutal tidal urge of violence, the oppressing algae of anonymity, the breeding ghettos, the complacency, the erupting in war. It is all men as new, as young, young in age as well as young in spirit, stalwart in simplicity, gathering and moving. It is a gaining awareness, for the unaware, of the possibility of man.

It is the world Event of Roncalli's dream.

It means a cessation of fear between peoples because any desire to aggress others ceases, because suspicion ceases, because distrust ceases. It is Russians who desert the dictates of their imperialism. It is Soviet satellite countries that begin to orbit in freedom and in hope. It is Americans who achieve the ideals of republican democracy through their multiplex society and find no need to insist on world leadership. It is Chinese who desist from the creation of hate and egotism. It is French, Germans, British, Belgians, Dutch, and Spaniards who stop fomenting economic patriotism, Swiss who renounce their smug isolation and amoral internationalism, Scandinavians who exit from their isolation and the development of cultivated human anthills, Indians and Africans who come to their untutored senses. It is all men as one man, and each man as all men, smiling, confident, seeking truly the impartial decision on the border problem, on import and export regulations, following the wishes and all the needs of each few. It is a community of men's hearts, a consensus in men's minds, and a common understanding in action by men in favor of men.

Roncalli, in effect, set up his Ecumenical Council as a stage for a human drama, a theater of the Spirit and of living man. Cold reason told him he had to begin with the Greats of Christianity. How could you get all of them together in close proximity and together in spirit, if they were not together in one place? Only by a Council. The Council was literally a *deus ex machina*, a theatrical gimmick, a machine for God's action among his sons, all men. This was Roncalli's Machine.

Bea, now his confidant, Bea with the trained mind, with his independence of an intellectual, with his eidetic memory—Bea never forgot either the details of ensconced powers in the Vatican and throughout the Church or the shored-up imperialisms and fierce independence of government administrations. At each step, he asked himself over and over again: What if all this is an illusion? What if the Spirit does not breathe its inspiration? A negative answer produced shivers in his being.

23

The Machine

For three and a half years, from January 1959 to late spring of 1963, Roncalli tended his Machine. The Machine in its effective reality was a complex or a series of actions and dispositions he took and movements he started from his first public announcement of the Council on January 6, 1959. In the light of his Council's failure, it is almost startling to follow his thoughts and actions, to examine the dynamisms he originated during that time. According to any human judgment in December 1962 or in the spring of 1963, Roncalli's Council had failed. We find, however, a totally different spirit and persuasion in Roncalli. Either he perceived deeper realities than we now can, or he did not realize what had happened, or he continued hoping against hope. But there was in his words and government a calm confidence. He spoke from a clear vision and he acted in view of that vision. Actions, words, movements, when sifted, give us the outline of the Machine as Roncalli saw it. The actual happening at the Council was another thing and occupies the next chapter.

On January 6, 1959, Roncalli announces serenely to his assembled cardinals that he will hold an ecumenical council. They are dumfounded, surprised, taken aback, unbelieving, cold, frightened, amused, everything in fact but enthusiastic. Roncalli notices the reception but covers it over with a gentle phrase. One Vatican official remarks afterwards that the Pope must have been mad. But Roncalli has set the wheels in motion. The timetable is drawn up. Originally, the opening date for the Council was set for not earlier than 1963. Roncalli then advances the date to 1962, having become more mindful of his mortality, and also because of the (sometimes baleful) urgings of Vatican officials who wish to put the opening of the Council off indefinitely. Procrastination always provided possible means of avoiding what most officials regarded from the beginning as a nuisance and a pointless flourish.

Between now and the time his Council opens, Roncalli has a huge task to accomplish on five levels: to arouse interest and enthusiasm among the Church's bishops, among the ordinary people, among non-Catholic Christians, among non-Christians, and in the governments of peoples. It is for this that he builds his Machine. Furthermore, there are to be four distinct stages in the building of the Machine. From January 1959 to the autumn of 1960: an "introductory, exploratory, ante-preparatory" stage. From the autumn of 1960 to the autumn of 1962, a directly preparatory stage. The third stage begins with the opening of the Council. The fourth stage is the planned Event.

There was no haste in Roncalli's movements. But a deliberate speed was noticeable in the orchestration of events. That orchestration must not be understood as a PR campaign, an artificial creation of emotional interest. Roncalli wanted to awaken into quickening life the three unities already existent, to provide them with a forum in which all major divergencies could be sunk into one unity. These three unities were: "the unity of Catholics among themselves . . . the unity of Christians separated from Rome but desirous to be united with it," and "the unity arising out of a common esteem and regard for the Catholic Church among those who profess different non-Christian forms of religion." Roncalli calculated that he could build on these three.

Roncalli's first stage, the "introductory, exploratory, ante-preparatory," was well named by him. The idea of the Council was to be introduced. He himself had to explore and determine the various mechanisms needed to achieve his purpose and incidentally to demonstrate to himself and his Vatican officialdom what were the logistical needs of any modern meeting of Catholic churchmen. He had to rationalize his inspirational decision to hold a Council. Catholics, Christians, and non-Christians had to explore the idea of a council, find it worthwhile, and achieve an enthusiasm for it. Finally, he had to crystallize the substance of their thinking (Catholics and non-Catholics) in order that the immediate discussions be carefully prepared. All would depend on how the Council discussions started as of October 11, 1962.

In 1959, he sets about determining the logistical needs of his Council and deciding on its required mechanisms. He organizes a synod for his own city and diocese, Rome. The ostensible purpose of the synod is to assemble the data of social, cultural, political, and religious life in Rome, and then to draw up norms telling Catholics how they can successfully lead a Christian life under these conditions.

The synod aroused little interest in the Church and none at all in the outside world. It was in itself a thankless job. Obtaining collaboration and prompt execution by Vatican officials and the clergy was very difficult; it was weighted down by the burdens of vested interests and fears that any changes would imply loss of positions and of prestige.

The facts gathered were gargantuan in number. The collaborators were many and varied. There was no real enthusiasm and no desire to seek any great truth. The clerical and theological work resulted in 755 "articles." These were supposed to express how Christians in Rome should live with the facts of their day. Nothing new, sensational, soul-stirring, fresh, or encouraging came from those articles or from the official sessions of the synod held in January 1960. It was to all intents and purposes a foregone conclusion, a rubber-stamp meeting, and an interminable bore. Roncalli spoke five times, stressing the purity of basic Christian teachings, and the need of Catholics and clergymen and laity to adapt to modern conditions.

But Roncalli had seen, in microcosm, all he needed to see: the reactions of Vatican officials, the latent dangers in the bureaucratic handling of theologians and of practical proposals, and the open-ended mentality of the mass of the people who desired change and adaptation—even though in this case that desire remained unfulfilled.

By January 1960 he had also formed a close working bond with Bea. Bea started with merely an initial intellectual assent to Roncalli's proposals. Anything to do with power Bea knew instinctively was fraught with inertia. Rapidly, he changed. He found Roncalli fired and burning with an overwhelming necessity to achieve a vast change, but that necessity was undulled and unmonitored by any self-consciousness of being helpless in the face of entrenched power. Roncalli was undaunted. Besides, Bea found, he filled a vital role for Roncalli: he could conceptualize Roncalli's impulses because he could embrace the data of preceding history, the quality of present practical difficulties, and the articulation of future plans. Roncalli's perceptions never shifted away from the immediate and confining present. His mind had not been molded by intellectual exercises and discipline. He could not move back and forth from one end of history to the other. He had not been supplied with a notation so large and so wide-embracing. He did not see things in pieces. He had his ironies, but his cosmos never creaked with them.

Bea could do all this. Bea could go from one thing to another, in his mind and in practical activities, tranquilly and efficiently (*"eine nach der anderen und ganz ruhig,"* was the way he described his multifarious activities), and still keep one main objective in mind. It was an invaluable talent for Roncalli's undertaking. The fire of soul in one man slowly caught on in the mind of the other.

Roncalli and Bea immediately sought the instrumentalities needed to achieve their purpose. They had to think, plan, and work on two levels. One level was the mechanical level of the Council, Roncalli's Machine. The other was the spiritual and mental level of Roncalli's Event. If all went well, by the time the third mechanical stage (the opening of the Council) was reached on October 11, 1962, the first two spiritual stages of the Event should have been achieved.

By the end of spring 1959, Roncalli had made up his mind concerning the instrumentalities. Bea would undertake a leavening of non-Catholics and non-Christians—in easy stages. He would be put in charge of a new creation, the Secretariat for the Promotion of Christian Unity. This would enable him to set up official relations with non-Catholic bodies. The Secretariat was to be enlarged later; or, as needs be, other secretariats would be created, in order to concentrate on the other great religions (Islam, Buddhism), and on atheists and nonbelievers as such.

For the authorities of the Roman Catholic Church, a notification would be sent out as soon as possible, and feasible to all bishops and major authorities, asking them for their ideas on the subject matter of the Council. Roncalli would establish a special body (the Ante-Preparatory Commission of the Council) to sift, classify, abbreviate, abstract, and synthesize these ideas. The resulting document would be enlarged with a series of regional reports and statistical data in order that a picture of the condition of the Church would be at hand. An elenchus of the problems common to all parts of the Church would also be drawn up. Roncalli would appoint a Preparatory Commission to study this document. Once the Roman synod was over, in January 1960, Roncalli would set up the necessary body of men in Rome who would do this vast work of sifting and preparation.

In the light of modern communications systems, Roncalli decided to use the written word as effectively as possible. He decided on the composition of at least two universal letters destined to conceptualize, crystallize, and set forth the rationale of the Event. One, later emerging as *Mater et Magistra* (published on May 15, 1960), would set forth a social doctrine of the Church and touch on the central problem of modern international life in terms of the individual. The second (subsequently published on April 11, 1963, as *Pacem in Terris*) should follow immediately on the heels of the first session of the Council and become a landmark in his great Event. For it would examine the machinery of international peace and the bases of the comity between nations, and make concrete proposals that would be feasible only in the light of Roncalli's Event.

The Soviet world and the rather remote world of Communist China presented another gamut of problems. Roncalli had to take into account the sensitivity of the United States on both points. And he could not even give the impression of venturing into an area as touchy as this. It was a mine field alive with the vital interests of great powers. Yet some steps had to be taken, and they could not be dictated essentially by the economic stance or political needs of any government. In his *Pacem in Terris* letter of 1963 Roncalli spoke abruptly and to the point concerning relations with Russian and Chinese Communists, outlining the principles he had followed since 1959 in this matter:

> It must be borne in mind that neither can false philosophical teachings regarding the nature, origin and destiny of the universe and of man, be identified with historical movements that have economic, social, cultural or political ends, not even when these movements have originated from those teachings and have drawn and still draw inspiration therefrom.

This was not meant to draw the teeth out of American opposition to the totalitarian regimes of Russia and China or of American disapproval of their economic systems. Roncalli had concluded that Marxism in Russia was undergoing profound changes. "These teachings, once they are drawn up and defined, remain always the same, while the movements, working on historical situations in constant evolution, cannot but be influenced by these latter and cannot avoid, therefore, being subject to changes, even of a profound nature."

For these reasons, he went on, "it can happen that a drawing nearer together or a meeting for the attainment of some practical end . . . might now or in the future be considered opportune and useful." Roncalli himself considered that a drawing nearer and meeting was opportune and useful. He had his own avenues of approach, his own sources of intelligence both in Eastern Europe and Russia and in China. But he put a severe brake on any rash of public contacts, discussions, and meetings. For the next three or four years, he would nurse along initiatives in this area. He would govern them, keeping a sharp eye on relations between Russia and the United States and on the bitter forest of sharpened knives that separated the United States and Communist China in the Far East. He would earn the respect of Nikita Khrushchev and some definite traces of affection in the onetime master of All the Russias. He would obtain permission for Russian observers to attend the Council. Khrushchev's daughter and son-in-law, Alexei Adzhubei, would come to visit Roncalli in the Vatican. These were icebergs moving above the surface; the major initiatives lay hidden.

A cautionary situation existed in the Vatican and in Catholic circles in this respect. The anti-Soviet and anti-Communist stances of Vatican officials and Catholics in Italy were based to a very large extent on the real fear of a Communist political, constitutional, and peaceful takeover in Italy. It used to be whispered in political and clerical circles of that time that only the Socialist split between Nenni and Saragat, obviating any strong accord between a unified Socialist Party and the Communists (an irresistible force at the Italian polling booth), had saved Italy from an election victory for a Socialist-Communist alliance. It was further said that the Nenni–Saragat split was the fruit of American intervention and of continual subsidy by American funds. Vatican political interests were closely allied with Italian Christian Democrats (or *Democristiani*), and together they represented the great financial cartels and groups, the big corporate investments of Italy, and the backbone of the Italian stock market.

These vested interests were of course the first and most zealous in giving haven and providing assistance to the innumerable refugee clerics and nuns and Catholics who had fled before the Sovietization of the Eastern European countries. Rome was full of Hungarians, Rumanians, Serbs, Croats, Slovaks, Lithuanians, and others, who maintained organizations near the Vatican and lobbied continually for Vatican opposition to the U.S.S.R. and her satellite governments in Eastern Europe. Roncalli had to contend with this general miasma of genuine suffering, exile, and broken spirits. He had to take cognizance of the enlivened anti-Communist stance of the average American, Catholic or otherwise, who had grown up in the shadow of the Cold War, lived through the Berlin airlift, the Korean War, and the revolts in Berlin and Hungary during the fifties. Besides, throughout the Western Church Pacelli had sown an undying distrust, hate, and fear of the Soviets. Any overt and unguarded move in their direction by the new Holy Father would be taken as a sign that he was a weak man, that he and his collaborators were either crypto-Communists, anti-capitalistically inclined, or at best simple-minded clerics who did not recognize the fire when they thrust their hands into it.

But even with all due care, Roncalli incurred great wrath and not a little scorn. Described by one prominent and fuming official as "that Danubian peasant of a diplomat" and, by one foreign ambassador accredited to the Vatican, as "an incredibly stupid choice as pope just right now"; caricatured by a rightist paper as having "his hands dripping with the blood of Christian martyrs in Hungary, Poland, Czechoslovakia, Germany, Lithuania, Estonia, and Latvia" (because he had shaken hands with Khrushchev's daughter and Khrushchev had personally supervised the liquidation of about three million people under Stalin), he was the object of hampering efforts. One example will suffice here. Many initiatives had been taken by 1962 and the beginning of 1963. Suddenly, in March 1963, Alexei Adzhubei, editor of *Izvestia*, and his wife, Rada, daughter of Khrushchev, appear as "tourists" in Rome. A sort of panic takes hold of Vatican officials. To all questions, Bea is close-mouthed; Capovilla, Roncalli's secretary, smiles with a special futurist gleam in his eye; and officials at the Secretariat of State wave their hands with a "why-ask-me-I-am-only-working-in-the-kitchen" air of deprecation.

Some hours before the Adzhubei interview, Vatican Radio broadcasts an unannounced editorial entitled "Forgetfulness," in which it states that "Communism is just what it is, atheist, materialist, in theory and in practice. John XXIII himself has had to complain about it." It was meant to tie Roncalli's hands. It did not. On the seventh, the Adzhubeis, Alexei (in a dark suit) and

Rada (her head covered with a dark veil, as was the custom for female visitors to the pope), appear among thirty other guests at a reception in the Vatican Throne Room. Roncalli listens to the speeches, says some inconsequentialities about modern communications and the love of God, and departs precipitately; the guests disperse, all except the Adzhubeis. They join Roncalli in his private library for eighteen minutes. *L'Osservatore Romano* did not report the interview. It had frightened even the Soviet embassy, which put out a denial with that ingenuous stupidity of which only doctrinaire Soviets are capable: "M. Adzhubei did not meet the Pope, but he did enter the Pope's library." The anticlerical press hooted with laughter. Roncalli himself was tickled.

As of June 18, 1959, Roman Catholic bishops and authorities were sent a letter by the appointed head of the Ante-Preparatory Commission, Cardinal Domenico Tardini. In it, they were asked to submit in writing their suggestions for the Council. In all, 2,812 bishops and prelates, together with 101 heads of religious orders and Roman Catholic academic centers, received this request. They responded with a tidal wave of 8,972 written suggestions (or *vota*, as they were called in Rome). The work of classifying these into a usable form was carried out by Tardini's Commission. On June 5, 1960, Roncalli announced the creation of Bea's Secretariat and of a new commission, the Preparatory Commission. The latter was to work on the document drawn up by Tardini's Ante-Preparatory Commission and to write the actual texts which could be used as discussion sheets in the Council itself.

Roncalli assigned a definite and limited function to such discussions and discussion sheets in his Council. When the first session of the Council was over and done with and the participants were about to leave for home, Roncalli addressed a farewell speech to them all. It was December 7, 1962, in St. Peter's Basilica. Do not be surprised, he told them, if some lapse of time has been required in order to achieve an agreement on certain subjects. Differences of opinion are not to be wondered at, but they do cause some of you a little worry. He then spelled out in a few words the function of such discussions and differences in his Council assembly: "This [discussion of differences] has happened through a providential plan of God. His purpose was that the truth should be known and the whole society of man could see plainly what a holy liberty flourished for the sons of God in the Church."

It is capital for an understanding of Roncalli's Council, and while it may be hard and go against the grain for many to recognize it, the "truth" in this case was not any particular doctrine or teaching about Catholic liturgy or the Bible or anything else. The "truth" was simply: the Spirit of God is with us, at least this time in the organized Church. See! We are all acting in complete liberty. Come and join us.

For the success of Roncalli's Event, it was necessary that he attract the interest of non-Catholic Christians. He needed to create an opening in their minds, for these were shut. The ordinary non-Catholic and non-Christian was persuaded that the Roman Catholic Church was a monarchic, monolithic, and centralized regime of religious and spiritual totalitarianism, in which one could achieve peace of mind and security of soul only at the cost of precious freedoms. Americans in particular had been used to the distorted image provided by prejudiced and bigoted writers such as Paul Blanshard, who made it his life's crusade to establish the obnoxious, hateful, dictatorial, and undemocratic character of the Roman Catholic Church. Blanshard did not realize it but he said the correct thing about the wrong people.

By Roncalli's time, there was working in the Church a group of clergymen who intended to have just that: a totalitarian and dictatorial regime. Pacelli had allowed it to flower. But this was not the nature or the character of the Roman Catholic Church. It was to offset this deleterious condition, the ice-age condition of which we have spoken, that Roncalli called his Council and planned his Event. At least in this, he succeeded to some degree. In fact, during Blanshard's visit to Rome and the Vatican during the Council, it was obvious to those who chatted with him that he was thoroughly and distressingly at sea, confused, warring in himself, and at a loss how to judge the situation. He arrived during the height of acrid discussions between Council participants, when foreign bishops and Americans in particular were engaging in verbal battles and sometimes quite rough treatment of some sacred cows of the Vatican bureaucracy. This should not have happened, as far as Blanshard was concerned.

Roncalli had no chance to create his forum for the Spirit, and Bea had no chance to establish worthwhile relationships with non-Catholic Christians, if such an adverse cast of mind persisted among non-Catholics, whether Christian or non-Christian or governmental agencies. Bea set out to create a wave of interest, to loosen up congealed attitudes, to dispel prejudices based on lack of contact and ignorance, to conquer hearts in order to reach minds, to arouse expectation where before there were closed minds, and to light a lamp of hope where none had existed. The norms of Bea's activity and its goals were fixed by Roncalli.

Roncalli's attitude to relationships with non-Catholics, while unequivocally clear on the fundamentals of belief, nevertheless carried enough appearance of dissimulation to cause eyebrows to be raised. He was explicit about the past: "We are not conducting a historical trial. We do not seek to determine who was right and who was wrong. All share the blame." This was dangerous talk already, and from the Pope! Roncalli intimated much more. Speaking to the non-Catholic observers on October 13, 1962, he said: "Now as for you, please read in my heart. You will find there much more than I have said with words." The message was clear. Roncalli was seeking the true stature of the Church he believed Jesus to have founded, and that stature was not filled by the Roman Catholic Church alone. Bea's job was to make sure that this message reached the hearts of the authorities and the principal people in the main non-Catholic groups. Roncalli set the pace; he received notables of non-Catholic groups: Dr. Fisher, the Archbishop of Canterbury, Dr. Lichtenberger, head of the American Episcopal Church, and Mr. Jackson, president of the National Baptist Convention. At that time, these events were unbelievable.

Bea's plan was to cover all of Europe with a web of travels, personal appearances, and lectures, to publish directly and indirectly on the Council and on the problem of Christian unity and the unity of all men, striving above all to reach the educated classes and the leaders of the various Christian sects. A list of his lectures alone, prior to the Council, reads like a travel guide. In 1959–61: New York (United States); Milan, Rome, Genoa, Turin, Chievi (Italy); Bern, Basle, Fribourg, Zurich, Lugano (Switzerland); Saint-Odile (France). In 1962: Paris (France), Heidelberg, Hanover, Essen, Tübingen, Munich (Germany); Vienna, Innsbruck (Austria); East and West Berlin; Padua (Italy); Heythrop, London (England). In 1963: Copenhagen and Roskilde (Denmark); Harvard, New York, Baltimore, Washington (United States). He published several articles and completed at least two books in this period, took active part in all sessions of the Council from October to December (seven major speeches), headed more than one commission, was at hand for private consultations with Roncalli, conducted plenary sessions of his own Secretariat, interviewed scores of delegates from other religions. He was indefatigable.

He visited the Archbishop of Canterbury, Dr. Ramsey, in London; held top-level secret talks with world leaders in religion and politics such as Dr. Visser 't Hooft, General Secretary of the World Council of Churches; received delegates and personages from Jewish-American organizations and other religions. He succeeded in arousing the desired interest and creating an expectation allied to a new respect, reverence, and the beginnings of a shy affection on the part of those once acridly critical of, and alien to, the Roman Church.

Meanwhile, the interest of local Catholic churches and their members, clerical and lay, was aroused and grew throughout the world. Popular articles in Europe and the Americas, some of them deliberately fomented from Rome, some of them spontaneous, carried for the first time direct criticism and even jibing remarks about highly placed officials in the Vatican. It was the first time this could happen in some hundreds of years without any fulminations from Rome striking down the offenders. Local prelates and theologians who went to Rome during the preparatory period of Roncalli's Council brought back stories of disputes, the flaring of tempers, contretemps between Roman cardinals and cardinals from the local churches, plotting and counterplotting, all of which opened up to the public mind a new possibility: perhaps, after all, there would be a change. It was not so much that a rather formidable god-figure suddenly seemed to have a weak stomach. It was rather that the total image of the monolithic Roman bureaucracy started to fade.

Roncalli immediately attained a new image for himself by going outside the Vatican. His picture appeared as he walked in the streets, talked with prisoners and hospitalized people, as he traveled in trains and preached in the open air. He even thought of traveling to New York for an appearance at the United Nations, to Jerusalem in order to worship at the Holy Places, to travel via Moscow (and thus greet the Patriarch of Moscow) to Constantinople to greet the Patriarch Athenagoras. At one stage, there was tentative talk of his visiting South America. Affairs of state, his deteriorating health, and the constant harassment of his frightened (and sometimes sullen) officialdom obviated such major moves. But he had created a new impression. A "new thing" was moving in his Church, and people were daily more aware of it.

On January 6, 1962, Roncalli addressed a letter to the priests of his Church and he could already speak of the "general satisfaction" with which his Council idea had been received. In his own private notes about that time he spoke of "that complete agreement of minds for which the Council is awaited and being prepared." In his letter to his priests, he continued: "We may say that we all feel we are within sight of a new era."

The last line along which Roncalli pursued his clear intent was in the area of governments and world powers. Roncalli's Council, the preparations for it, the coming and the going of Vatican diplomats, couriers, visitors, Bea's interventions, the increasing interest in the Council which was manifest among large numbers of people in every country in Europe and the Americas, the daily conversation in Rome among the diplomatic corps and in chancelleries around the world, all this could not but create a wave, first of interest, and then of expectation.

The situation, however, was confusing. This congenial and fast-talking man with the wide girth, deep voice, ready smile, mischievous eys, expressive hands, and waddling gait was apparently organizing a religious meeting in Rome for bishops and theologians and members of other religions. But there was some (not much) evidence that at least his preparations for the religious Council were touching questions of vital interest to all powers, great and small. We have already mentioned Roncalli's interest in Soviet Russia, its satellites, and the Far East. It struck government observers that any leader, religious or otherwise, whether he was a Roman Catholic, an Indian guru, or the Dalai Lama, was worth watching—indeed, needed watching—who could alone and without asking for it get his statement about the Cuban missile crisis published on the front page of *Pravda;* receive a lengthy and warm telegram from Nikita Khrushchev on his birthday and have his own valet stay to listen to its contents; maintain inner lines of communication with Russia itself and every satellite country of Russia and even with Albania; have accurate information about the interior of Communist China; arouse such enthusiasm in South American countries (already a sore spot for the United States); have a strong influence with Italian Socialists and attract definite respect from Italian Communists (both of whom could wreck parliamentary democracy in Italy, a vital member of NATO and part of America's defense posture in Western Europe); extract from a Siberian concentration camp a prisoner whom everyone had forgotten (Bishop Slipyi); entertain a 1,959-year-old and purely religious issue (the crucifixion of Jesus) and by that fact set most Arab countries in a turmoil, with Nasser agents and Israeli representatives vying for information in Rome. This man did bear watching. For there always was an unpredictability about Roncalli. In the final analysis, he did not answer to anyone but the God he served.

Besides, certain policy decisions and actions intrigued foreign governments. His effect on the Near East, for one. Was he going, say, to recognize Israel diplomatically? And if so, what would be the Arab reaction and how would this ricochet on American policies in that area? And the quiet, behind-the-scenes talks with Soviet representatives and Soviet satellite representatives: was he planning another and unexpected statement which would throw the defensive attitude of the United States and of NATO out of kilter, making them sound like warmongers? Then, again, Bea came to New York in 1963 for what was called an agape meeting. He had been there already in 1959 and conducted high-level talks with several religious leaders and personages. This time he met and talked with Secretary General U Thant of the United Nations and with the president of the General Assembly. It all seemed so natural, so innocuous. Yet one never knew. Roncalli, it was realized, kept lines of communications open with Adenauer, de Gaulle, and other world leaders.

The total effect of all this was, first, to create a definite interest on the part of governments and governmental agencies. The Machine was succeeding in doing what Roncalli intended it to do. The interest was on the whole benign; no world leader and politician could gainsay the positive role played by Roncalli in the Cuban missile crisis or by the Vatican in extending its help in normal difficulties—if only as a safe and neutral meeting place for parties who would not be seen dead together in public. Besides, the problems confronting most major powers at that time were such that they were willing to accept help from whatever quarter it came from. There was, therefore, a general expectation and hope that the Council would redound to the cause of peace. After all, an international gathering of such representational character should have an effect, especially if its leader had expressed such explicit intentions as entering "the marrow and essence of human affairs," as providing men with a chance of finding political peace and international tranquillity, as establishing the solid basis for an international comity that had not existed in Europe since it was a fiefdom of the Roman Empire or the spiritually dominated realm of the Roman popes for a brief period of history.

But Roncalli kept his deepest counsels for himself, and even joked with outsiders about their assessments. Speaking with about three hundred journalists after his election as pope, he poked fun at their reports and at the general opinion they expressed of his proposed Council: "You truly know many things! You have already found out the secrets of the Conclave [in which he had been elected]. You have also written that I was a pope of transition. I don't quite understand what you mean by that. Well, perhaps, you are right . . ."

When Roncalli opened his Council on October 11, 1962, he resumed the main themes: his Event, his Council, the expectation and the hope. As to the state of the world: "After almost twenty centuries, the most serious matters to be solved by the human race have not changed." There is no question of distorting our traditional faith, he stated. But we must "with alacrity, without fear, tackle the work which our age demands." This is primarily a question of "examining and explaining our certain and immutable teaching in that particular way which is demanded by our time." He then made his oft-quoted distinction. "The deposit of faith or the truth of our sacred teaching, this is one thing. The way in which these are proposed (keeping the same meaning and opinion), this is another thing." On that distinction and its application would depend to a large extent the outcome of Roncalli's central hope—attainment of the "full truth" of Christianity in thought, word, action—and this would constitute the core of the Event.

His Event he again described in quasi-mystical terms: "as a day of the most brilliant light." Yet the beginning of the Council is the "dawn only; already the first rays of the rising sun suavely possess our spirits." Looking at the diplomatic corps and the government representatives, he reminded the Council participants that they were going to act in full view of an expectant world: "We see around us men of the greatest dignity who have come from the five continents to Rome to represent their nations and who are here with all reverence and a most human expectation." Speaking to the diplomatic corps on the following day, he remarked that the Council, "over and above its properly religious signification," had a social aspect of interest for the life of all peoples "because it will surely bring a luminous answer from God to the painful problems of our contemporaries and thus truly help both individuals and nations."

Roncalli could take encouragement from the letter which the Council participants composed and addressed to all men: "Whatever concerns the dignity of man, whatever aids in building a true community of nations, this we make ours." There was yet no flame apparent among the participants. But mentally and as a group they seemed to be perfectly disposed for the labors of the Council as he foresaw it, and for the Event. He had his own view of the first, unexpectedly slow session which began October 11 and ended December 7, 1962. Speaking in his farewell address to the departing Council participants, on December 7, 1962, he said: "The first session, in a certain slow and solemn way, opened up as it were a door to the very big work of the Council. It was, in other words, a beginning. By it, the Fathers could enter with eager spirit into the very heart and deepest reason of this matter, this divine plan."

You come from all over the globe, he continued. The Council was composed of men who came from distant regions. They had never spoken with each other, never established any bonds. He describes this bond-forming process: "They [the Council members] have had to look at each other together, in order to make clear their mutual ways of thinking. Each one has had to communicate fruitfully and deliberately with the other the knowledge which he had gained by experience, thus bringing out what is important for the apostolate in various places for various kinds of men."

Now, as to the ultimate goal of his Council, the Event, Roncalli speaks effectively. First of all, this first session has not yet yielded the standards (*normae*) or principles which he expects from it, which all men expect from it. In his eyes, the direct result of Council discussions would be such standards and principles. They would be applicable to Catholics, to other Christians, and to non-Christians. These principles would be applied to all fields of human activity. But at this point of development the Event itself would be taking place.

It will without any doubt, he said, be a new dawning Pentecost, giving a tremendous surcease of spiritual force to the Church. In virtue of this force, all men will be affected. The Event, thus emerging full-blown from the labors of the Council, will be recognizable because the Council will have caused a new efflorescence of belief, hope, and love among all men. Roncalli could not be more explicit.

He was well aware of the effect of his Council on the general public. He had noted the mounting interest not merely in non-Christian religious bodies such as Jews and Moslems but as well in most of the major non-Catholic Christians. He had followed closely the interest of foreign governments, had been informed of their fears and their hopes, their interests and their difficulties. All of them felt an apprehension. In some, it was great. In others, it was less. It was, in general, a sort of fear that, truly and effectively, the Council men would take some giant step rather suddenly and unexpectedly; that some movement would be born from the Council; that it would outstrip their individual analyses and projections for the present and the near future; that it would engulf the tidy confines of their individual national rationales; that they would wake up some morning in their chancelleries or return from lunch to their offices, or be interrupted one day at a meeting of state, and be told of news which dwarfed any matter in hand. The one lurking danger for the machines of state, for the diplomatic mind, for the bureaucracy of government, and for the day-to-day caretakers of national affairs is, briefly, the unexpected, the surprising, the imponderable.

Roncalli sees in the attitude of leaders both in other religious bodies and in government a foretaste of his Event. He knows that if the Event arrives, any trace of real fear will disappear. We have traveled, he wrote in a letter of January 6, 1963, a long way from the beginning of this Council three years ago. "In the beginning, the summoning of the Council did not seem to occupy the thoughts of civil society." Now it is obvious that "the Council's work has aroused up such a respect even among those who differ between themselves in religion, philosophy, and politics that we can justifiably ask ourselves whether or not the light of divine grace has not already entered men's spirits."

His eyes are on Americans, on Russians, on French, on British, on Arabs, on Jews, on all who were watching and listening carefully, ausculting the heartbeats of the Council, entertaining Council members, talking with Vatican officials, seeking the rationale of this decision and the signification of that move. For Roncalli, the entry of divine grace was the signal: the Event was in the offing. He saw the new attitude to the Council as a beginning of that universal effect, the Event. As always, when talking of it, he has recourse to quasi-mystical terms. It is perhaps the only occasion, however, where he almost explicitly attributes to his Event a theophanic element, a "showing of God's face."

To do this, he uses a word found in the Fourth Gospel where, the night before he died, Jesus prays to his heavenly father. Jesus had said: "Father, the time has come. Glorify your son, in order that your son glorify you." And, as a consequence of this "glorification," Jesus prayed further: "I have prayed for the men you gave me. They are yours, Holy Father. Preserve those you gave me by your power, so that they may be one, just as you and

I are one." Christians, and Catholics in particular, had always understood "those you gave me" and "the men you gave me" as *themselves, Christians* as distinct from all other men, or *Catholics* as distinct from all other men. Roncalli does not take this view. It is all men. The "glorification" mentioned is expressed by a technical term (Greek *doxa,* Hebrew *kavod*) in both the Jewish and the Christian Bibles. It is always used to express an appearance of God, a theophany, a moment when the veils of flesh and blood and mortality are drawn aside, when the immortal and eternal being of the Beyond, of God, shines forth with that eerily unhuman but humanly all-desirable sheen of awesomeness, of limitless beauty, ineffable peace, luminous truth, and heartfelt satiety mortal man has always felt in his religious experiences of God.

Roncalli likens the respect for the Council and the wave of expectation and of hope it has aroused to the beginning of a "showing of God's face." Many people, he says, are now turning once more to that prayer of Jesus, endeavoring to understand it in the light of Council developments.

In April 1963, Roncalli releases his charter of world concept and organization, *Pacem in Terris.* It immediately provokes that kind of interest which betokens a great event. Read as carefully in the Kremlin as in Washington, Paris, London, Jerusalem, Cairo, and Peking, commented upon avidly, giving birth to congresses, meetings, discussions, and written studies, *Pacem in Terris* is a landmark. Without the Event, it is just a brilliant analysis and proposal. Inserted in the Event, it would be the basis and source for a conceptualizing of a world community of men in action.

He settled down to wait out the inter-sessional period and to deal with the day-to-day problems. His Machine was working; the Spirit was effecting the Event. But Roncalli's health was slipping. In March 1962 the first rumors had circulated about a malignancy. Cardinal Léger, one of the Council participants, on his return from the first session for Christmas 1962, said flatly: "The Pope is tortured by a disease which does not let go; he will not last another year." By May 31, all hope was gone. And on June 3 he died, the victim of peritonitis consequent on a gastric tumor.

In the last few months of his life, as well as during the first session in the fall of 1962, the clamor of chaos had made itself felt faintly. Sometimes, indeed, it seemed to be budging ever so slightly from the dark outer periphery to which it had been relegated. He had, from the beginning, abdicated any reliance on power, relying on compassion to exorcise chaos, compassion with the smile of friendship, compassion with the look of understanding, compassion with the instinct of love. Roncalli knew that his own Church was a tightly sealed container of bottled liberties, enslaved wills, drumming and shaking with end products of grave dissatisfaction, disillusionment, hopelessness, a kind of desperation, and a desire to be free. To unseal that container, to let all loose and rampant, to give rights to those whose rights had been nonexistent for centuries, to let the perpetually silent speak their mind, to ask the professional receivers to be givers, to acknowledge deficiencies, faults, errors, and heartlessness in high places, to consort with those who had been previously damned as erroneous, vice-ridden, inimical, ungodly: this, in practical terms, was to smile invitingly at chaos, to cry "Holy! Holy! Holy!" and let loose the dogs of confusion.

24

The Happening

What happened at the Council can be summarized in a relatively short space. The significance of what happened as well as of what did not happen can be suggested but, as yet, cannot be fully assessed. For we are still living in its aftermath, and the throes provoked by the Council are still wreaking pains and dislocations and confusion in the Roman Catholic Church. We are still in the post-Conciliar period.

In all, the Council held four sessions: October 11 to December 8, 1962; September 29 to December 4, 1963; September 14 to November 21, 1964; and September 14 to December 8, 1965. The conclusions and statements of the Council concerning Roman Catholic teaching and attitudes to world problems and conditions were contained in sixteen documents or "decrees," the result of 544 rounds of voting. The most important of the Council's decisions can be briefly stated.

The Roman Catholic Church, headed by the pope, is indeed the true Church founded by Jesus. The bishops of the Church have the right to participate with the pope in the government of that Church. The division between the Church and the other segments of Christianity was deplored. Catholics are allowed to pray with the others and all must strive to achieve unity. All men have a right to religious liberty and to worship as they see fit. Atheists are no longer to be anathematized. Jews are declared innocent of the crime of deicide.

Some new provisions affect the internal life of the Church.

The diaconate, a Church function, is restored. It means that married men can baptize, officiate at marriages, bring Communion to the dying, and perform certain ceremonial functions. Mass may be said in the ordinary vernacular languages. The lay folk can participate actively by singing, answering the priest's prayers and invocations, and by symbolic gestures. Marriage is no longer described as destined solely to produce children. But any decision about birth control is left to Paul VI.

On the face of it, and theoretically, there was no decision of the Council which could not have been taken by the pope himself —whoever he was—alone or perhaps in conjunction with his cardinals, his papal offices, and the major ecclesiastical authorities of the whole Roman Catholic Church. A good case can be made for the statement that, as things were developing in the Church after Pacelli's death, most if not all of these "liberalizations" would have had to come anyway. Pacelli himself had seen fit—indeed, it was a necessity—to relax the laws of fasting and the hours at which Mass could be legally attended by Catholics.

Advocates of the Council will always return with what appears to be an irrefragable answer: "The Council did much more in an imponderable and unquantifiable area of human relations." It opened up the Vatican and the Church bureaucracy. It aired difficulties and exposed weaknesses. It launched a new spirit of inquiry and zeal. It brought Catholics and other Christians closer. It also resulted in the bishops having a somewhat more official say in Church government; since the Council, they meet regularly, if infrequently, with the pope in Rome as a whole synod. Finally, the actual Council opened up the Church to the world, showing that Catholics did not condemn out of hand those who differed from them, and stretching out a willing hand for collaboration in mutually beneficial ventures. Were not some of the proposed changes so earth-shaking that a staunch conservative like Cardinal Ottaviani cried out at one instance: "May God give me the grace to die in the bosom of the Catholic Church"? Without the Council, in other words, there would be none of the spirit of renewal which swept the Church in its wake; the shoulder-rubbing of bishops from all over the world, and the free exchange of wishes, views, needs, and principles.

There is no gainsaying the emergence of a new spirit as a result of the Council. But it is precisely this spirit which still prompts the fundamental question about the Council. Over against the situation of man today and the invading structuralism which threatens to reduce his life to unbearable conditions, the Council's achievements seem to be assessable in two major ways.

First, it did produce a series of new decrees ordering changes in ways of worship and certain ways of internal government. No one of these represents a stunning breakthrough or a historic step of huge proportions. In the same vein, the Council refurbished some old ideas, notably by elaborating on the members of the Church as the "People of God" and on the concept of what the Bible signifies.

Second, it opened up several doors, mainly by decrying certain age-old prejudices: all men have a natural right to worship as they please; all Christians should work for Christian unity, and let past mistakes take care of themselves; Jews are not to be hated; Catholics should actively work for the economic, social, cultural, and political betterment of all mankind.

A line must be drawn at this point in the list of the Council's achievements.

The Council produced nothing that was not in the logic of events. What it did produce, it produced with one eye on existing models outside its own boundaries, models exhibited by other Christians or by non-Christians. Its newly adopted attitudes to the Bible, to the Mass, and to religion reflected a good deal of Protestant thinking and a measure of contemporary man's thinking, with no reference to a supernatural salvation or a divine Church. In particular, two well-known and flourishing concepts of the circumambient world gave the Council a falsely roseate hue. One was a rather old one and its extreme form used to be called Gallicanism, the notion that a council was superior to the pope. Vatican Council II did not go this far, but the Gallican spirit moved among many. It was a disinterred ghost from a previous century when Pius IX thought he had buried it forever with the decree of papal infallibility promulgated at his prodding by the First Vatican Council in 1870.

The second innovation was almost exclusively an American import but readily adopted by the French, the Dutch, and the Germans. It was the idea that if everybody can have his say, if no holds are barred, if a true forum for a democracy of free speech is permitted to function, then all will be well. This principle of republican democracy is inviolable in the political arena. When it is applied indiscriminately to matters of the spirit and to truths which depend for their integrity on a traditional teaching authority, it can wreak havoc.

The net result of these two dominating ideas was, of course, an inevitable structuralism. Truth was born on the computer machine tallying up votes, the ayes and the noes. The Council itself, not as Roncalli's Machine, but as any other Church council or parliament, was structured into commissions, discussion groups, press conferences, vote-taking, lobbying, and all the paraphernalia of a normal getting-together of men. The decretal results of the Council have this structuralist mark. They said nothing effectively salvific to men of that age. Above all, the Council itself did not create a "new thing," a fresh "charisma," for all men or, for that matter, for Catholics or Christians. The Spirit did not shine out. There was no Event. There was born a spirit animated by the old and threatening chaos masquerading in a watered-down Gallicanism and protecting itself behind the principles of republican democracy. Let the representatives of the people speak. But this belongs to the context of post-conciliar madness and the wisdom peculiar to the age, and is discussed in a later chapter.

A similar conclusion emanates from a consideration of ecumenism. There is no doubt that the Council started Roman Catholics talking with other Christians. The Archbishop of Canterbury came to the Vatican; he and Paul VI made a common declaration which more or less relegated what was past to the past and promised mutual good will, prayers, joint activities, and a search for the unity lost four hundred years ago. The Patriarch of Constantinople, Athenagoras, came to the Vatican, celebrated a new era of friendship with Rome. The Orthodox and the Roman Catholic Churches had mutually anathematized each other in centuries past. Each had said of the other that it was execrable, unholy, erroneous, and condemned by God. They now lifted this ridiculous and utterly meaningless anathema. A measure of its significance for men at large with all their acute problems is this: it had about as much effect on those problems and the mind of the ordinary man as if the present Dalai Lama, a stooge of Communist China, met the former Dalai Lama, now an exile in India, and they declared that they would be friends in future. Roman Catholics now took part in the ecumenical activities of the World Council of Churches.

But as regards any real unity, all this has meant nothing in the effective order. Nor has it meant the lighting of any great illumination for all men. Bea's Secretariat for the Promotion of Christian Unity became an inter-agency for maintaining relationships between Catholics and other Christians. The desired unity has become a matter of compromise, of finding the phrase all will subscribe to, and the act of worship all can perform in common without feeling that they are being violated in their sectarian beliefs. Ecumenism's total effect was to consecrate a new structuralism, as if paper measures could make a church; as if the putting together of two dead weights could produce a lightness of spirit and a forward movement.

Within the Event on which Roncalli counted, there would be no need for ecumenism as such. Ecumenism presumed divisions. It bogs the participants down in a morass of negotiations, a spiked jungle of self-guarding egotisms, and it engages them on a long endless road along which, as mutually independent caravans, they have agreed to travel, not too far from each other (for protection) but certainly not too near each other (for fear of contamination or encroachment). The Council provided no religious experience, forged no new unity. What had begun as a means to an end became the sole end of the Council.

This negative result is seen more vividly as regards non-Christians. When the Council tally was over and done, Roman Catholics and Christians were not any nearer to non-Christians. In sum, the Council told non-Christians: you have a right to believe as you like. It was, in effect, telling them that they were as good as Christians, except that Christians did not quite agree, but would do nothing about it and certainly would not think badly of them, much less act subversively in their regard. But the Council lit no beacon for non-Christians. Nothing flowed from the Council to unify all other believers, to leaven their minds, to weld their hearts together. The Spirit did not manifest itself. There was no Event.

A prime example of what happened to Roncalli's Council on particular issues affecting non-Christians is provided by the Jewish Declaration. Christian anti-Semitism had persecuted Jews for over sixteen centuries. It became a more crucial question between Christians and Jews after World War II, because of Pacelli's wartime decision not to attack Hitler's "final solution"; in effect, he had not done all he could to prevent what later became the mass murder of about six million Jews. In general, and apart from the Holocaust, no blot is greater on the history of Christianity than the horrors occasioned by its officially fostered anti-Semitism.

In the summer of 1960, Roncalli received a French professor, Jules Isaac. Isaac, author of *The Teaching of Contempt*, wished the forthcoming Council to do something effective about the bases of anti-Semitism in the modern Catholic Church. To the credit of that Church, it, and not the Lutheran, the Episcopalian, the Anglican, the Greek or Russian Orthodox, or any other church, was willing to consider some concrete action. Roncalli, sensing an opening, referred him to Bea. After discussions, it was decided that Bea would draft a text about Jewish-Christian relationships to be considered by the Council. In Roncalli's perspective, any step toward one non-Christian religion should be part of a general approach within the ambit of the Event. There thus was born what came to be known as the Jewish Declaration.

The Declaration had a checkered career. Prepared and drafted in 1960–61, it was suppressed by June 1962, restored to the agenda by a letter of Roncalli on December 13, 1962, put off again *sine die* in November 1963, and finally restored in a more amplified document entitled *The Relationship of the Church to Non-Christians*. This was finally accepted by the overwhelming majority of the Council during its fourth and last session in 1965. Bea earned much praise and devotion from some Jewish circles, not a little obloquy and abuse from Arab sources, the anger of many conservative Christians, the contempt of many Orthodox Jews, and a final cloud of painful misunderstanding from many Catholics, together with some restrictions from Montini. But the Council declaration concerning the Jews was unequivocal in two vital points: the Jews cannot, as a race, be called deicides (Christ-killers) or an accursed race. The final version of the Declaration was, in certain respects, worse than nothing; in other respects, it was better than anything any Christian church had said on the subject.

For the Arabs, of course, this Declaration was tantamount to a betrayal: only the State of Israel stood to profit by it, they said. For many Christians and Catholics, it was a denial of historical truth: the Gospels and St. Paul in his letters speak of the Jews as deicides and as cursed with blindness by God. Or so they argued. "Cardinal Bea is the tool of Zionism," commented *Al Ahram*, the news organ of Nasser's government. "This declaration of Cardinal Bea's is nothing but a plot of international Jewry," Salah al-Din Bitar, the Premier of Syria, had brutally declared. "The declaration is most timely," said Richard Cardinal Cushing of Boston. "It shows what is the relationship of Jews and Christians." "Why, in effect, was there any need to define the relationship of Jews and Christians?" a Spanish rightist paper jeered. "We know that they killed Christ and that they have been rejected by

God since then. Scores of popes and saints have taught us this."
They had.

The Cardinal in his four-year struggle with the Jewish Declaration had to listen to many tones: the voice of Pope Innocent III
declaring in 1169, "The Jews are paying for their crime by God's
eternal banishment, and through them the truth of our faith is
confirmed"; Pius XI declaring in 1938, "Spiritually, we all are
Semites"; and in 1963 Pope John XXIII approving a draft text
which stated, "Christ, our Peace, reconciled Jew and Gentile,
making the two into one body." What reconciliation? What one
body? In these two words "one body" lay the entire Jewish-
Christian difficulty.

Jew and Gentile in one body: Christ our Peace. Between these
antinomies, as between the jaws of a pincers, the fate of the
Jewish people has been inexorably caught, held, twisted. Not to
be Christian meant they could not possibly be of one body with
Christians; to be Jews meant they refused the reconciliation of
Christ, for he was not their peace. Contrariwise, to accept the
Christian reconciliation meant betrayal of their Jewishness; to
retain their Jewishness meant the refusal of Christ. In this historical paradigm and in pre-twentieth-century history, to refuse
Christ had meant persecution by anyone who chose to be, or who
was regarded by Christians as, an incarnation of Christ's wrath.
That incarnation could be and was any of the Hitlers of history:
a Tamerlane, a Philip II, a Peter the Great, "Christs" who spoke
in the pogrom-preaching tongues of St. John Chrysostom, St.
John Capistrano, and Martin Luther, the "Christs" who sharpened the sword blades for any Jewish massacre in Seville, in
Pomerania, in Cracow, or in Naples, or the "Christs" who blessed
the rack and whip of Torquemada. The Gentile could be any
historical agglomerate of human beings who associated with the
alien Jews only on the condition that their Jewishness as a historical entity be liquidated: the empire of Justinian I, the medieval papacy, the Roman Church from the fourth century onwards, the German National Socialists of the thirties and forties,
and the Soviet Bolsheviks of our day.

In Roncalli's mind and in Bea's opinion, the problem of Jewish-Christian relations could be solved only within a wider
framework. That framework was the large one of international
comity. In the Event, Christian anti-Semitism and Jewish anti-
Christian attitudes would dissolve. It is in such a context that a
Jewish Document could find meaning. Roncalli had no intention
of leaving the solution of the problem to the exegetes who pored

over the tortuous sentences of St. Paul as *he* tried to reason his way past his own Jewishness, his newfound Christianity, and the hate he had been subject to everywhere from Jewish communities. In the twentieth century, there was no use in flogging a dead ass.

Two thousand years of history have finally culminated in the end of an era. The mental and moral attitudes of the millions of people who share the worn-out Jewish-Christian heritage of the West have been dislodged from well-set grooves. At present, we are living in the almost imperceptible time lag before a new era becomes an obvious reality. It is not merely that during World War II Christian anti-Semitism reached a paroxysm unparalleled in past centuries, or that Jews finally achieved a return to their homeland in Palestine, or that the traditional home of Diaspora Judaism was obliterated forever and that America now houses a newly developing form of Judaism, or that, finally, the twentieth-century Roman Catholic Church has faced this question in an oblique way in her Ecumenical Council, has lived past the violent reactions provoked by her questioning, has spoken all she purports to know for the moment on the subject. The history-making element lies not merely in what the Church has or has not declared, but more in the historical context of our day.

The ultimate aim of any Jewish Document, in Roncalli's mind, was a very well-defined one. He did not envisage merely a declaration by a Church council to the effect that "now you Jews can be assured that we no longer think you killed Jesus; we will not call you a cursed race any more." This would, in the first place, be an otiose gesture, an end flourish of a fading dogmatism. Roncalli and Bea thought along other lines. The real problem lay in a mentality of opposition between Jew and Christian shared as ardently and nourished as vividly and deliberately by Jew as by Christian.

Christians were taught to despise Jews. Jews taught each other and their children to hate and condemn Jesus and Christians; Jesus, because he was, in their eyes, the apostate par excellence; Christians, because they followed the apostate Jew and they persecuted Jews. It is naïve to think that Jews disliked Christians merely because the naughty Christians first hurt the Jews. The only historical evidence we have indicates that hate and persecution first came gratuitously from Jew against Christian. Unfortunately for Jews and Judaism, Christians succeeded in becoming stronger than Jews.

However, two wrongs do not make a right. Two claimants to

be right were and are both wrong, Jew and Christian. This was the essence of the idea entertained by Roncalli and Bea: the righting of a double wrong. But this wrong was not a question of words, or letters, or decrees. It was a question of a change in heart, of a coming together in mutual esteem. Jews continually hampered Bea's efforts by a "give-us-our-Jewish-declaration-or-we-will-not-believe-your-sincerity" attitude. Christians continually hampered his efforts by their "let's-do-something-for-the-poor-Jews" attitude. Over and above all this, there was a noticeable shrinking on the part of many Jews from the whole matter of the Jewish Declaration, notably among the more orthodox and religious, as if too much contact with Christians would derogate in some way from their Jewishness or their Judaism. There was here a real fear and, sometimes, a supercilious contempt.

Besides, Christian theology and Vatican politics did as much damage as Jewish theology and Jewish politics. The Vatican had many interests in the Near East; it did not wish to hurt these by appearing to support Israel against the Arabs. In that quarrel, neither side permits anyone to be neutral: "he who is not with me is against me." Most Catholics in the Near East lived in Arab lands, were in fact "Arabs." Finally, Catholic theology, from St. Paul in the first century on, taught, indeed, that the Jews were cursed.

On the other hand, Jews in Europe and America with their heads on their shoulders had a vital interest in seeing that the Vatican made a pro-Jewish declaration; it undoubtedly could be used to clobber a good deal of vile Nasserist anti-Israeli and anti-Jewish propaganda, while offsetting the residues of anti-Semitism in Christianity. In addition, Jewish theology was explicit about the apostasy of Jesus and the hatefulness of Christians, his followers. In the normal course of events, the kindliest thought which Jews could have of Jesus was some version of Klausner's outmoded Germanic theories about Jesus, the innocent and quite virtuous countryman from Galilee, a pious Jew at heart but subject to innocuous decisions, whom the clever and duplistic Hellenistic Paul, an apostate, built up into a marvelous image of a god descended on the earth, after some models drawn from his newly adopted Greek mythology.

Now Bea fell between two stools. He had committed himself to a Jewish Declaration within the framework of Roncalli's Council and planned Event. The Event did not come off. Yet the need to produce a Jewish Declaration of some kind had been created within the expectation and the plans of many Jews and many Christians. There had to be a declaration of some kind or other. Bea also published a book, *The Church and the Jewish People*. In certain ways this book seems to detract from the fullness of certain statements in the final version of the Jewish Declaration. The outside world could not know that Bea's hand was held by others in the final redaction of that book. His achievements still displeased his Vatican opponents and the conservative members of the administration.

Bea continued with his tours, his lectures, his contacts, his writing. He saw his decree on ecumenism approved overwhelmingly by the Council. His travels and lectures in the years 1964–67 took him to Frankfurt, Cologne, Munich, Würzburg (Germany), Madrid (Spain), Harvard, Philadelphia (United States), Geneva (Switzerland), Milan (Italy), Taizé (France). He was in Constantinople in April 1966 to see Patriarch Athenagoras. He prepared new books: *We Who Serve, Christ and Mankind, The World of God and Mankind, Ecumenism in the Council*. He still seemed indefatigable. He never lost his apparent tranquillity and never betrayed to outsiders any disillusionment or loss of trust; nor did his sense of humor desert him. At odd moments, his long dormant sarcasm (nurtured in the years he walked with power) took its head and he demolished in some throaty remarks the hypocrisy of those who justified what he called euphemistically their spiritual *Fleischwerk* (sitting down and doing nothing) with a pious self-righteousness but whose sly cunning and persistent worldliness threw them into a febrile opposition to all and any change.

In a conversation with a former associate some few weeks before his death, he was asked what moment in his Roman life he treasured most. It was, he said, in April 1966. It was, he added, a blessing from Pope John. And it lasted a brief few minutes. He was at the head of a papal delegation at Constantinople to greet the Patriarch Athenagoras in the name of Pope Paul VI. He recalled the old city across the Golden Horn, the shabby suburban location, the gateway entrance to the residence of the Patriarch, the gardens, the steps, the stark hallway, the dowdy, narrow, high-ceilinged workroom, the big table, and the aged kindliness and Abraham-like countenance of Athenagoras sitting beneath a Byzantine icon of the Virgin and the Child and a photograph of himself and Paul VI shaking hands. His mission accomplished, both men went to the church and took part in a Greek Orthodox ceremony. Afterwards, as they emerged together, the stooping, five-foot seven-inch, eighty-five-year-old

Cardinal and the erect, six-foot one-inch, seventy-nine-year-old Patriarch, Bea's precious moment came.

In Athenagoras's presence, he had been reminded of Roncalli. It was not so much the impression of a large physique. Athenagoras had the most powerful and magnetic personality of any of his contemporaries in any Christian church: a white mane of hair, large brown-black eyes of piercing light, cadaverous face, long curving Byzantine nose with small flaring nostrils, a flowing beard, quick, delicate but long hands, a gaunt frame looking taller than it really was because of the conical *kalimmafki* he habitually wore, and a deep, unhurried voice. It was rather that in his presence there was a breath of the dream which Roncalli had invoked for Bea, something of the infinity which shines briefly through the chinks of all human finiteness when man is seized by the eternal, and something of God's greatness which filters through the lattices of flesh and bones when man has walked with God in the quiet evening of life.

As the two men passed through the people assembled (more than one Christian group was represented), the officious importance of the papal delegation Bea headed that day vanished. Athenagoras was smiling and saying: "Pope John smiles with God now and salvation is ours." The rush of the years overtook Augustin Bea, carpenter's son, scholar, cardinal, old defeated man. For the first time in many years he yearned for death and an end to all the botheration. "See! They are all Christians," Athenagoras was saying. Bea knew that, although Roncalli's gamble had failed, success was yet to be measured by another yardstick. "Bless them! Bless them!" Athenagoras told him. Bea did so, immediately feeling that the blessing of Jesus was wafted out from Constantinople, across the Golden Horn and the Black Sea and the White Sea to the wide world beyond where the hammer of the Galilean carpenter would hammer at the hardened heart of man, telling him of the wisdom he needed to find his happiness. It was Bea's fondest moment, it lacked all particularisms, he said.

Without Roncalli, he was a lamp without a flame, a judgment without a will to make it lightsome, a body without a soul, a book without a leading title. But he had faith enough to sustain him when the bleakness of routine ceased to be enlivened with the passion of Roncalli's vibrant trust in the future. His hope in God never flagged, even though the substance of that hope was severely strained in the crucible of power struggles after Roncalli's death. And because Roncalli's brief example had reapprenticed him to the art of loving God in men, he could take refuge in an inner sanctuary of his spirit where faith had both poetry and subtlety, where hope had still its passion even amid the ruins, and love remained gentle and transparent, even though its strands ran thin and he became toward the end, like all great men, the knowing subject of whispered conversations and "after-he-dies" plans.

Within that sanctuary he could enjoy persistent memories that hovered unceasingly over his life, murmured to him in the silence of his sleepless nights, and accompanied him during his last hours. "My death will not be lonely," he had written sometime earlier. When he came to die, Bea was ready in more ways than one. He had for a long time past conquered both the fear of death and, more importantly, the fear of dying. Moreover, he had been purified. Anything of contempt and anger for the opposition his wishes encountered, his onetime compromises in dilemmas, his fear of human respect, or the occasional wisps of vanity—all this had been purged from him by the abuse of his detractors, the heartbreak he suffered at the hands of those in the Vatican administration who undermined his position, the contradictions thrown at him by his enemies and opponents, the frustration of his good intentions, and the painful obligation he had to shoulder responsibility for decisions that he was not allowed to make but whose consequences he was obliged to bear. Surely, within the Catholic optic of time and eternity, God took Bea at his death and invited him to rest forever.

25

The Death of Roncalli

In the last weeks of May 1963, John suffered from internal bleeding. The public then learned that he had a tumor. In spite of transfusions, coagulants, morphine, and medication, the hemorrhaging started again on May 26. Then peritonitis set in. On Friday, he received Communion and confessed his sins to Monsignor Giuseppe Cavagna. The Last Rites were given him by the granite-faced Dutchman Monsignor Peter Van Lierde, the ideal papal confessor, whose Latin, according to popular report, was limited to "si" and "no." From now until his end on June 3, John went in and out of comas, as he lay on a low wooden bed on the top floor of the Vatican Palace. His heart ("as strong as a horse's," remarked Dr. Piero Mazzoni) fought a long, losing battle with a lethal infection. It was as if the first egregious victim of compassion's failure was John himself in his three-day effort to die.

The Church he inherited from Pacelli had undergone for too long the discipline of survival. Both its structure of government and its methods of teaching religion were dictated, not by an understanding of circumstances as they were, but by an insistence that circumstances be as they were ideally desired to be. The prime casualty in this discipline of survival was the individual: power required him to measure up to an established norm. And the principal element sacrificed for the sake of that chosen insistence was realism.

The brute fact concerning Roman Catholicism's condition at midcentury was trebly painful: as a cohesive group spirit, it

250

was finished and spent; as an organization, it had no mooring
lines with contemporary society; as a great religion, it no longer
participated in the culture and civilization of its day. It had been
replaced, ousted, drained. The pathos of this end could not be
obvious, however, to the myopia of power. The suffering caused
by the discipline of survival was invisible for the idealism of
power. Only compassion had eyes open for the suffering, and
honesty available for admission of the pathos. I say that this
realization of pathos, of suffering, and of imminent death was
the first characteristic of John as Prince of Compassion.

He received visitors sporadically; sometimes he recognized
them; sometimes he did not. Sometimes he communicated.
Sometimes a dumb horror seized those trying to interpret his
feeble efforts to make himself understood. Battista Roncalli, a
nephew of John, standing in front of him, was terrified by
John's distress and labored effort to communicate, until he realized that, standing as he did, he blocked John's view of a crucifix
hanging on the opposite wall. Archbishop Josyf Slipyi, recently
released by Nikita Khrushchev at John's request, after seventeen
years in Soviet prison camps, came and prayed. The cardinals
assembled to hear John speak hoarsely for eight painful minutes
telling them to unite all Christians. One cardinal, John's sincere
arch-enemy, reportedly told the dying old man that his death
was "the hand of God." In the Cardinal's opinion, John had
nearly ruined the Church.

John's three brothers arrived with his sister Assunta to nurse
him, not to help him die. He would live, even if it required special intervention by God. "He cannot die now"—this was the
phrase.

They and the thousands of onlookers in the square below and
the millions beyond the seas surrounding Italy could not give up
hope. But the doctors knew otherwise. "The life of His Holiness
is indeed slipping away," reported the R.A.I. commentator. "The
game is up," Monsignor Parente of the Holy Office muttered to a
companion as he left. *Finità la commedia.* For John's closest ones
and his adherents, this vain expectation, this almost childlike
belief that the apparently impossible was not only possible but
necessarily true and bound to happen, this was born directly
from the compassion which John had engendered. It was as vain
as the gamble which the same compassion had dictated in the
policy of John. For he, in his turn, had arrived at the bedside of
an expiring Church organization. Voices he heard agreed per-
functorily that its demise would be "the hand of God," ridding

the world of an incubus too long on men's backs, too long triumphant, too long anti-man in its demands.

There was one difference between the hope of John as pope and the hope of those waiting for the outcome of his illness. John had realized that, without some special event or intervention, the Church as he knew it was finished as a religious organization and as the vivifying force of its carrier civilization in the West. But he believed that the seemingly inevitable could be exorcised. He hoped against all hopelessness. On one condition: that a renewal take place. Not a renewal of Church rules or even of doctrine. Such was not required. The kind of renewal that only his God could effect. He had hoped, in other words, for an Event, an outpouring of a new spirit in Christians, in Catholics, and in all believers. God must once again show his face. All John proposed to do was to provide a forum, a setting for that special event. It was, as I said, a gigantic gamble. The second characteristic of John's compassion was, then, this substantial hope in the teeth of apparent impossibility.

John's pain was now intense and constant. It wrung from his lips pleas to God that he be allowed to die and "be free." His brothers knelt and prayed. Monsignor Loris Capovilla, John's secretary and confidant, wept quietly in a corner. On Monday, June 3, Roncalli's pulse began to fail. Assunta wiped the perspiration constantly from his face. They all heard the death rattle in John's throat. But he still lingered. It was the end of a warm golden day in Rome's twilight. The sun was just setting, dulling the earth-brown sheen of the buildings and graying the cupolas. Luigi Cardinal Traglia had just finished saying Mass in St. Peter's Square for the crowds who waited and watched. Suddenly, as night fell, John gave a sharp cry. There was a quick shudder. All was still. No one heard him draw a last breath. It was 7:49 P.M.

Outside in St. Peter's Square, more than ten thousand people knelt and looked up at the bedroom window. For the first time in three days, the shutters were open. The curtains were parted. A bright light shone within on the doctors, cardinals, officials, and attendants. After death was certified, the body was ceremonially washed and clothed, as Pacelli's had been. The silence of the settling night was broken only by the splashing of the two fountains down in the square. A full moon rode overhead. Three days later, John was buried with his predecessors. Nikita Khrushchev had to comment publicly, even if with an agitprop phrase. John, he said, had "won the respect of peace-loving peoples." "An incomparable pope," remarked Giovanni Battista Cardinal Montini. Both tributes seem, in retrospect, to be niggling. The truth is that both judgments missed the point of John's single-minded effort during his short years as pope.

As pope and in his papal policy, John was a failure. He won love forever; but the respect Khrushchev spoke of will never be his. There had been better popes than John. He had organized his desired forum, the Ecumenical Council. He had reached out and touched the hearts of believers in all religions. He had drawn the curious and puzzled gazes of those who would have nothing of religion. So far, he had succeeded. Everyone was dressed up, at his bidding. But, lamentably, they never had anywhere to go. John awaited the outpouring. There was none. He hoped for a new birth in the spirit. Nothing was born. The gamble failed. The jig was up. *Finità la commedia*. The era of compassion was over.

As always, when compassion dies, there is born an inevitable illusion. The spirit of man is stubborn beyond all knowing and pigheaded beyond all the limits of reasonable hope. John's religious enemies within his Church were cackling piously of God's will. But his friends, deprived of his vision, would refuse the cold appraisal of which John had been capable. They would become fascinated with their own actions. Mistaking bureaucratization for progress and continuation, persuaded that their own febrile activity was inspired, they would transform John's forum for renewal into a fantastic eccelesiastical amusement park littered with the debris of paper resolutions and official documents, overshadowed by the ferris wheel of ecumenism, resounding to the marionettes of clerical castes. The voice of his entire hope was changed to an insular crescendo of inbred clericalism, stitching and patching the ragged ends of worn-out ideologies and "isms," much as the marooned and destitute do in their desire to maintain the illusion of human continuation.

Part V

———✦———

THE FIRST UN-POPE

26

The Wisdom

After the Council, it is as if Roncalli's Event has happened, but in a remote place. Far from the humdrum trails of ordinary Catholic life. A great light had burst into brilliance. Relayed messages told of its healing incandescence. Returning messengers, bishops, theologians, writers, inculcated its panacea brightness: it lit the future, all the dark corners of the future; it blotted out the past, every hoary relic of dormant uselessness. Daily, it was expected. Universally, it was hoped for. It was so far away, however, that there was a time lag. You had to wait awhile. The Event was a light-star. Its rays were racing through interminable space. The star was finished, dead, gone, recalled to the silent womb of treasured moments. But messengers and messages, dispatched before it ended, told of the newness borne on those rays. And it would not be long in coming. When it came, so burned the expectation, thus shone the hope, all would be new.

The expectation and the hope were real, and due to many things. Partly ignorance. Partly desire. Partly the end pangs of a patience too much tried by waiting. Partly the illusions of a faith too much tested by commands to hold, stand firm, and trust the darkness. Chiefly, the ineradicable memories of Roncalli and trust in him who promised them Pentecostal newness with compassion they had never known before, and who had made them live for some short moments in a smiling landscape trod and tilled by all men as the sons of God and brothers to each other.

257

This expectation would not die. The hope refused all quenching.

One day, when an ordinary dawn displayed an unchanged world, familiar grayness, and all the old defeating obstacles and bogies, it was too much. It was refused. To do otherwise would be to panic. The Event must have taken place. Surely. All had really changed. But you had to live it now, make it now, change things now. The long-tested faith took the ignorance as a mystical instruction giving innate knowledge for action. The tried patience took the desire as irresistible movements of the Spirit. And there was born a wisdom and a madness specific and peculiar to the post-Conciliar age.

The "new age" is Genesis all over again, a formlessness best described in the first few verses of the Bible, with not a little touch of chaos. The Roman Catholic universe used to have clear and definite contours. The authoritative heavens above: pope, Vatican, cardinals, bishops, priests, religious. The solid earth below: the "good Catholic people," docile and faithful, supplying moral support, babies, money, candidates for church offices, and never ending trust. The Spirit, the Holy Spirit, not only hovered over the whole thing; he whispered in the heavens, so that what the authorities said and decreed was literally the voice of God. All in all, a clearly defined universe, and no nonsense about where anybody stood.

Now, there is no longer a recognizable firmament of heaven above men's heads. Or, at least, so men begin to think and reflect in their words. There is, instead, an elected official traditionally called the pope and served by a backtracking, dyed-in-the-wool, inherently conservative bureaucracy trying to restrain the spirit and the wishes of John XXIII's Council. The *dramatis personae* of the heavens have been reduced in number: many priests are out of it, have ranged themselves against those heavens; some bishops also, even a cardinal or two, and many theologians, canon lawyers, and writers. There is no longer a solid earth. It has become a tohuwabohu of voices clamoring to be heard as holy above all others, some as the voice of John XXIII's Council, some as the futurists predicting woeful things and nasty cataclysms for all religion. The Spirit is the most extraordinarily changed of all the original elements. It is now a complex of wild winds rushing over shaking institutions, making them unfit to house what man has hitherto held as sacred. There is, in fact, formlessness due to ever changing forms, and in between the new heavens and earth a subtle chaos enveloping the vast body of Roman Catholics. They find they no longer know what should be held, who should speak authoritatively, where the truth lies, or what is happening. This is the darkness.

The wisdom of the post-Conciliar age is claimed by the remnant of the ancient heavens. The madness is the moving force which has stirred up the inhabitants of the earth. Both wisdom and madness are facets of the same thing: a frustrated Roman Catholic mind which refused to admit cold reality. Roncalli's gamble had failed. The Spirit had refused. It hovered for a while above the chaos broodingly. Both the wise and the mad claim to be possessed of the Spirit Roncalli did, indeed, invoke, and to move within the shadow of its wings. Heirs, therefore, of the newness and the renovation promised originally by the great Event. For the wise, the "others" are mad. For the mad, the "others" are not wise. But the wise claim continuity in power and in authority to preserve an ancient deposit of faith. And the mad claim continuity in power and in authority to preserve the "spirit of John XXIII." There is in the making, therefore, a model of disintegration, a tech manual on how-to-tear-an-institution-apart-without-having-really-tried. The unity of the Roman Catholic Church, then, as an organization is a done thing. Montini, as Paul VI, presides over a fragmenting body. He is the Prince of Agony, straitened by the wisdom, beset by the madness, haunted by the futurists.

No doubt about it. Montini sees it all in 1963, when he becomes pope and shoulders the responsibility for Roncalli's Council. Five days after his election on June 22, 1963, he announces that the second session of the Council will open on September 29. In the meantime, he revised the Council rules in order to facilitate greater speed in getting through the proposed Council discussions and a greater freedom for the participants. Better get it all over and done with as quickly and as cleanly as possible. His opening address on September 29 swings Roncalli's Council into the mainstream of all Church councils. The Council's purpose now, he declared, was to define more clearly the role of bishops in Church government, to introduce new meaning into Church functions, to work for Christian unity, and to start a dialogue with the contemporary world. Montini's decision was clear: while he had the prelates assembled together, he wanted to get some unanimity from them in order to preserve the structure of the Church, threatened as it was by the increasing isolation of the papal office and by the growing indifference of Catholics to the functional life of the Church. He saw that some start must be made in establishing meaningful relationships with men outside the Church. The wisdom of the post-Conciliar period is embodied in this mentality.

The essence of that wisdom is that certain concessions must be made in order to cope with the situation. Each of those concessions has but one purpose: to involve more people—innocuously—in the existing structure: bishops in the overall government of the Church, priests in the government of dioceses, lay people in the government of parishes (and to some degree in that of dioceses). It is, thus, that synods of bishops meet in Rome periodically: these have a purely advisory capacity. There are senates of priests in dioceses to advise the bishops. In each parish, there is a council composed of laymen, religious, and priests, again with an advisory function. Some of the pope's ministries in Rome (the Congregations) are opened up to a wider membership: the Congregation for the Propagation of the Faith, which is in charge of all missionary activity, receives representatives of missionaries actively working in mission fields.

Within the ambit of that wisdom, according to the decrees of the Council, and sometimes in accordance solely with the spirit of the Council, Mass is said in vernacular languages, Communion of both bread and wine is permitted to the laity, several priests may concelebrate Mass. People need no longer kneel when receiving Communion. In some places, the laity receive Communion into their own hands. National offices of the Roman Secretariat for the Supervision of Publications and Entertainment are established, and lay experts from foreign countries are appointed to the center in Rome. Other "liberalizations" concern annulment procedures for marriages: local ecclesiastical courts around the world are now conceded greater freedom in deciding such annulments and need less recourse to Rome.

Thus, the total *juridical* effect of the Council is to permit a greater participation (passive rather than active) in Church government and functions to those who hitherto were excluded on various levels. The total effect on the *morale* of the members is only measurable by the results. Insofar as these are already visible, there is no evidence that this participatory wisdom of the Council has resulted in any renewed vigor, or that it has brought the Church as a church nearer to all men or some groups of men in particular. The contrary seems to be the case: the very principle of this wisdom seems only to whet the appetite of madness.

It is not so much the evidence of statistics which counts here, although there is some significance in the fact that the number of young men studying for the priesthood in the United States has been reduced nearly by half since 1966. It is, more importantly, that there is no evidence that the Roman Catholic Church has been thereby introduced more actively into the common problems of human society as a religious body. A greater structuralism has certainly resulted, and with that there comes the usual consequences of inertia, spent efforts, disappointments, and restricted goals. In a sense, the procedures of this wisdom have been boring for Roman Catholics.

An analogous result of greater confusion with no tangibly positive result is to be noted in the case of the well-known Dutch Catechism. This was published in Holland in 1966. Cardinal Alfrink, Primate of Holland, and the Dutch bishops had given their permission. Romans reacted very unfavorably and vigorously. Montini appointed, first, one commission of cardinals, then another cardinalitial commission. One of them recommended that at least a third of the book be revised and emended in order to bring it into line. But the authors and patrons of the Catechism refused. By then it had been translated into at least three languages.

Montini makes his own stand and in his own way. He takes the opportunity to publish a Credo on June 30, 1968, which repeats the ancient truths of the Catholic faith integrally and in the ancient order . . . "We believe in God, Father, Son, Holy Spirit, creator of visible things in the world . . ." It is hailed by conservatives and reviled by progressives. But the juxtaposition of the Credo and the Catechism baffles the majority of Catholics.

Actually, the Catechism slurs over most of those points of Catholic faith which today are difficult to explain in the light of science and archaeology: the creation of man, original sin, the original conception of Jesus, the Trinity, for example. If the Catechism errs, it errs by omission, by opaque statements, and by vague definitions. The net result of this exercise of wisdom on everybody's part was clear: Rome could not prevent the publication and dissemination of a document it considered erroneous; the ordinary believer had two formulae of his faith to contend with; clearly, the Dutch cardinal and his bishops in their wisdom would not comply with the Pope and his Vatican officials in their wisdom.

Again, when Hans Kung, Swiss theologian and thinker, published his *Infallibility? An Enquiry,* the same result was noticeable. Kung questioned the pope's infallibility (in a newspaper article he stated that he really had "nothing against the pope personally; I have always respected his good intentions"). His main contention was that no one person or group in the Church has the privilege of infallibility in proclaiming dogmas of belief. The German bishops, gathered at Munich, refused to condemn the book or to declare that the pope had the privilege of infallibility. They stated that the book does not uphold "several fundamental elements of the Catholic understanding of faith and of the Church." The nearest they came to saying anything about infallibility was a statement which for sheer involution, mental gymnastics, verbalizing subterfuges, and open-ended meanings is difficult to beat. It went: "The possibility exists, in principle, of declarations which are true and recognizable as such, and the sense of which remains unaltered and unvaried in value within the historical changing of the modes of thoughts and expression."

This is a statement which could be applied to any human science and be appropriated by any human being of any creed, outlook, philosophy, or culture. There is nothing specifically Christian or Catholic about it. It can literally mean anything, including that the pope is infallible, perhaps. But it could also mean what Kung later contended: "The bishops thus allow margin for further constructive discussion about this highly important question for the Church today." The net result of this exercise of wisdom on Rome's part and by the German bishops was to confuse the ordinary layman further. Was the pope infallible or not? Was the First Vatican Council wrong or right in declaring his infallibility?

The wisdom of allowing a participation in the structure reduces itself then to the concession of more liberal provisions. But each of these provisions has the air of a concession, a privilege granted from on high. None of them can be construed as a reaching out in compassion and understanding for the persons of the Church. They are the conclusions of a deliberate compromise. Compromise can go so far. Both Rome and the bishops of the Church have found it necessary to draw a hard line at one point or another. Some years ago, fifty-nine priests of the Archdiocese of Washington signed a public statement supporting the right of individuals to follow their own conscience and thus perhaps contravene the Church's anti-contraception laws which Montini had outlined in a special letter, *Humanae Vitae*. In a final recourse to the Vatican over the head of their cardinal, Patrick O'Boyle, the priests were told to comply with the teaching norms laid down by the Cardinal and by the Church. The American affair had to end like that.

In Europe and elsewhere, the wisdom intervened to create further confusion. It had all started off with the creation by Roncalli of a pontifical commission in 1963. Its eight members were demographers, and they were supposed to study the possibility of some evolution in traditional Catholic doctrine concerning contraception. Montini increased its membership to fourteen, then to sixty in 1964. In 1966, he added to the existent commission another super-commission composed of sixteen cardinals and bishops. This super-commission acquired twenty specialists immediately. Cardinal Ottaviani was made chairman of another small, eight-member committee in 1967. A majority of all members were in favor of some change in Roman Catholic law. It is reported also that 80 percent of the delegates to episcopal synods in the year 1967 were of a like mind. Paul, however, decided to bypass all this. He issued his letter *Humanae Vitae*, which restated the traditional prohibition of all and every kind of artificial contraception, contraceptive device, or action.

Episcopal reactions to the letter were predictable. The Austrians asserted that the letter created problems of conscience. The Germans advised the priests to respect the decisions which lay people took. The Belgians declared that all were bound by the letter, but, of course, nobody was bound by it as by a dogmatic definition. The French said that, of course contraception was a disorder, but you must realize that this particular disorder is not always culpable. The Canadians said of course the Pope was right but those who do not obey him must not be considered as outcasts. The English and Welsh declared their spirit of obedience to the Holy Father but added that nobody is bound to violate his own conscience. Both the wisdom of the bishops and the wisdom of Montini resulted in making a laughingstock of any claim of theirs to represent a *teaching authority*. It was all a matter of words.

The one bridge which the Council would seem to have thrown across the gulf to non-Catholics is that of ecumenism. Since the Council, Roman Catholics have been authorized to consort with non-Catholic Christians in prayer and study activities. Into this ecumenism there has also been introduced a further note which at first sight seems to savor of Roncalli's original idea: ecumenism is not being restricted to Christians: Jews, first of all, but also other non-Christians, are coming into the movement. After all, this ecumenism has nothing to exclude them. We find that the same post-Conciliar wisdom is at work within the same impossible limits. There are manifest the same incipient signs of the madness always consequent on the niggardliness of that wisdom and its impossible position as a halfway house.

Originally, in Roncalli's concept, there was to be no such hybrid as Catholic ecumenism. Indeed, there would be no more need for ecumenism as such, Protestant or Catholic. Ecumenism had its roots in the Protestant mind with its inherent tendency to so respect individual idiosyncrasies that any form of unity really amounted to an amalgam, a collection of non-warring but distinct bodies. The principle of that ecumenism allows of nothing but a polite permissiveness and a turning away of the eyes from whatever displeases us or whatever we cannot share in the other man. No ecumenical merger or union has created or could create a living spirit and a veritable church. Ecumenism need not end up as a cocktail religion; its grandest aim is the religious smorgasbord, something for everybody, everybody for something, all for everybody, provided anybody can be himself and still belong.

At most, it can dispose people to receive the Spirit—provided that their ecumenism is built on the principle that nobody is right, all are deficient, and all must sink their deficiencies as well as their differences. The ecumenism of the Council, however, is a process resembling the attempt of the Ugly Sisters to fit that beautiful glass shoe of Cinderella on ungainly feet: pare away an inconsequential toenail, slice a bit of the heel, suffer a little pain and loss. It attempts to level all distinctions while maintaining the most important distinctions. In the end, to achieve any "unity," it must make all religions the same by reduction to a common level if not to the lowest common denominator, and each religion becomes just a facet of the one, same, grand, unknown, and unknowable Blob of Loveliness.

There is, in principle, a thing called Christian ecumenism. In practice and to be logical, it should be called human ecumenism. For its principles allow any religion of any source or character to be part of its undistinguished and inoffensive whole. This is the tendency and the practical effect of what is called Christian ecumenism today, into which Roman Catholics may now enter under certain conditions. But this is where the gleam of madness appears. It does not stop with Christian children participating in a Jewish Seder, nor should it—in principle. Nor is there anything inherently wrong in the consecration of Episcopalian Bishop P. Varley of Salisbury, Maryland, in the Roman

Catholic Cathedral of Omaha. There is a certain satisfaction in seeing General W. Creighton Abrams, Commander of American troops in Vietnam, standing beside Roman Catholic Bishop Paul Nguyen van Binh and Ellsworth Bunker, U.S. Ambassador to Saigon, as lay readers at the Ecumenical Service of Prayer for Peace, Brotherhood and Christian Unity in Saigon Roman Catholic Cathedral, on June 27, 1971. But the wisdom which allows this has no plan of action able to curb the madness which eventually takes over such a movement.

For half a loaf will never satisfy the human hunger for sinking differences—if that is all there is to it. Ecumenism is the most marvelous system by which those differences can be sunk, and all can come together, somehow or other. It fixes the Star of David on the arm of the Cross, stands the Cross in the Buddhist Lotus which sprouts from the Altar and Fire of Zoroaster in the Sacred Shinto Gateway of Torii, hangs the Moslem Star and Crescent with the Tao symbol for Unity of All things in the sky above, and embroiders the floor with a mosaic of the Hindu Wheel, Yin and Yang, the Hexagrams of China, and the ideograms of Kung Fu-tzu. A dizzying amalgam. A meaningless juxtaposition. A syncrisis of irreconcilables. A Babel of Languages.

The latest expression of this syncretistic confusion leading to the Most Unsatisfying Nothing of Unobjectionableness to All and Sundry was presented at the Graymoor Ecumenical Institute (Garrison, N.Y.) in 1971. "I prefer to speak today as a Hindu, which I am," said Raymond Pannikar, an Indian Jesuit priest, "and not as a Christian." He outlined the Hindu ascent to perfection. First, *puja*: "concentration by taking an icon to serve as a meeting point between me and what is not yet me, what I am seeking to discover." Then comes *java*: concentration through a vocal prayer or a name. A name "indicates that man is not fully himself, if he fails to recognize that which is outside." Then there is *dhyana* (Chinese *Chan*, Japanese *Zen*): you concentrate yourself, "gathering all the centrifugal forces in you; you don't strip off things; you concentrate them." Finally, one arrives at *samadhi*: "liberation takes place, so that the world has reversed the process from creator to creature and it has come back to creator. You now literally do what you like to do. You are liberated. You no longer need to concentrate, because everything is centered in harmony."

Declaring that India has seven million gurus, and that Christianity is the only cause of atheism there, Pannikar commented that it is so important to get to *samadhi*, that if LSD achieves it for someone, then LSD is the answer for that person. Pannikar was succeeded by Brother David Steindl-Rast, a Benedictine monk, who summed it all up: "Buddhism expressed the theology of the Father, Hinduism the theology of the Holy Spirit, and Christianity tells about the word." Father Theodore Stylianopoulos put the entire philosophy of the post-Conciliar madness in a nutshell: prayer is experience, response, and action, rather than thought.

Fundamentally, the wisdom of the post-Conciliar age is an exercise of power. Unfortunately, in the period of Roncalli's pontificate there was a dawning of compassion and, born from that, an expectation that all the structures of power as known hitherto would be dissolved or bypassed in a new wave of belief and fresh activity. Thus, any concession by the wisdom of the age is taken as a meager remnant of what should be granted. For there is alive in the Roman Catholic Church a religious faith of enormous proportions and of burning depths. It is hungry and isolated, frustrated and fuming to be "with it." But the wisdom of structuralism merely frustrates that faith.

It induces a madness of frustration and a fecklessness that truly savors of iconoclasm. As affairs stand today, the tug-of-war between the wisdom and the faith is going to vary back and forth, seesawing between the iron-clad resistance of entrenched power centers of the Church and the volatile, directionless, and, in the final analysis, self-disruptive forces loose in the Church, at bay with the Church's authority, and impermeable to any allurement, blandishment, or concession of power.

27

The Madness

There is some mysterious element in religious faith. It is something that defies rational analysis, is not governed by logic, is deaf to all contrary appeals, is always right in its own eyes, is not consequential. It has always frightened civil governments and the holders of political power, because it has an irrational appeal which inflames the will but numbs the mind, and can therefore be impervious to reason. It defies their laws in the name of a higher law. It scorns their threats, imprisonment, exile, death. It will violate those laws and feel justified. It will adopt violence to spread its creed, because "the Kingdom of Heaven suffers violence and the violent bear it away." It will even shed blood to achieve its purpose, because it believes that it shall live here on earth until the end limit of time and hereafter forever in the endless grandeur of eternity. Just a change of scenery. At least the three great religions, Judaism, Christianity, and Islam, were baptized in blood: Judaism in the slaughter of the Pharaoh's Egyptians, Jesus on his cross, Mohammed with his holy wars and ruthless armies. A pacifist way of life such as Buddhism which lacked this faith never created a great civilization.

When that first form of religious faith is let loose and housed within an ordered structure, one of two things can happen. It can pour into every part of the structure. It can infuse every nook and cranny, covering every inch of its extent. It will renew any aging members, soften, lubricate, and liquefy hardened joints. This is the faith which moves mountains. It is not hypocritically

267

passive, nor is it wearingly active. It provides good taste as well
as good morals. It nourishes harmony, culture, peace. It evokes
the poet, because it sanctifies nature without sinking man to the
level of nature: and lyrics are born. It inspires the mystic, because it shows him how all things are in God and not merely how
God is in all things. It does not conform to its surroundings or,
chameleon-like, adopt the color of passions and the texture of
desires which rack those surroundings. It makes its surroundings its own, kneading, molding, transforming all with a newfound plasticity. It revivifies, rejuvenates, enlightens, and
makes young again. It does all this because it has a monopoly
on enthusiasm, is primarily borne on the will, and has an unerr-
ing instinct for what is good, what is proportionate, what is fitting. It thus sees the mysteries brooding over all things human.
It is forever looking to the dark periphery of things unknown, of
emotions untried, to the heart of matter, the heart of man, the
heart of the universe, and the heart of God in its highest peak
and in its deepest fathoms.

It seems, however, to be a condition of its high efflorescence
that it be housed in a structure as its naturalized and adopted
environment. Religious faith only lives, survives, and is perpetuated in a living condition by generations of living men. Men
themselves have different characters, differing needs, diverse
tendencies, habits, heredities, and constitutions. Religious
faith of itself has no order, no instinct for the priorities of survival in the conditions of physical life and the demands of material progress. It needs a structure. If religious faith becomes at
variance with its chosen habitat, it can refuse the principles
which made possible the unifying of different men and diverse
human trends beneath one roof. It can, in fact, arrogate to itself
the functions which only the structure can discharge. The consequences are dire. For the faith now conforms to its surroundings, and in so doing undoes itself.

The religious faith, or, properly speaking, the men of that
faith, will be gripped by a contrariness. They can turn on themselves as religionists and commit spiritual suicide. The faith that
once united them will end up diseased, afflicted with elephan-
tiasis of the spirit, gone stark mad, mounted against itself. The
former inhabitants of the structure will splinter into warring
groups.

They can become like the members of a once united family
who are now riven by suspicion, frustration, and fear: breaking

the furniture to demonstrate their independence, violating house rules and flaunting established customs, shouting and gesticulating insanely at each other in order to fill the void they cannot bear to contemplate calmly; self-dramatizing, scattering poison among themselves, proposing and disposing according to the wild whim of the moment, dashing off under any impulse that comes, without orientation, without a lodestone to guide them. The members of that faith can end up as merely lost people, wandering in a hopeless and homeless universe in which God at the end kills himself because man went mad on him. God is dead. The post-Conciliar madness of the Roman Catholic Church shows the incipient signs of such tendencies.

The madness is born, as was said, from the firm expectation that the Event had really taken place, that all was changed, that they now had to go forth and take possession in the name of God. To some this will seem akin to the aspiring pride which flung Satan from the face of heaven. To others it will be the surcease of disappointment or the issue of ignorance. But, in truth, there is such sincerity and such a patent confidence and hope that a form of madness best describes it. For the behavior of the afflicted plunges them into a troubled sea to search for a desperate and unfounded hope. The pathos does not lie in the delusionary character of this search; such a will-o'-the-wisp hope is much like what the wisping fata morgana was for delirious Norman sailor eyes in search of a friendly shore in alien seas. The pathos lies rather in the fact that men of religious faith thus surrender the very birthright of the faith: its transforming power.

They and their faith no longer transform anything. They are transformed by this world, conformed to its conditions, its ideals, afflicted with the universal problems, hemmed in by the same insufficiency of solutions and of light for solutions, that afflict the rest of men. They no longer are unique because of a unique spirit, and no longer special because of a specially made solution of which they are the bearers. Man's weak solutions and troubled spirit are uniquely theirs. They share in the democratization, the facile activism, the intellectual structuralism, and the false sense of mystery characteristic of the age.

The democratization of the Roman Catholic Church is a onetime thing. It could only happen in the present socio-political conditions of the United States and the world over. It cannot last for very long. Bishop Maurice Dingman of Des Moines expressed the central idea of democratization very well: "The whole Church is looking for the democratic experience, and the U.S. Church has this democratic experience, because of its political, cultural and social life."

The democratization already is an ongoing process. A bevy of new organizations have sprung up: the National Association of Catholic Laymen, the National Federation of Priests' Councils, the National Association of Women Religious, the Young Priests' Caucus of Chicago, the Association of Chicago Priests, the National Office of Black Catholics, the Association of Mexican-American Nuns. Some of these are not very representative. The Association of Chicago Priests represents only 900 out of 2,400 priests in the archdiocese of Chicago. The National Association of Women Religious represented only 4,409 out of 160,000 American nuns in its first year of existence. But the National Federation of Priests' Councils, for instance, draws its representatives from 122 out of 148 American dioceses.

Opposing these new progressive associations are arrayed organizations such as the Pastors' Associations (of older priests), the Sons of Thunder (militant conservative youth), Catholics United for the Faith, the National Wanderer Forum, and others. The lay folk thus organized have taken to heart, and more literally than the Pope intended them, what he wrote in his encyclical letter *On the Development of Peoples*: "It belongs to the laity, without waiting passively for orders and directives, to take the initiative freely and to infuse a Christian spirit into the mentality, customs, laws, and structures of the community in which they live." The actions and mode of procedure employed follow a strictly democratizing trend.

They advocate a compulsory retiring age for bishops, the ministry of women, the end of mandatory celibacy, wider experimentation in the ministry with "non-geographical parishes," a bill of human rights for priests, the removal of all military chaplains from the Armed Forces (in protest against the war in Vietnam). The Association of Chicago Priests proposed to censure their archbishop, Cardinal Cody, and his auxiliary bishops, for failure to afford them adequate representation in Rome. At the annual United States bishops meeting in Detroit, in 1971, seven women delegates from the National Organization for Women protested at a press conference against the "sexist" character of the Church; the National Federation of Laymen stated at their news conference that the bishops had failed to deal effectively with the critical mistakes in catechetical teachings; the Young Priests' Caucus opened a "hospitality suite" on the seventh floor of the hotel, inviting the bishops attending the annual meeting to drop in to discuss such relevant things as mandatory celibacy. One did.

The democratization principle is extended quite far. Father J. Meyer, assistant in Pontiac, Detroit, filed charges to remove his pastor, Father R. W. Thomas, from his office as pastor. In Bridgeport, Connecticut, a poll was taken among lay people concerning such things as lay participation in the election of bishops, non-mandatory celibacy, and the ministry of women.

The new activism of Catholics carries them into varied sectors of public interest: civil rights, environmental pollution, the war in Vietnam, drug addiction. The activism extends to all levels. Young girls wish to act as altar girls, as they did for a while at St. Matthias Church in Philadelphia. Forty-two children in Genoa, Italy, refused to accept the sacrament of confirmation from their Bishop as a "sign of solidarity" with other children who had been refused the sacrament because, the Bishop maintained, they were inadequately prepared. Nine members of a large American Catholic inquiry group were arrested trying to say Mass on the steps of St. Peter's Basilica, in Rome, in protest against the silence of the Vatican about the Vietnamese war. Father Gerard Lutte, a Belgian, stayed on as chaplain of the Roman shack dwellers in spite of an order from his superiors and the relevant authorities of the Vatican to leave the Eternal City. He is still there. Father J. Manseau, a censored priest, became pastor of the Congregational church at Dunstable, Mass. Father Duryea, married secretly for seven years, functioned as pastor in Pacifica, California, until his bishop found out; he was excommunicated and removed from his post.

More and more priests and nuns are entering the area of socio-political activity. Nuns are withdrawing voluntarily from "racist schools"; they wish, in all events, "to be deeply involved in the problems of war and peace," as was stated at the last meeting of the National Federation. Priests run for Congress and state legislatures. One has become a speech writer for President Nixon. Father Groppi makes headlines for his stand on housing and job rights. The White Fathers, a religious order, are withdrawing from Mozambique, in protest against the colonialist policies of Portugal, the occupying power.

The Vietnam War has claimed a lot of attention. Some nuns and priests signed the People's Peace Treaty with North Vietnam in its initial form. Forty-five American clergy and laymen went to Paris, spoke with the Vietcong representatives (the Provisional

Revolutionary Government), with the representatives of the Democratic Republic of North Vietnam, as well as with clergy from North and South Vietnam and with the American delegation, finally issuing an appeal to halt the war and for Americans to return home "now." Another group of Catholic priests tried to say a Mass for peace on the steps of the Pentagon, but they were arrested. At Fordham University, at the annual ordinations of new priests, one of the priests refused to give the kiss of peace to Cardinal Cooke of New York, on the ground that the Cardinal was the Military Vicar of all the Armed Forces. The Berrigan brothers, noted for their antiwar stand, have drawn strong endorsements from religious, priests, and nuns, and from lay people.

In South America, the involvement of the clergy, of laymen, of nuns, and even of some bishops is more extreme. There are cases such as that of Father Camilo Torres, a Colombian priest killed on February 15, 1966, while fighting as a guerrilla against government forces. He stated before his death that a "socialist revolution" was needed "so that the hungry would be fed, the thirsty given drink, and the naked clothed, and to bring about the well-being of the majority of our people." There are a sufficiently impressive number of priests and nuns who have taken up guerrilla arms.

Usually, the energies of Roman Catholic activism are channeled into political avenues. The new political liberalism of the Church in South America draws its inspiration from the views ascribed to John XXIII. In Chile there is a "Christian Marxism" among members of the Jesuit order. The Dominican order are noted for their anti-government stand in Brazil and Bolivia. The bishops of Chile called on the Socialist-Marxist regime of President Salvador Allende to aid them in their fight against contraception, alleging that it was Karl Marx who stated that "marriage is above the whim of the individual by virtue of its social dimension." President Allende himself gracefully returned the compliment, saying that some bishops at least had identified with the poor, and adding: "Before, for centuries, the Catholic Church defended the interests of the powerful. Today the Church, after John XXIII, has become oriented toward making the Gospels of Christ a reality, at least in some places."

An echo of the "Christian Marxism" beginning to show its face in South America was sounded in, of all places, the diocese of Bolzano-Bressanone, Italy. Eighty priests and seventy-five lay people composed a document supporting Marxism against capitalism (at least, they stated, Marxism did not facilitate the exploitation of the working classes).

Other issues have come up to plague the Catholic Church and the Pope. Montini has been asked by the people of Worms, where Martin Luther was condemned four hundred years ago, to rescind that condemnation. Women's Lib has also entered the arena. Nuns demand equal rights with men: they wish to attain diaconate and even priesthood in the Church. Doctrinally, some go further. Dr. Elizabeth Farians told a conference at the Synod House of St. John the Divine that she envisioned a second coming of Jesus, but this time he would come as a black female divine principle. Thus, she concluded, our human idea of God would be complete. "If Jesus was not a feminist, then he didn't come from God," she added.

The structuralism of the post-Conciliar age takes many forms. It is manifest, for instance, in the recent discussion about mandatory celibacy for priests. In 1970 alone, there was a loss of 1,476 priests, and there was a drop of 12½ percent in new priests. In the United States in 1966–70, the number of enrolled candidates for the priesthood dropped by almost fifty percent. The polls were quite definite: of the priests under forty years of age who were polled, eight out of every ten were against mandatory celibacy; of those over fifty years of age, about 50 percent were against it. One half of those under thirty years of age were thinking of resigning in order to get married; 44 percent thought of resigning for other reasons (dissatisfaction with their work, status, etc.). This post-Conciliar intellectual process is modeled on a structuralist premise: the majority are in favor of doing away with mandatory celibacy; therefore, it must be done away with. But the principle behind this reasoning, if applied overall to the doctrines and practices of the Catholic Church or, indeed, of any religion, would do away finally with the need of a fixed theology or a precious tradition. All would depend on the statistical poll and the inductive conclusion drawn from figures.

Another aspect of post-Conciliar structuralism is provided by the recent action of the Canon Law Society of America. The members studied a draft of a new constitution for the Roman Catholic Church which had been composed in Rome. They then drew up a sharply worded letter of criticism, recommending that the draft be rejected on the grounds that it is regressive and would erode the already diminishing respect for law and ecclesiastical authority. There is little doubt that the proposed constitution was drafted by minds out of tune with the concrete con-

ditions obtaining in the United States, for instance. But the
Society went on to state what it thought should be produced: "a
declaration of essential rights and government principles in the
light of the experience of Vatican II." Hans Kung, the Swiss
theologian and author of *Infallibility? An Enquiry,* which has
been already mentioned, codified the stand of post-Conciliar
structuralism under five headings: (1) demythologize and deideo-
logize the teaching office of the Church; (2) abstain from all infallible decisions and develop a more constructive form of
preaching the Christian message in the modern world; (3) protest against the official Roman stand against birth control, abortion, optional celibacy, the Dutch Catechism, and such matters;
(4) "push on toward a solution of infallibility," the chief obsta-
cle to an ecumenical union of the Churches; (5) rethink the historical character of the Church, seeking a better intellectual
foundation for faith, renewing Catholic teaching, and allowing
the reality of Jesus Christ to shine in a refurbished ecclesiastical system.

This stand of Kung's is echoed, with some nuances, in the
opinions and statements of Cardinal Suenens, the Primate of
Belgium. Suenens declared shortly after the Council that "there
is no longer any question of the pope governing the Church without the bishops." He further outlined how the Church would develop, never asserting, always suggesting, sometimes using a
rhetorical question to make a point without seeming to affirm it.
He condemned any view of the pope's function as "a right to be
exercised at will (*ad placitum*), a 'whenever-I-like' style of
thing." The good of the Church could require a lesser number of
papal interventions. He spoke of a "certain pluralism on various
levels" of the Church. "The more active bishops are, the quicker
local churches will have their own physiognomy, the better the
Christian people will expand in a diversity of rites, of theologies,
of studies, and of customs."

Along with Suenens of Belgium, Cardinal Alfrink of Holland
and other northern churchmen have voiced similar opinions, always adding an affirmation of their allegiance to the Pope. There
is, in other words, a new form of ecclesiology coming into vogue
in certain parts of the Roman Catholic Church. It intends to di-
lute the centralist power of the Vatican and the dogmatic infallibility of the pope with other equalizing elements in the
Church.

This same idea was made clear in the aftermath of the criticism of the Dutch Catechism. The six cardinals appointed by Paul were a mixture of progressive and conservative: Jaeger and Frings (Germany), Florit (Italy), Browne (Ireland), Lefebvre (France), Journet (Switzerland). They listed more than a hundred places where, they said, the language of the catechism was inexact and of doubtful meaning. Their critique was attacked by a blue-ribbon list of such theologians as Kung and Rahner (Germany), Schillebeeckx (Holland), Tucci (Italy), Chenu (France). "Any form of inquisition, however unobstructive, injures the development of a healthy theology and hurts the Church's credibility in the world today," these men wrote.

The false sense of mystery and of mystical involvement, a characteristic of this age, can be illustrated in two ways: the new theological mystique of blacks, and the Roman Catholic revolutionary mystique. The new theological mystique of blacks is called by its advocates "a functional black theology." They seek to fashion it by fusing the feelings of black consciousness with the traditionally strong Negro religious feeling. It is the National Committee of Black Churchmen who are most vocal about the new mystique. On the Committee are grouped Roman Catholic priests, Protestants of different kinds, black Jews and black Muslims, and black "humanists." Together they produced the Black Declaration of Independence last summer.

Father Lucas, a Roman Catholic black pastor in Harlem, has voiced the new mystique in his book *Black Priest, White Church*: "For years white Catholics have been talking about a colorless Christ who was savior of all men and open to receive and relate to all men. And the more they said this, the harder they fed black people a lily-white Jesus, concerned only with white interests . . . This white Jesus loved black people who desired and strove to be white."

The blackness of God and everything implied by it in a racist society, stated Dr. James H. Cone, is the heart of black theology's doctrine of God. Another member, Calvin O. Pressley, stated bluntly: "Theology is by definition what one does, not what one thinks." The Committee aims at doing away with the idea of a "spiritual white Jesus," which never existed. It aims, instead, at reconstructing "the historic black Jesus who was a revolutionary leader attempting to build a black nation." And Father Lucas commented on his own mission as a priest: "I am preaching to blacks the Gospels of Christ. Not the Gospels of Christ as distorted by white people for white interests." The mystical aim of the new theology is, "not the abstract, the universal, the infinite, but the fulfillment of black people in this life, by all means appropriate."

The Roman Catholic revolutionary mystique is an altogether *ad hoc* thing. It is put together to suit the concrete situation of the moment. For Thomas and Marjorie Melville, the issues are clear. "Pope John XXIII changed things . . . He spelled out Catholic responsibility in social matters and launched the process of making the Church relevant to twentieth-century consciousness of war, racism, and poverty." The Melvilles have lost faith in "the ideal of propagating an institutional church." Catholics have been blocked from implementing John XXIII's wishes by the weak Pope Paul VI and his retrogressive Vatican officials. The only recourse, then, is revolution, which implies counterviolence.

Both the Melvilles and Daniel Berrigan speak ominously of the near-future struggle. "The struggle is only beginning," state the Melvilles. "We are in the dark preliminary stages of a new humanity," states Berrigan. "The conflagration is rising . . . We are called to grow new organs by new conditions of life and death." Berrigan, however, has sought justification and rationalization of his stand in the writings of St. John of the Cross. The latter confined himself exclusively to describing an inner conversion of the soul which ascends to God by means of a purification. Saint John had no eye whatever on the social institutions of his day. He was not concerned with wars, poverty, racism, military-industrial complexes, student protest, or revolutionary arms. Berrigan, however, translates John's spiritual instructions into his own context. In the process, Berrigan likens himself subtly (perhaps unconsciously) to John.

"John," wrote Berrigan, "wanted a community in which men would choose for themselves how they would live and where." John is "guru of the absurd." In another place, speaking *sotto voce* of himself, he states that "guru John was generating a storm, predicting it, welcoming it." Although Berrigan protests that, in speaking as he does, "one is not thereby being apocalyptic or self-fullfilling or screwed up," there is throughout his statements a sense of imminent danger and cataclysm, an insistence on the need to gird ourselves for great and bitter trials. This outlook we can only describe as apocalyptic.

There is, in addition, a note of death-wishing, a messianic strain issuing in statements that claim absolute adhesion, and an imperative call to action along the lines followed by Berrigan.

The imperative for him, as for the Melvilles, is to resist by new revolutionary means what America has become—ugly, imperialist, corrupt and corrupting—and thus aid in inaugurating a new era. It is all there, as in the old manifestoes: the forces of darkness, the nobility of soul gripping the enlightened sons of light, the evil of the sons of darkness, the inevitable triumph and apotheosis. "Who will translate the imperative into action?" he asks. "Can my friends and I?"

It all finds an echo in the death stab of the ancient Jewish sicarii sure of dying when they caused dying. It is a post-Christian response to the barbarous barbecues of self-immolating Buddhist monks in Saigon. It has a horrible presumption that human blood is as salvific as the blood of Jesus. And it sins excessively by evacuating the divine from all human nobleness. It is dogmatic, intolerant, derogatory of all opposition, and persuaded that whatever might—spiritual or material—it has is on the side of right. It finishes, as it must, with a slight grin of that irreverence which frightens. Daniel Berrigan summed it up: "Men normally win the kind of eternity for which their lives prepare them, Socrates said to his friends. Indeed."

A few conclusions are evident concerning the above manifestations of post-Conciliar madness. All democratization procedures are inspired, as Bishop Dingman said, by the political models of the twentieth century. There is nothing inherently religious, supernatural, Roman Catholic, or Christian about those democratic models or the policies and actions flowing therefrom. To attribute such democratization to Pope John's Council is laughable. It simply means that the socio-political ambient of the Roman Catholic Church has transformed the Church, and not vice versa.

In the area of activism, we are at grips with the chief manifestation of the malaise which afflicts twentieth-century human society. The activism into which clerics, nuns, religious, and lay folk are plunging has no professedly or professionally Christian intent, purpose, or scope. It only means that there will be more politicians, more civil-rights workers, new Congressmen, fresh Presidental speech writers, more anti-Vietnam war demonstrators. Nor can it be construed as a carrying out of the clerical or religious injunction and undertaking to spread the Gospel of Jesus as professionals. It is a reduction of the Church's role to a purely secular one. The secular has transformed the religious role into being part of it.

The structuralism of the post-Conciliar period is, perhaps, the most dangerous trait of the madness. There is here a dual danger: a genuine and fatal division of the Roman Church due to the aggressive liberalism of northern churchmen; and a gradual secularization of the theology of the Word. Only for a time and to a certain extent can non-Roman churchmen attack, limit, and lampoon the administration of the Vatican and papal interventions. No amount of added professions of allegiance to the pope can help. It is about as sincere as saying that we love art but cannot really put up with the Mona Lisa, the Taj Mahal, and the Sistine Chapel. The two statements cannot stand together.

The day will have to come when the central teaching authority of the Bishop of Rome has to be asserted. As things are going, the voice of that authority will fall on ears and into minds whose owners will have already been de-Catholicized in order to be "freer," "more democratic," "more conformed" to their non-Catholic ambient. Any stress on rights and on freedom has to be made within a juridical framework. The anti-Roman stand of the northern churchmen echoes faithfully the mind of decadent Western Protestantism. This is a fatal transformation.

The same one-way conversion and transformation is noticeable in the false sense of mystery and mystique. A black Jesus, revolutionary leader, guerrilla fighter, a divinized Che Guevara, is as intellectually palatable and historically acceptable as a bearded baby or a talking skeleton. A black female divine principle is as reasonable as an IQ of 120 in a mechanical music box or a cure for German measles in Scottish porridge. It is sheer rubbish. If theology is only what one does, and not what one thinks, then there have not been many theologians in any church. In fact, robots and computers and kitchen blenders are, by definition, theologians. Theology is reduced essentially to action.

The falsity of Berrigan's grating martyr-complex is all the more potent in that he and those like him unjustly implicate the Roman Catholic Church and Catholics in general in a revolutionary movement which, to say the least of it, lacks judgment and piety and good taste. Above all, it has nothing to do with the wisdom and the sanctity which lie behind any Catholicism. Those of their clerical brothers and others who have saluted the Berrigan brothers in print and in the spoken word will not take this critique lightly. But they should reflect that at a later date the old bogy of Roman Catholicism in the United States may return to haunt the Church: is Catholicism as such irreconcilable with the American thing, as Paul Blanshard and others contended? In their efforts to prove the contrary and to be "with it," have they relinquished the essential of the faith which molded their spirits and minds in the first place? The Berrigans, the Melvilles, the National Black Committee, the intellectualizers, the activists, and the democratizers of the post-Conciliar period are, thus, people profoundly affected by their physical and socio-cultural ambient. Whatever judgment must be passed on them as men and as citizens by a later generation, it is clear that the madness which has gripped them has nothing essential to do with attaining the purposes that originally animated Roncalli or gave rise to his Council. Godfathers, perhaps, of tomorrow's Lumpenproletariat of world-citizen protesters, cosmic kibbitzers of the world's growing pains in politics and economics, disillusioned lovers of yesterday's ideal, and fascinated into a practical paranoia by the blood-drenched tomorrows they foresee, they all share a responsibility for the decline and fall of the Roman Catholic Church as a spiritual power. They have accepted being transformed by their ambient. They do not transform it. To acquiesce in this is the ultimate step in the religious madness we are describing.

28

The Futurists

Any review of Montini as the Prince of Agony must take into account the human scene as he now finds it and the *de facto* situation in his Church. It should cover the situation at the Vatican, in the Roman Catholic Church at large, and in Christianity as a whole. There can be no firm predictions, but the analysis should expose the main elements that compose Montini's world. Most useful for a summary, too, is a consideration of the views of the future which lie at the back of men's minds, which are the presumptions of national and international policies and which inspire the attitudes and actions of individuals and peoples. These are, to a large extent, the views of the futurists. And over against the backdrop of their views, the agony of Montini comes into final focus.

Within Montini's Church there are two predominant concepts of the future. One belongs to the conservative, the other to the progressive mind. Neither is free from apprehension, but while the conservative mind is naïvely at peace and eschews any real fear, the progressive mind is foolishly fraught with a doomsday persuasion. The conservative mind relies ultimately on the promise of Jesus that "he would be with his Church unto the end of time" and that "the gates of hell shall not prevail against you." To this main theme of the conservative futurist mind are added other and ancillary themes. Principal among them are: the number of the saved will always be restricted ("Many are called but few are chosen"); the world will always be against the truth of Christ's Church ("You are not of the world, as I am not of the world"); there will be continual plots and attacks against the Church until the last days when apocalyptic happenings will usher in the final sufferings of the saints and Jesus will appear in the clouds of heaven to judge both the living and the dead.

The practical consequences of such a mind are patent. There is in it a persuasion that truth is of a particularly immutable and unchangeable kind. It does not agonize very painfully over defections, opposition, diminished numbers, human miseries, and the ravages of time. After all, such a course of events was foretold. It lays much store by the repetition of actions, the exact reproduction of particular modes of behavior which have been handed on from previous ages. It has a snobbism all its own. All others may approximate to the precious truth which it possesses. None but the initiate and the elect of the Church can know it or possess it or practice it so that it lead them to eternal life. It has, finally, an ultimate source of consolation in all human vicissitudes and a palliative for every one of its victories: the only victory ultimately permitted the Church of Jesus is the entry of individual souls into the glory of Jesus after death.

The progressive mind is of a different cast. Generally very sensitive to ambient opinions and currents of thought, it is saddled with a feeling that the Church is out of date, that it is not "with it," is "old hat," and that it can contribute nothing—as it is—to the immense problems and prospects which confront mankind. It sees the future as a challenge. It seeks primarily to "adapt" the Church to the new conditions of human life. It draws inspiration from its surroundings. It draws even the principles of its judgment from the ways in which men judge their own affairs in politics, economics, humanism, and psychology. It does not draw much consolation or firmity of purpose from the past. The strength of its action comes primarily from a sense of urgency, for it is gripped by the same malaise, the same feeling that time is running out for the human race as agitates a great mass of human beings today. It shares, therefore, the live fear we find flourishing like a baleful mushroom on the human scene.

The progressive mind does not stay at peace with this fear. As in other human affairs, its general and definite tendency is to change what appears to be either a standstill element or a hindrance or a source of retrogression. Its norms in this matter are not drawn primarily from religious doctrine or traditional beliefs. They come from what suits merely the surroundings and what seems to cohere with but in no way to leaven the mentality of the majority of men they serve. The democratization and the mystical tinges of the progressive mind are thus explicable. For each of these represents a manifest tendency of the modern mind of man. Over all there is the pall of fear. Fear, first of all, that the world will blow apart and end with a big bang of atomic war or a whimper as it chokes on its environmental waste and is crushed by unbeatable waves of hunger and economic misery. Fear, in the second place, that around the corner of man's road there is some event about to arrive, something much more earth-shaking than the discovery of America in the fifteenth century, something more transforming than the splitting of the atom in the forties. It is either a complete genetic mutation in the human species (in that case, the present race of Homo sapiens will be an inferior and subject alien in its own earthly home) or the arrival of some new and utterly superior civilization from beyond the Milky Way (the human race would be prostrate before its highly evolved technology and its superhuman intelligence).

Outside official circles of the Roman Catholic Church, the geography of opinion about man in the present and in the near future falls into a distinct patchwork of ideas. There is general acknowledgment that man has created a world intrinsically different from what he inherited, so different that the methods of reasoning and the principles which governed his progress hitherto are otiose and rapidly falling into total desuetude. Men predict that within the foreseeable future the world will be inhabited by from five to seven billion human beings—beings caught in a dilemma. They will possess a polished technology for peace and for war; they will demand the good life; they will lack any comprehensive understanding of each other; and they will not be able to understand the transformation they have undergone as a civilization. At that point, when all previously known and acknowledged reference points have been obliterated and there no longer exists a commonly recognized scale of values or commonality of ideas, the human race cannot but wreak irreparable harm to itself.

This common framework of thought about the future is colored by ideology, religious belief, or economic intentions. The Marxist inspiration of the Soviet empire and of Communist China will blame the capitalist world and the United States in particular for any ultimate failure of the human race to cope with its critical situation. The religious conservatives will blame the irreligion of man and the pernicious effects of original sin. The progressives will lay the fault at the door of conservative religionists who did not or could not read the handwriting on the wall and who therefore let things slide beyond the point of recall. The ideological opponents of Marxism will blame Marxism and the Communist world in general for the lack of progress in the making of human peace and the harmony of man's world society. Each ideology and each philosophy will have its own interpretation of events.

In America today there are many varied views of the future. Some have a quasi-religious concept of man. Such is the Westernized Buddhism of Scientology, teaching that man is inherently good but that he has to undergo a transformation in order to realize that potential. Others spring from some professional bias and principally from the practitioners and theoreticians of psychology, who ascribe to their science the potential of being able to curb the deficiencies of the free enterprise system, the warring instinct of man, and his overriding nationalism.

Pessimism is the usual note both of futuristic writings today and of the analyses on which those writings are based. There is the typical science-fiction horror world of the future such as George Lukács painted in his film *THX 1138:* human society will be regulated within a quite inhuman law and a most immaculate order by a set of steely robots, and men will live in an underground city, vast, sunless, joyless, where their lawful happiness consists in being clear-skinned, hairless, germless, and abstinent from the disruptive thing called human love.

Notes of panic are struck by specialists and technicians in various fields from time to time. Architect and city planner Buckminster Fuller issued an appeal for some solution to the overspecialization of human society today. "We have so many specialized abilities, we can blow ourselves to pieces, but we have no ability to coordinate ourselves," he stated. Our society is so powerfully conditioned by its reflexes, with very, very tight ways of functioning, that unless man starts thinking globally, "we may not be able to continue on this planet." A rare note of optimism is struck by writers such as Leonard Gross, who condemns the "affluence of dismay," lauds today's "humanistic revolution," and concludes that there is still hope.

An occasional religious writer like R. F. Capon dips into the treasure chest of Christianity and comes up with a new version of the old optimism we find in the *Chanson de Roland* and the

writings of Chesterton. "The world," he writes, "is not God's sur-
plus inventory of artifacts; it is a whole barrelful of the apples of
his eye, constantly juggled, relished and exchanged by the persons of the Trinity." God is in love with being, Capon states.
Therefore, nothing in man's world is superfluous. His solution,
then, is a theology of delight: to love to laugh, to have confidence, and, perhaps, to avoid the pitfalls of extensive theologiz-
ing. Many have written of the need to treat the world in a godlike
way and to play in it as God's children. But none of them attain
Capon's optimism, Kahner in his *Man at Play*, Caillois in his
Man and the Sacred, Keen in his *Apology for Wonder*, and
Zucker in his *The Clown as the Lord of Disorder* underline the
childhood of man in the universe, but there is throughout their
thought a pessimism and a foreboding, capped with lively recommendations to man that he improve. The note is pessimistic: God is inclined to be dead, man, unless you buck up . . .

The most pervasive and vocal of futurist views concerns what
is commonly called the "revolution." By this term is not meant
generally or necessarily an armed uprising or rebellion. It is a
much more subtle process and affects the very essence of society
as we know it today. It is remarkable in that under this rubric we
can group many progressive theologians, many young writers
and thinkers of the New Left, as well as many popular enter-
tainers. In recent years, leaders and trail-blazers in these sectors
have met and cooperated in the field of political activism. The
most oft-quoted authorities of the "revolution" are philosophers
such as Herbert Marcuse, popularizers such as Charles Reich,
and social commentators such as Theodore Roszak. But of late,
theologians, priests, and nuns have come to the fore: Ivan Illich,
Daniel Berrigan, Harvey Cox, Thomas and Marjorie Melville,
among others.

The basic assumptions of the "revolution" theory are two.
First, the present system, the Establishment—economic, financial, cultural, political, military, and religious—is rotten, is op-
pressive, and is about to end. Second, there will follow a new era
in which all the old deficiencies of society will not exist. It is a
new heaven and a new earth. Our concept of human reality and
human nature will be completely changed. For man will attain
that perfect freedom of thought, of feeling, of outlook, of action,
of cooperation, without which he cannot be genuinely happy and
lacking which up to this point in history he has not attained true
happiness.

It may be a source of amazement to some people, but there is already in the United States a sizable number of people who are rearranging their social, religious, political, and sometimes their personal lives in view of this revolution. A. J. Waskow gives a vivid picture of how he and his children will spend their lives as "organizers-workers-intellectuals building new institutions . . . sometimes in jail, sometimes in exile, ultimately dancing and singing across from the White House, or from GM, or from Fort Jackson, as the old government dissolves and abdicates." The new conditions will be ushered in by the emergence of such things as a transnational religious underground and by the creative power of the individual communities. The title of Waskow's book indicates this theme graphically: *Running Riot: Official Disasters and Creative Disorders in American Society.*

J-F Revel, in his *Neither Marx nor Jesus,* makes the blank assertion that "the twentieth-century 'revolution' will take place in the United States. It can take place nowhere else. In fact, it has already started. It will spread to the rest of the world, only if it is successful in North America." Revel sets down five conditions for the realization of the "revolution": criticism of injustice, of the way things are run, of political power, of culture, and of traditional Christianity. For Revel, the level and volume of disputation and debate in the United States regarding these elements of its fabric warrant the conclusion that the "revolution" is taking place. Although his conclusions are not substantiated by the facts he adduces, there is at the back of Revel's thesis the same persuasion concerning the nature of the "revolution" and of the human condition which will emerge from its throes.

There is another, less violent, more benign, rational view of the "revolution." It is based on the promise inherent in man's newfound science and his developing technology. One of its most pointed descriptions has been set down by Dr. Harvey Wheeler. He assumes that man does not exist without religion and that religionless cultures, though theoretically possible, are unlikely in the practical order of things human. He does not think, therefore, that man will ever become "post-religious," though he may well be on his way to becoming "post-theological." If man does continue on his present development of culture and civilization, he will eventually furnish it with a "god-like, or logos-like, principle of order." For man and God, according to Dr. Wheeler, have always existed in a dialectical relationship. He considers the Christian episode in human history to have been "just plain bad luck for mankind." Attila could have done something about it, if his logistical support system had not petered out at Châlons. Man will have to furnish himself with such a principle because he has to resanctify his life and the nature of his world.

A new theocracy will be inaugurated: God will descend "from heaven to live and work among men," thus becoming the essence of peace and freedom but especially of democracy: "the symbol of a democratic theocracy in which the principle of the holy is infused throughout culture." Science will also be sanctified. There will emerge a new age of wisdom: "reason will be enthroned and reinforced by science." "We shall need a god capable of helping us to re-create man," states Dr. Wheeler. In fact, the world may at that moment be inhabited by neo-men requiring not a god but a neo-god, something quite different from all the previous god-figures which caught man's attention in the past.

It is obvious that this view of the future is irreconcilable with both the conservative and the progressive Roman Catholic view of the future. Nevertheless, today where we find some concrete hope among Americans of something good emerging from the present malaise, we find that some version of Wheeler's view reigns. The basis of Montini's agony can be understood in the light of the above views.

It is clear to him that the view of the future in vogue among the progressives of 1971 could by subtle metamorphosis and gradual shadings be changed into some form of the futurist views we have just sketched. This would mean the end of Christianity as Montini knows it. This is what makes the conservative view of human history, of revelation, and of the Church so attractive to him. On the other hand, he sees that the general trend of the members of his Church is away from the conservative viewpoint. He cannot see himself even attempting to impose that viewpoint on the Church at large. For one thing, it would provoke a rebellion far more divisive than the sixteenth-century Reform. For another, even if he succeeded, he would only have staved off a fatal decision which would confront one of his successors in a more acute and intractable form.

The basis of Montini's agony lies here. He must contemplate the coming and going of the forces which Roncalli's Council and its aftermath let loose in the Church. He does not know precisely where to lay the emphasis. He has no trump card to play. If he turns to contemplate and pray to the Jesus whom he serves, he finds no parallel in the latter's life. For at the end, when failure bent over his entire undertaking, Jesus as the man-God and Saviour had a trump card: by failing summarily in human terms, he succeeded beyond all human dreaming. So Montini's faith tells him. He has no such alternative.

29

The Agony

The concrete situation of Montini as Paul VI is unparalleled at least in the history of the popes since the sixteenth century. Other popes suffered more direly in their persons. Others underwent greater humiliations. Others still were beset by greater internal ills in the Church of their time. All had clear-cut situations. Choices were imposed by circumstances or forced on them by events. But no pope felt the grip of history as sorely as Montini. His situation calls for a compassion which is lacking in our age. And his dilemma should command a greater love than most men today can muster for any non-charismatic leader.

In Montini's Church there are about 600 million faithful, about 3,000 bishops, 230,000 priests, 320,000 religious men, over one million nuns, about 150,000 seminarists, without counting contemplatives the world over. The facts regarding the condition of the Church are patently clear. Within the Vatican, Montini's own domain proper, he has a house divided, partly by his own doing, partly by chance. His closest collaborators have minds of their own, different from his and from each other's. The lower echelons are split accordingly.

Cardinal Villot, his Secretary of State, French, sixty-six years old, six feet four inches tall, bespectacled, with a full head of hair, exasperatingly courteous in the French manner, insistingly righteous, efficient, with his own lines of communication to France, progressive, tolerant of weakness, humanistic. In 1968, Montini placed all his Vatican ministries under Villot's direction. Next to the Pope, Villot exercises the greatest power over the internal and foreign affairs of the Church. Villot measures his loyalty. Opposed to Villot in theology, political principles, personal tastes and ambitions, there is Monsignor Benelli, Under-Secretary of State, medium-sized, husky, balding, fifty years old, nicknamed the "Gauleiter" and the "Berlin Wall" by the Italians, not perfect in tact, ruthless in rooting out corruption, conservative, combative, a disappointed aspirant to the post of Secretary of State. Benelli was and is a good balance to Villot; between them, two poles of thought and manner, two ambitions.

In the Vatican there is a large bureaucracy of Italian clerics, minor and major, but only two of the major posts remain in Italian hands. Montini appointed foreigners to the nine others. Again, a house divided.

On the next level of the Church, where the national bishops and prelates are located, Montini is faced with a similar division. As of today, a poll count would separate those of Italy, Spain, Portugal, Ireland, Australia, the United Kingdom, and the Soviet satellites as sharing the mainstream of Montini's views. They are moderately progressive in sociological matters, conservative in theology and philosophy, prudent in politics. Those of France, Belgium, Holland, Germany, Austria, fall into a progressive category: progressive in sociology, progressive in theology and philosophy, progressive in politics. The bishops and prelates of the United States, Latin America, Africa, and Asia are hopelessly split. It is difficult to speak of any corporate unity in these areas. More and more, those of Africa and Asia are swinging over to a progressive position on the three counts.

The intellectual life of the Church depends, as always, on the work of thousands of theologians, philosophers, priests, lawyers, writers, thinkers, teachers, lecturers, popularizers. At present, the centers of this intellectual life are precisely the countries governed by the progressive bishops—France, Holland, Germany, and Belgium, notably. No other section of the Church has the same vibrancy, the same stubborn diligence, the same scorn of dogmatic limitations, or, not to mince words, the same readiness to experiment dangerously, combined with an intellectual ability to rationalize, defend, and justify both the experimentation and the daring. They can canvass every quiddity known to philosophers and muster every theological reason to support their arguments.

In every country there is a malaise among the ordinary priests. In the last seven years, it has been calculated, about 25,000 have left the priesthood.

In the practice of the Catholic religion (and this is now the level of the ordinary man and woman), the most enlightened but the least faithful in practice are the Catholics of France, Germany, Holland, Belgium, and Austria. The most ignorant and the least faithful in practice are the Italians and the Spaniards. The Irish and the Portuguese exhibit all these traits. In their number they have some of the most enlightened and the most faithful, a goodly number of the most ignorant, and some of the most rebellious, sons of the Roman Catholic Church. The practice of Catholicism in the United States is going through the doldrums. Vulnerable now to every wind of change, susceptible to any infringement of their democratic rights, provided with no genuine indigenous Catholic intellectual class or tradition, just emergent from a ghetto mentality imposed originally by the dominant Protestant ethic and Establishment, ridden by a bench of bishops who can administer better than they can think, but who can rule more efficiently than they can govern, hamstrung by a Catholic education with no intellectual roots and no indigenous religious tradition, alive to injustice and dogmatism and to high-handed autocracy by virtue of their Americanism, American Catholics catch the backwash of every movement started in the European Church. They are caught also in the helter-skelter malaise—economic, social, political—of their huge country. Ill-led by the charismatic few who appear from time to time and by non-charismatic bishops, the American Catholic Church is split between conservative, moderate progressive, and liberal tendencies.

The anciently established faith of Latin America and the newly founded faith of Africa and Asia are both beset by an economic situation that is not improving substantially. Part of the Third World in economics and industrial development, these countries have material problems that are making severe inroads into the cohesion, the loyalty, and the faith of Roman Catholics. There is here no theorizing about the Logos, no intellectual ballet dancing with ecumenism, no liturgical communications, and none of the sometimes senseless falderal of European theology and its antics. Men, women, and children are starving, disease-ridden, ill-housed, short-lived, neglected, persecuted, worn by guerrilla wars, oppressed by economic masters, or all and every one of these things at one and the same time. The Catholic faith has been consistently associated there with colonial powers, foreign capitalists, or exploitative native oligarchies in the shape of big families, ruling dynasties, or bands of military dictators. The danger there is not intellectual schism but political Marxism as an answer to all their difficulties. In Latin America, for instance, if the Allende experiment in Chile persists and succeeds even moderately, government in the hemisphere will rapidly be of two kinds only: socialist-Marxist, like Allende's, or by military dictatorship. In either case, the Catholic faith stands to suffer.

The Church of Montini, then, is a house divided. Let loose in that Church since the appearance of Roncalli is a gamut of forces which tear and pull and tug at the massive entrails of a onetime monolith now unprepared for the stresses and strains, ill-fitted to adapt in the pressure cooker of modern events. This ferment of ideas, clash of opinions, irreconcilability of political ethos with religious principles, and the irredentist trend toward liberalization contending with a long-entrenched and prejudiced conservatism, have rendered Montini's position as pope theoretically untenable, practically tortuous, and prospectively of dim outlook. It has, in a true sense, unpoped him. For he cannot act as popes have acted before. This forced inaction has nothing inherently conservative, nothing of craven fear in it. Montini does not know what to do. Nobody alive can tell him.

His alternatives are clear but in their entirety unacceptable. He could, theoretically, demand and exact under severe sanction obedience and submission of all bishops and prelates. He could come down hard, personally and through his administration, on all progressives and liberals in his Church. But any foreseeable result of this is forbidding. He would stand to lose major portions of the Catholic population intellectually, politically, and in practical religion; he would risk too many defections among priests, religious, nuns, as well as among bishops, and destroy whatever bridges have been built to non-Catholics and non-Christians. He is not willing to answer for such consequences. Besides, he would need to act with an authoritarianism which is not his. For Montini is of a different cast, can never flash in the human firmament as a crystallized embodiment of greatness, is not made for contentious dealing, for argumentative approaches, for vociferous imposition of his views, for any muscular expression of his Catholicity or any strong-arm advancement of Christianity. The conversation is suave; the manner is cool; the accents are measured; the mode is pianissimo. The motto is: be stubborn. The hope is: that they understand. Belief, yes. Love, yes. But, Lord, please that they understand the impasse today.

He could, on the other hand, decide to encourage the progressives beyond the limits bearable to the conservatives. In that case, however, two eventualities might severely impair his Church for several generations. A quicksilver series of spasms would run through the conservative Catholic population, churches, and churchmen, producing what would amount to local schisms, regional divisions, and separatist mentalities. Second, any concession on a disciplinary or theological level could open up the insides of his Church and let chaos enter there. Running through the present ferment he rightly detects a simply human element of potential danger in an organized religion: the existence of a feeling in men that they should reach for the top of the world, become what they want, do as they please. He understands that this emphasis on self-realization springs partly from a genuine need felt by man in today's world to demonstrate that he exists in reality, that his life is not merely a cry of anguish or the muted sound of naked feet running from danger but a human story told in accents of peace and triumph. Montini knows that it is his immediate successors who would pay for any mistake in this direction.

If, however, he does nothing or little which is significant, he runs a further risk. He knows that human society is moving toward a series of historical denouements in which some basic and perennial human problems must be solved, if the international community of men is not to survive merely as scattered remnants of a sundered civilization. By doing really nothing, his Church and Christianity would miss a high tide in human affairs. The Roman Catholic Church would surely lose heavily in such a case, because great numbers of its membership will refuse to be held back from striving to attain the possible ideal of the human situation.

His interim solution, therefore, is a holding operation. He will do nothing to alienate the reasonably progressive; he will not stifle the protests or reactions of the conservatives. He will not innovate; nor will he regress. On capital points such as abortion, contraception, divorce, priestly celibacy, theological unity with other churches, female ministry, he will restate traditional doctrine but endeavor to do so with sweetness, with light, with harmony, with calm precision, and with a cool head. He wants no crisis, no confrontation. He trusts the future with a trust that exceeds all his botherations, and he hopes with a hope which goes beyond the transient misunderstanding, the occasional diplomatic *gaffe*, the hurt pride of intellectuals, and the ignorance of individuals. His trust and hope are laid up for later times, when he is dead and buried in St. Peter's with Roncalli and Pacelli and their predecessors, when the contentious northerners have learned to lighten the dark fire of their brains with a little less theological logic and somewhat more with a genuine love of the heart, when the conservative heart has been as profoundly touched by human problems as its mind is now by abstract formularies, when the world has grown old, not in its sins, but in the good lessons learned through sinning and repenting. Then there is a possibility that Christianity may create a new society which has not yet taken even a shadowy shape. It will be a veritable City in the world which is God's because he dwells there and man's because God built it for him in the labors of his Spirit. It will be less theological than the Christianity of the Roman Emperors, more genuinely pious than medieval Europe, and somewhat more human than the Catholic Counter-Reform and its arguable strictures. It will be based on what lies before, above, and beyond man, but it will be immersed in the here and now like a flaming wick in a candle or like songs that fill all the valleys that lie between tall mountains.

It will have nothing of the irreverent or falsely democratic; but it will lack the rough-edged rigidities of classical dogmatism. It will claim no domain on the planet earth in virtue of what lies beyond human life, but it will be constituted of men, women, children, cities, nations, and races. Its culture will be the flower of its sacredness. Its civilization will be a framework of human perfection. This is the trust and the hope of Montini.

He has, therefore, no illusions left but at the same time is the victim of no delusions. He is the conscious captain of a fragile unity which, under the circumstances, he manages quite admirably, but it does not resemble the unity of the Church in former days. As the Prince of Agony, he has accepted his role and the limitations of his character. He knows he cannot re-create the Roncalli image or better it in any way. As pope, he stood once in front of the member nations of the United Nations Organization, the first pope in history to address so many representatives of so many nations in one place. Yet he could not evoke a new ambient of feeling, could not inspire a leadership, could not unite them. He was there as one ruler among other rulers. He knows also that he cannot afford to tamper with the forces Roncalli let loose in his Church. He takes up no heroic stands, therefore, does not pose as a hieratic figure, watches a crowd surrounding him with the quick appraising eye of an experienced leader and the quizzical look of an expectant schoolboy, can smile at the huzzahs and *evvivas* while reflecting on their meaning, is tender and soft-spoken with his family, can shed tears in his distress over policy failures, human suffering, and unnecessary misunderstandings. Montini's low-key performance is so effective that even his really significant pronouncements pass unnoticed. He has, for instance, stated the ideal of all progressives, religious and political, but with quasi-understatement and in such sane terms that it passed unnoticed. Here is Montini's masterful description of what modern individualism is all about, whether it is in Harlem, New York; Dacca, Pakistan; Rio de Janeiro, or the Bantustans of South Africa:

> There is urgent need to remake, at the level of the street, of the neighborhood or of the great agglomerative dwellings, the social fabric whereby man may be able to develop the needs of his personality. Centers of special interest and of culture must be created or developed at the community and parish levels with different forms of associations, recreation centers, and spiritual and community gatherings where the individual can escape from isolation and form a new fraternal relationship.

He is describing an ideal as dear to the heart of American hippies, blacks, Chicanos, as it is to the poor in city ghettos and underdeveloped countries. He abstains from the romantic idealization and utopian liberation images which some modern "revolutionaries" depict. Modern man is a distinct entity from man of any other known period in human history. But in Montini's view there is no use in deluding him with false promises. He has decided to leave to later men the realization of the ancient promise of former days and the newfound dream of the modern "revolution": the transformation of the world beyond man's imaginings and making it lustrous beyond measure.

Like all men of thought and all leaders of great populations, Montini has dreamed of events capable of molding a genuine fraternity of all men and creating a community of peoples linked not merely by economic interdependence or technological needs but by a newly acquired cast of mind, a commonality of feeling, thinking, talking, fantasy, dream. In such a community, the line of demarcation would disappear between reason and unreason because unreasonableness would never hold sway. There would no longer be an alienation of body from mind, passion from beauty, one man from another, or one man from himself.

It is the dream of the Islands of Hesperides and the Land of Perpetual Youth, but translated into the concrete terms of this world. Man's capacity for experience would be enlarged in the world of God. He would learn again festivity and celebration, how to value his experience of people and of things for their own sakes, and to find himself again with the assurance of ease and a lively instinct for the timelessness of human life when liberated from the anguish of self-ignorance and the preoccupation of hidden guilts.

For Montini all this is laid up for a later time. For the nonce, there is the daily grind, the seesaw struggle in his government, the round of public and private audiences, the daily decisions affecting men in many nations, the petty problems of Church politics, and the sleep of each night as a foretaste of the sleep for which he has already started yearning.

Index